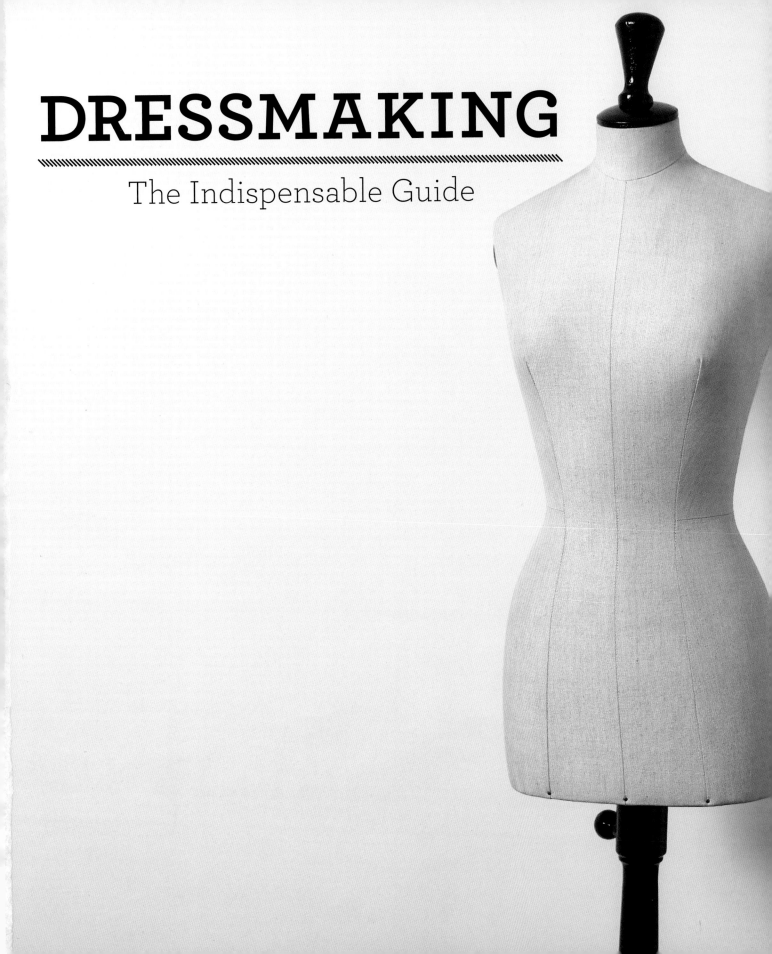

DRESSMAKING

The Indispensable Guide

DRESSMAKING

The Indispensable Guide

Jules Fallon

FIREFLY BOOKS

A FIREFLY BOOK

Published by Firefly Books Ltd. 2017

First printing

Publisher Cataloging-in-Publication Data (U.S.)

Names: Fallon, Jules, author.
Title: Dressmaking : The Indispensable Guide / Jules Fallon.
Description: Richmond Hill, Ontario, Canada : Firefly Books, 2017. | Includes index. | Summary: "A guide for dressmakers new to the craft, and for those who want to take their skills further" – Provided by publisher.
Identifiers: ISBN 978-1-77085-938-8 (hardcover)
Subjects: LCSH: Dressmaking. | Tailoring (Women's)
Classification: LCC TT515.F355 | DDC 646.404 – dc23

Library and Archives Canada Cataloguing in Publication

Fallon, Jules, author
        Dressmaking : the indispensable guide / Jules Fallon.
-- 1st edition.
Includes index.
ISBN 978-1-77085-938-8 (hardcover)
        1. Dressmaking. 2. Dressmaking--Handbooks, manuals, etc. 3. Women's clothing. 4. Tailoring (Women's).
I. Title.
TT515.F35 2017   646.4'04   C2017-900388-7

Published in the United States by
Firefly Books (U.S.) Inc.
P.O. Box 1338, Ellicott Station
Buffalo, New York 14205

Published in Canada by
Firefly Books Ltd.
50 Staples Avenue, Unit 1
Richmond Hill, Ontario L4B 0A7

Cover design: Erin R. Holmes / Soplari Design

Color separation by PICA Digital Pte Ltd, Singapore
Printed by Hung Hing Off-set Printing Co. Ltd, China

Conceived, edited, and designed by
Quarto Press
6 Blundell Street
London N7 9BH

Senior Editors: Chelsea Edwards, Victoria Lyle
Art Editor and Designer: Jackie Palmer
Step-by-step and author photographer: Charlie Budd
Model and garment photographer: Nicki Dowey
Studio photographer: Phil Wilkins
Illustrator: Kuo Kang Chen
Editorial Assistant: Danielle Watt
Copy Editor: Sarah Hoggett
Proofreader: Caroline West
Art Director: Caroline Guest
Creative Director: Moira Clinch
Publisher: Samantha Warrington

Contents

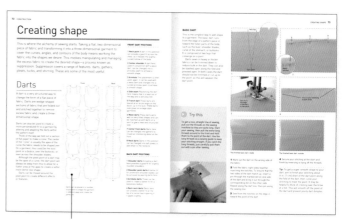

Illustrations
Line drawings clearly show the construction of garments.

Try this
Alternative ways of working or tips to make the technique easier are suggested in Try this boxes.

Step-by-steps
Clear step-by-step photographs are accompanied by concise instructions on how to achieve each technique.

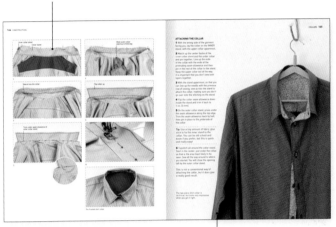

Help
If something has gone wrong, help boxes suggest the reasons why and how to fix.

Finished garments
Styled photography of finished garments offers inspiration.

Chapter 2
PREP

28

Chapter 3
CONSTRUCTION

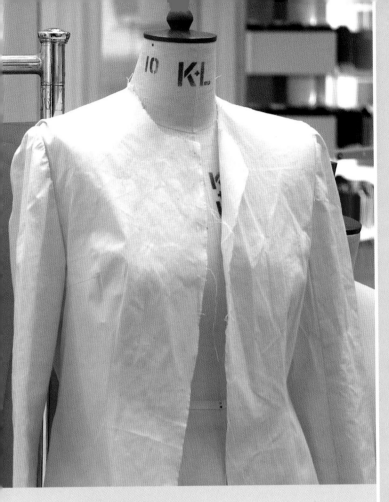

Meet Jules Fallon

Hello! My name is Jules Fallon. It is no secret that I enjoy sewing. I've been doing it for years and now run my own shop: Sew Me Something, in Stratford-spon-Avon, UK. During my day, I run craft and sewing workshops, design and produce dressmaking patterns, and help nervous beginners feel at ease in front of a sewing machine. In other words, I know what I am talking about! And now I'd like to pass on some of this knowledge to you.

I initially trained as a pattern cutter and worked in the fashion industry for over 15 years before falling into teaching when my children were small. I lectured for over 10 years, heading up a fashion design course in the Midlands. It was much easier to work during the school year, and spend my vacations sewing for myself and my children. Having learned to sew as a child with my mom and grandmother, it was wonderful to be able to pass this on to my daughter and show her how to make things for her dollies and then herself.

It is the wonder of sharing information that I really enjoy, the conversations it sparks, and the deep satisfaction to be gained from making something. This is the main reason I started Sew Me Something. Being able to share the knowledge and skills you have with other people and, in return, to learn from them is what enables us to grow both in terms of our sewing abilities but also as individuals.

It is great to be able to just whip up a summer skirt, or to add a bit of sparkle to a cardigan to change the look of it completely. But sometimes it is the processes of creating something that is as much a part of the joy as the finished result. There is a real sense of haste in life today; taking time to enjoy what you're making and the skills you are developing as you work your way through a project will mean the next project you work on will be that much easier or better finished.

This is my first book and a place where I have tried to collate my years of sewing knowledge. I have included little bits of information not usually found in textbooks, the kinds of things we chat about in our workshops that help you sew better. There are also a few new ways of doing things that I have discovered while talking to professional colleagues or that I have used myself working in the industry. These techniques will help improve the finish of your clothing projects. This book should be the kind of thing you have next to your sewing machine to dip in and out of when you just need to know how to do something.

I hope this book will help you to sew better because there is no better compliment than when someone says, "I love what you're wearing, where did you get it?" And you reply, "I made it myself."

JULES FALLON

Equipment

1

When you start a new hobby, it can be tempting to surround yourself with all the equipment you could possibly imagine you'll want to use. But when you start dressmaking, all you need are a sewing machine, a sharp pair of scissors, and an open mind. You can decide on everything else when you have a greater understanding of your way of working and what will help you to sew better.

Essential equipment

Once you have started on your sewing journey there are all kinds of specialty tools and pieces of equipment to help make your life easier and to enable you to give your clothing a professional finish.

ESSENTIALS

Choose good-quality tools and equipment that allow you to make or adapt accurate, well-fitting patterns. Take care of them and you will never need to replace them.

Sewing machine

Although hand sewing can be therapeutic and is in some instances essential, a sewing machine (see pages 20–21) will make sewing your own clothes much easier and quicker. It is worth spending time with your machine, getting to know all of the stitches and functions it can provide. Look after it, keep it lint- and dust-free, and have it serviced regularly.

Scissors (1)

A good pair of sharp, long-bladed scissors is essential and will make cutting fabric much easier. A small pair of embroidery or needlework scissors will help to snip off threads and get right into corners that need snipping. A pair of paper scissors are also a must for cutting patterns and templates, as fabric scissors will blunt if they are used for cutting paper or cardstock.

Pins (2)

Pins hold fabric in place before basting and stitching. Glass-headed pins are easy to see and the heads won't melt if accidentally placed under a hot iron. But long, thin, steel dressmaker's pins will last longer and are easier to work with when using finer fabrics.

Tape measure (3)

Tape measures are necessary for accurate work and making sure that garments fit the wearer perfectly. Their pliability makes them ideal for measuring curves. When placed against an edge, a measuring tape can follow lines to give accurate sizing. You should, however, try and find a good-quality one, as cheaper ones can stretch over time and will affect accuracy.

Iron (4)

An iron with a bit of weight behind it and controllable steam will improve the finish of your sewing. Use it to open seams, press hems, and create folds and creases (see page 70). An iron can often reduce the amount of pinning or basting between steps. It also improves the finish of a piece of clothing, sharpening edges, smoothing creases, and reducing bulk. Pressing effectively throughout the sewing process is essential to a well-finished garment

Tailor's chalk (5)

Tailor's chalk is a good choice for marking most fabrics, as it is easy to brush away. It is important to keep the edges sharp—you can do this by drawing the edge of the chalk through a part-opened pair of old scissors, making sure to collect the dust in a trash can underneath.

Needles (6)

Always use the correct needle for the fabric you are working with. You will be surprised at the difference it will make to your sewing.

Seam ripper (7)

This small tool is shaped to make it easier to undo stitches sewn in the wrong place. It is a sad truth, but even experienced sewers will make mistakes, so a seam ripper will come in very handy. Find one with a little bobble on the shorter point, as this is the bit you insert under the seam to zipper through the stitches.

Marker pens (8)

Fade-away pens are a good choice for plainer fabrics, but you will need to work with them immediately as they fade over 48 hours. Wash-away pens stay in place until the fabric is washed or cleaned with water.

Space to sew

Once you have the equipment you require, think about the space you are going to work in. A large, flat surface at the correct height is the ideal, but not always possible. Cutting fabric often happens on the floor. If this is the case, try and use a smooth piece of hardboard under your fabric to protect your flooring and to keep the fabric from catching.

A lot of work needs to be done at waist height so, if you don't have a large table, an ironing board is the next best thing.

Storage is important, too, as most projects are created over a period of time rather than all in one go. A safe place to keep a work-in-progress is essential. If you are not lucky enough to have a separate sewing space, then a cabinet, box, or even a zipped-up bag will keep all the components of your project together and sharp pins away from children.

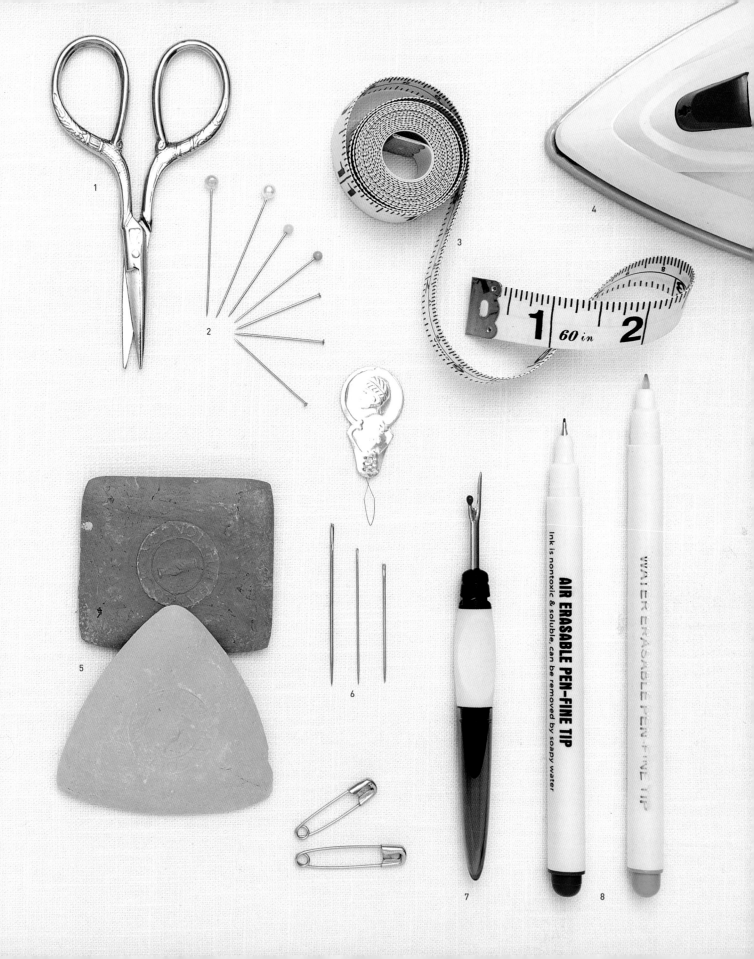

AIR ERASABLE PEN–FINE TIP

Ink is nontoxic & soluble, can be removed by soapy water

WATER ERASABLE PEN–FINE TIP

60 in

1

2

3

4

5

6

7

8

NICE-TO-HAVE EQUIPMENT

Overlocker

If you are making a lot of your own clothes this is the one piece of additional equipment that will increase the quality of your sewing dramatically. These useful machines (see page 20) are for neatening raw edges and giving clothes a professional finish. However, they also perform many other decorative functions and, although not essential, are a great asset. They also make sewing jersey fabrics a dream. They can seem a bit intimidating at first but, as with your sewing machine, make time to get to know the functions and it will pay off in the end.

Tailor's ham

This is a tightly packed, ham-shaped cushion, which can be used to support a garment as it's being pressed. The rounded shape of the ham allows a curved seam to be pressed without compromising or creasing the rest of the garment. The sleeve roll provides the same support on difficult-to-press areas such as sleeves or pants legs.

Dressmaker's dummy

When making your own clothes, it can be quite difficult to fit yourself correctly. Having a dummy that is as close to your size as possible will be extremely helpful. Adjust the dress form as required and check the fit of your garment as you sew.

Pattern-tracing wheel

Used in conjunction with dressmaker's carbon paper, this tool marks a line of dots. It is more useful for heavier-weight materials.

Dressmaker's dummy

Point turner

You can make do with the point of your scissors for only so long. A measuring gauge has a useful point, or a specific corner and edge shaper will do the job nicely, and the point won't go through the fabric like scissors are prone to.

Magnetic pin holder

This will keep all the errant pins in place when they're thrown in the rough direction of the pin pot as you are sewing. It's easy to make your own with a couple of flat magnets, some glue, and an old bowl.

Measuring gauge

This is a handy plastic or wooden gadget that has various measurements marked on it, so you don't need to count all the little lines on a tape measure.

Fashion ruler or French curve

You may wish to alter the pattern you have to accommodate a figure or style alteration. These rulers enable you to create smooth curves to alter patterns effectively. If you need to draw a straight line, then always use a ruler.

Pattern paper

Use this paper to make a pattern alteration or to trace a copy of a pattern. It is weighty enough to be effective, but you can still see through it to trace your pattern. The dots and crosses on the paper make it easy to draw straight lines and match up grain lines.

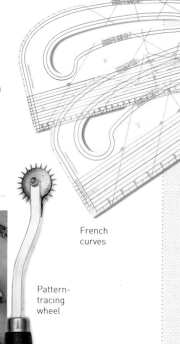

Measuring gauge and point turner

Corner and edge shaper

Measuring gauge

French curves

Pattern-tracing wheel

Pattern paper

Needle know-how

The needle is the principal piece of sewing equipment—you must have one if you want to sew! Originally whittled from bone or wood, needles are now made from high-quality steel in sizes for every application.

CHOOSING NEEDLES

It is important to select the correct needle for the task at hand, whether for hand or machine sewing. Neat hand sewing is easier to produce with the correct size and type of needle and, although machine needles may all look the same, subtle differences tailor them for particular threads or fabrics.

Hand needles

Hand needles come in a range of types and sizes to suit different tasks. Short, fine needles are ideal for sewing small, functional stitches, whereas larger-eyed varieties are needed to take thicker embroidery threads. Keep a range at hand, and select the one most suited to your current sewing project.

Eye

Body

Point

Machine needles

Modern machine needles are adapted to suit particular fabrics and threads to give better results. The points vary from sharp points that sew most fabrics without causing skipped stitches or damage to the fabric, to a rounded ball that slips between the yarns of knits without splitting them, and wedged points for cutting through vinyl or leather.

Groove: When the needle is in place, the groove faces forward. The thread lies within it. This enables the needle to slip through the fabric, carrying the thread in the groove so that it causes less drag.

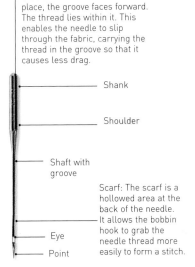

Shank

Shoulder

Shaft with groove

Scarf: The scarf is a hollowed area at the back of the needle. It allows the bobbin hook to grab the needle thread more easily to form a stitch.

Eye

Point

 Try this

Can't thread your needle?

- Cut the thread at an angle. This makes it easier to fit through the eye.

- Place a piece of white paper behind the eye of the needle to make it easier to see the hole for the thread to go through.

- Use a needle threading wire or gadget. There are many of these on the market (see right), ranging from a simple diamond-shaped wire on a handle to tiny hooks that pull a thread length through the eye of the needle.

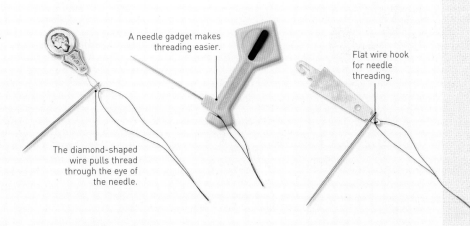

A needle gadget makes threading easier.

Flat wire hook for needle threading.

The diamond-shaped wire pulls thread through the eye of the needle.

THE RIGHT NEEDLE FOR THE JOB

Use the chart below to select the correct needle for your sewing task.

Hand
Generally, sizes range from 1 (largest) to 12 (finest).

Type	Embroidery (crewel)	Beading	Tapestry	Bodkin	Sharps
Description	Medium length, with a long eye to take embroidery threads	Long and very fine; thin enough to pass through the hole in a bead	Blunt needle, shorter than a darner, with a large eye	Long and broad, with a rounded point and a large eye	Medium length, with a small round eye for general sewing
Purpose	Embroidery	Beading	Tapestry, needlepoint, and silk ribbon embroidery	Threading elastic, ribbon, or tapes through a casing	General sewing projects

Machine
Generally, sizes range from 60 (smallest) to 120 (largest).

Type	Universal	Ballpoint	Stretch	Microtex	Denim
Description	Standard needle with a sharp point to penetrate most fabrics without causing damage	Rounded point to slide between the fibers rather than split them	Deep scarf to prevent skipped stitches	Sharp point for fine fabrics	Strong needle with a sharp point
Purpose	Most weights of woven fabric	Knitted fabrics	Stretch fabrics, including knits, Lycra, and synthetic suede	Delicate silks and synthetic microfiber fabrics	Denim and other strong fabrics with a dense texture

Betweens	Darning	Milliner's (straw)	Leather (gls)	Chenille	Self-threading
Shorter needles with a round eye	Long, with a large eye and a sharp point to take woolen yarn	Longer length, with a round eye	A sharp, wedged, triangular point to pierce leather	Longer in length, with a sharp point and a large eye	A sharp medium length, with a slotted eye
Detailed, precise work for tailoring and quilting	Darning	Basting, pleating, and hat making	For sewing leather, suede, vinyl, and other tough materials	For sewing thicker fabrics with stranded threads, wool, and ribbon	Easier threading

Metallic	Embroidery	Quilting	Topstitch	Wing (hem stitch)	Twin (triple) needle
Large, polished eye holds thread and prevents it from shredding and skipping stitches	Larger eye holds the embroidery thread, and the scarf allows dense stitching without shredding the thread	Sharp point and narrow, tapered shaft	Sharp, with a large groove and eye to take thicker threads	Wings on either side of the shaft push fabric threads apart; well-chosen stitches leave decorative holes in cloth	Two or three needles fixed to a single body for parallel rows of stitching
Metallic threads, including monofilaments	Rayon, polyester, and specialized embroidery threads	Sewing through several thick layers without damaging them	Topstitching	Decorative heirloom stitching similar to hand-sewn thread work. (Iron fabric with spray starch for a stiffer finish before starting to sew.)	Heirloom stitching, pin tucks, and imitation cover stitch

Cutting it

Blades of all shapes and sizes are available, and each has a task to perform in the sewing room. Get the best results by using the right tool for each job.

Type	Shears	Pinking shears
Description	Dressmaking shears or scissors have long, sharp blades and shaped handles for comfortable handling	Scissors with zigzag-shaped blades to make a notched cut
Purpose	Cutting fabric	Use these on fabric to prevent the edge from fraying

 Try this

- If you attend a class or sewing group with friends, tie a length of ribbon to the handle of your fabric shears to make yours stand out.

- Dropping scissors on the floor can knock them out of alignment. Place them in the center of the table when not in use, not close to the edge.

- Keep scissors dry and out of damp conditions where they may rust.

- Blades become dull through use. Sharpen them when they need it.

ALTERNATIVE CUTTING TOOLS

Aside from using scissors to cut fabrics and threads, there are other cutting gadgets in the sewing room. They are useful additions to your sewing box and will save both time and energy.

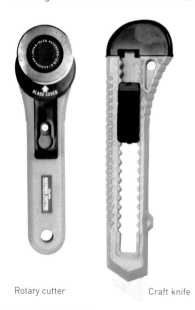

Rotary cutter

This has a circular blade with a handle and is used with a self-healing cutting mat placed under the fabric. It cuts fabric accurately and several layers can be cut at once. This makes it ideal for patchwork and small garment pieces. It is a fast method of cutting out. Here are a few useful tips:

- Buy two blades so that you always have a spare if one gets damaged.
- Buy the largest mat you have space for, especially if you are using it for clothes as well as patchwork.
- Keep the mat flat and away from heat, as it can bend and crack.

Rotary cutter   Craft knife

Needlework/embroidery scissors	Serrated shears	Curved embroidery scissors	Paper scissors
Short-bladed scissors with sharp points	Textured blades, not smooth	Small, sharp, pointed scissors with short and curved blades	Standard scissors with medium-length sharp blades
For cutting threads and snipping and notching seam allowances	The ridges grip fabric to make cutting soft and lightweight fabrics easier	Use these to snip thread ends close to your work	Use these for paper projects only, and keep your fabric scissors sharp for cutting cloth

Craft knife
Cut stiff vinyl or leather with a craft knife rather than scissors, as you will achieve a much neater cut. Keep the knife sharp. A blunt knife is more likely to cut you, because you'll be putting more pressure on the blade. A knife with a retractable blade can be stored safely in your toolkit.

Thread cutter
These little cutters hang around your neck, so they are handy when you need them. The blade for cutting threads is concealed behind a disc with slots. The thread is cut by the blade when it is pulled into a slot.

Thread snips
Thread snips have no handles, so they are easy to pick up quickly. Use them when sewing on the move and space for equipment is limited.

Buttonhole chisel
Opening buttonholes neatly without snipping the threads can be difficult—but not with a buttonhole chisel. Place over the center of the buttonhole and tap the end to cut through the fabric.

Thread cutter

Thread snips

Buttonhole chisel

Machine anatomy

With the help of a sewing machine and an overlocker, you can sew much more and much faster than you can by hand. Whatever machine you own or plan to buy, learn how to use it properly to appreciate its full potential.

SEWING MACHINE

Although the most modern machines have needle threaders and cutters, multiple buttonhole options and dozens of pretty decorative stitches, and may even create intricate machine embroidery, some still just sew! When buying a sewing machine, select one that carries out the functions you need and consider the areas you want to progress into.

Thread guides
Guides are positioned to route the thread through the machine to create the stitches. Consult your machine manual or follow the arrows marked on the machine to take the correct route.

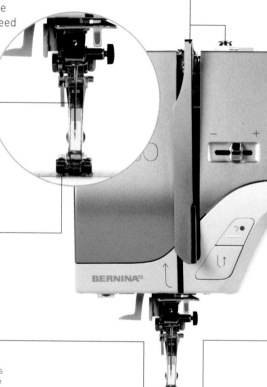

Needle
The needle fits into the machine with a clamp or screw to hold it in place. The position is fixed on some machines, but many allow you to adjust the needle position to the left, or right, and to work zigzag and decorative stitches, too.

Presser foot
This foot places pressure on the fabric around the needle to support and encourage the layers to progress with the help of the feed dogs below. On some models, the pressure or weight can be increased or decreased to suit the depth of the fabric.

Throat plate
This plate—normally made from metal—surrounds the feed dogs and has a hole through which the needle passes while it takes the thread down to meet the bobbin. There are generally guidelines etched into the metal throat plate to mark the most popular seam allowances. By feeding the fabric edge under the presser foot and along one of these guides, the line of stitches will be parallel to the edge.

Feed dogs
The jagged teeth that sit under the needle within the throat plate move in a circular motion to steadily move the fabric. This means that as the needle rises, the teeth move the fabric on—so when the needle lowers into the cloth, it produces a stitch. The movement of the teeth can be adjusted to alter the stitch length and can also be dropped down out of the way for free-motion sewing.

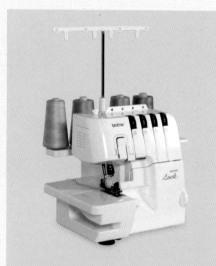

Overlocker

While an overlocker is not essential for dressmaking (see page 212), you might want to consider one if you are making a lot of clothes. An overlocker uses three or four threads and cuts, sews, and neatens seams all in one. Use it to construct garments made from stretch fabrics and to neaten the raw edges of most other projects. It also sews a range of decorative effects and uses interesting threads and yarns.

Thread spindle (hidden behind)
The reel of thread is placed on this before it is fed through the guides toward the needle. Additional spindles allow more reels to be used—for example, when sewing with a double or twin needle.

Bobbin winder
This winds thread quickly and evenly onto a bobbin.

Handle
The handle on the right of the machine rotates as the needle moves up and down through the fabric. Although the foot pedal or a stop/go button on the sewing machine controls the movement of the needle, sometimes it helps to be able to have fine control of the needle by using the handle.

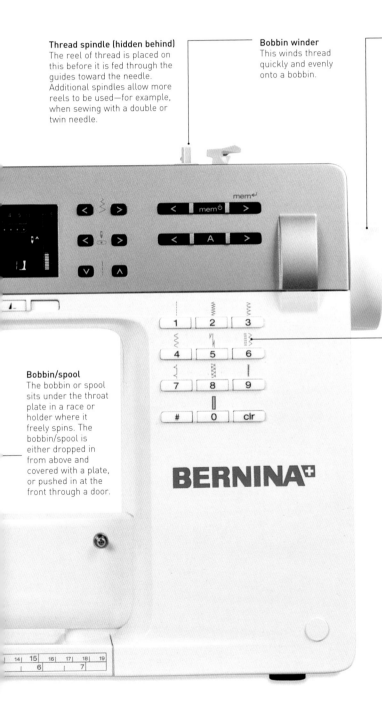

Stitch selectors
Select and adjust the length and width of stitches with dials or buttons. A manual sewing machine normally has dials or knobs with symbols, while electronic machines often have a window showing the chosen stitch, along with other information— for example, the presser foot to use with the selected stitch.

Bobbin/spool
The bobbin or spool sits under the throat plate in a race or holder where it freely spins. The bobbin/spool is either dropped in from above and covered with a plate, or pushed in at the front through a door.

BERNINA⊞

> **Try this**

Handling

Like any piece of equipment, it takes time to learn how to operate a sewing machine and get the best from it. Ideally, start sewing with stable, woven fabrics and simple shapes that are easy to feed through the machine. When you have mastered these, move on to fabrics that are more difficult to handle, like stretchy, lightweight, or thick ones. Through practice you will learn how to hold, support, ease, or pull, depending on the characteristics of the fabric you are sewing with.

Foot pedal
Most machines are powered by electricity, and this is generally by means of a cable and pedal that sits on the floor. However, some machines have a stop/go button on the front as an additional option. Use this for sewing automatic buttonholes or when creating a decorative stitch to ensure that it is regular and consistent.

Sewing machine feet

When you buy a sewing machine, it comes with a standard presser foot and a small number of additional feet for specific tasks such as inserting zippers and sewing buttonholes. However, there are many more specialized feet and attachments that may be fitted to your sewing machine to make tricky techniques much easier.

Some sewing machine brands offer a large number of specialized feet and attachments, while others have only a limited range. There are some universal feet available that may fit your machine if you are short of choice, but always choose those designed for your brand first before seeking an alternative. The most common feet are listed here, and are generally included when you buy a sewing machine.

Standard foot

For straight and zigzag stitching, this foot has a smooth base and it clips or screws in place. It is designed for everyday tasks like sewing seams and topstitching hems.

Tip: Although great for general sewing, this foot does not always work for decorative stitching where the stitch is bulky and the base is hindered by the buildup of stitching. Swap for a foot that has a channel in the base, such as the open-toe foot.

Zipper foot

These vary in design from brand to brand, but generally consist of a single prong with an indent at either side so that the foot can stitch close to the zipper teeth.

Tip: Zipper feet are very versatile and are great for sewing piping, too, since the needle can get close to the edge of the thick cord.

Buttonhole foot that calibrates length of buttonhole from button

Top

Bottom

Buttonhole foot

Blind-hem foot

A blind-hem foot has a vertical guide in the center to help when feeding the hem under the foot so that the stitches are placed in the correct position. The guide may be set or adjustable, depending on the brand.

Tip: Experiment with your fabric before sewing the hem to get the perfect stitch position and adjust the stitch length so that the stitches are farther apart for a less visible finish on the right side.

Overcasting foot

This foot has a prong or finger that sits over the cut edge of the fabric while you sew. The stitches are formed over this guide before sliding off and onto the raw edge without pulling and distorting it. The foot allows you to create a simple overlocker-style stitch, using your sewing machine and only two threads.

Tip: Trim the cut edge so that it is smooth before stitching; otherwise ragged edges may show through the stitches.

Buttonhole foot

These come in many different styles, but they all allow the stitches to be formed as two straight parallel rows of satin stitch with a narrow gap in between.

Tip: If you have an automatic buttonhole attachment on your machine, do not forget to lower the sensor, as this ensures that all the buttonholes you make are identical.

OTHER USEFUL FEET

Once you have mastered using the basic sewing machine feet, you may want to go on to using some of the many specialized feet available in order to take your sewing to the next level.

Concealed zipper foot

An invisible zipper cannot be inserted with a standard zipper foot, as it does not get close enough to the teeth. A concealed zipper foot has grooves in the underside that twist the teeth out of the way for stitching.

Tip: Sew the zipper tape with a standard zipper foot to hold it in place first and then use the concealed foot to stitch in the correct place. Insert the concealed zipper, then sew the seam afterward for a neat join at the base of the zipper.

Open-toe/clear-view foot

This foot is open in the center, giving an unhindered view of the stitching while you sew. It also has a channel in the underside to sit over bulky decorative stitching.

Tip: Use it for appliqué, machine smocking, attaching ribbon, and decorative sewing where you need to see the point of the needle as it enters the fabric.

Open-toe foot   Clear-view foot

Walking foot

This chunky attachment is screwed to the sewing machine with its lever placed over or around the needle bar. This allows the feet on the underside to raise and lower with the needle bar to "walk" over the fabric. This provides even feeding when sewing thick layers of cloth or stretch fabric. The angled bar slots into the walking foot and can be adjusted to suit the distance required between quilt lines. Once set in position, all rows of quilting will be equally spaced.

Tip: Use this foot when sewing a bold printed or striped fabric so that the pattern matches along the full length.

Free-motion foot

The free-motion or darning foot sits around the needle but does not apply pressure to the fabric below. It is long and slim, often with a spring, and is clipped to the ankle of the sewing machine. It circles the needle with a ring, horseshoe, or saucerlike guard. Use it with the feed dogs lowered for free-motion machine embroidery or quilting.

Tip: For machine embroidery, stabilize your fabric and place it in a hoop for easier handling.

Choosing your thread

All kinds of threads are available for sewing, and choosing the best one for each project is easy with a little help. Here we identify the various types, their characteristics, and the purposes to which they are best suited.

General-purpose thread (1)

Standard sewing thread is made from highly spun fibers. It may be polyester or mercerized cotton, or it may be produced as a polyester core covered in cotton to combine the best properties of both. It is ideal for general sewing projects such as making clothes, drapes, or soft toys.

Cotton thread (2)

One-hundred percent mercerized cotton thread is perfect for projects using cotton fabric. The completed garment can be boil-washed without fear of the thread deteriorating, and the thread and fabric will share the same properties. Cotton thread does not stretch like polyester does, so use it for decorative drawn thread work as well as for sewing functional seams.

Silk thread (3)

Use silk thread when sewing silk and woolen fabrics, since they are natural animal fibers and their properties are alike. It is ideal for machine sewing, although silk thread is also great for knot-free hand sewing, too. Silk thread is expensive, but for many projects polyester thread can be used as a cheaper alternative.

Machine embroidery thread (4)

These threads are normally made from rayon or polyester, as they have a high luster. The thread is very fine and can be used to fill blocks of color with machine embroidery. Use with a machine embroidery needle and specialty bobbin thread (see opposite). Variegated threads are available to give shading effects.

Metallic thread (5)

These threads are fine metallic filaments, or can be spun around a core thread for strength. They add a sparkle to your projects. Use with a metallic needle and bobbin thread to avoid shredding.

Topstitch thread (6)

Topstitch, button twist, or upholstery threads are thicker than standard sew-all thread. This makes the thread stronger and more prominent, so it is perfect for decorative topstitching, sewing on buttons securely, and when sewing upholstery fabrics. Sew with a topstitch needle with a large eye.

Basting thread (7)

Basting or tacking thread is loosely spun, with less strength than standard thread. This makes it ideal for temporary stitching, as it can be removed when it is no longer needed without damaging the fabric.

Invisible thread (8)

Invisible thread is a clear, fine filament that is soft and flexible enough to work like thread. Its lack of color allows it to blend with the fabric.

Hand embroidery floss/thread (9)

Skeins of stranded embroidery floss are wound into bundles. They are generally produced from cotton, silk, or rayon. Use them in their grouped strands or split them for finer stitching. Perlé cotton is twisted thread for hand embroidery. Hand embroidery thread is ideal for embroidery, embellishment, and couching.

Overlocker thread (10)

Overlockers use a lot of thread to sew and neaten seams, so threads are available on large reels or cones in lengths of 3,000–17,000 ft (1,000–5,000 m) for this purpose. The range of colors is normally limited, but adequate for overlocker seams.

Bobbin fill thread

A very fine white or black thread is available for winding onto your bobbin for machine embroidery. Since it is very thin, you can wind far more than usual onto the bobbin, reducing the number of refills you need to make. It does not affect the color you are using on the surface. This thread is also available on pre-wound bobbins.

 Try this

- Choose good-quality thread for every project and keep vintage reels, passed on to you by relatives and friends, as nostalgic mementos! Old thread will disintegrate or wear out long before the modern fabrics it is holding together, resulting in seams coming apart and pockets falling off.

- Choose appropriate needles (hand and machine) for your choice of thread. For example, a machine needle designed to sew metallic thread has an eye that will not shred it, and a crewel needle has a longer eye, making it easier to use with embroidery thread.

- Match the fiber content of the thread and fabric where you can. Use cotton with cotton, polyester with synthetic fabrics, and silk for silk and wool. If this is not possible, a good sew-all thread is a wise choice.

Special-purpose threads

Specialized threads are available for a variety of purposes. A few are mentioned here, but check out your local store or next large exhibition for new novelty and specialized threads coming on the market.

Smocking thread When used in the bobbin, this thread shrinks with the heat of the iron to give a crinkle effect to fabric.

Thread fuse thread Used in the bobbin and perfect for a facing. Once heated with an iron, the thread will melt and fuse with the layer of fabric below.

Glow-in-the-dark thread As the name suggests, when stitched, this thread is luminous in the dark and is great for embroidering novelty shapes and outlines.

Wash-away thread This is an ideal thread for basting to hold pieces in place while stitching.

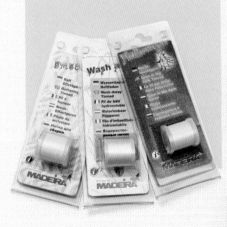

Dressmaking notions

"Notions" (also referred to as haberdashery) are items such as zippers, ribbons, tapes, and fastenings for finishing sewing projects. They are sometimes overlooked, but are essential.

If you are following a paper pattern, check the materials list on the back of the envelope. But if you are designing your own garment, consider what you will need and how much—for example, the number of buttons and their size, or the length of ribbon needed to decorate an edge. Select these when you are buying your fabric in order to get a good color match and to save having to make return trips to the store.

Zippers

Zippers are available in many forms and for all kinds of garments and projects (see pages 128–145).

Uses: There is a zipper for every purpose, from strong, blue in color, and metal-toothed for jeans to lightweight and open-ended for evening bodices.

Tip: Use the appropriate presser foot to make it easier to insert different zippers—for example, a concealed zipper foot or an adjustable zipper foot (see pages 22–23).

Buttons (1)

Buttons of all sizes, shapes, and styles can be sewn on to fasten and embellish garments (see pages 120–125).

Uses: Fasten garments and bags of all styles.

Tip: Choose buttons wisely and sew an appropriately sized buttonhole to fit the button.

Satin ribbon (2)

Ribbons come in a range of widths and are available in many colors to suit every purpose. Polyester ribbons have a high sheen and are fairly stiff, while those made from rayon are slightly softer.

Uses: Decorate collars, cuffs, and hems, or use narrow ribbons for hanging loops.

Tip: Sew in place by hand with tiny stitches, catching each edge, or use a sewing machine with a straight stitch or preprogrammed blanket-style stitch. Use a Microtex machine needle to avoid damaging the satin.

Petersham ribbon (3)

This stiff, closely woven tape is available as straight or curved and has a ridged edge. It looks like grosgrain ribbon but is more rigid and firm, and provides a stronger finish.

Uses: For waists and belts to create a strong, supportive band. Sew a length around the inside rim of the crown of a hat to help it keep its shape.

Tip: Some people prefer the curved Petersham to grosgrain ribbon because it gives a closer fit, since the waist band tilts toward the upper body.

Grosgrain ribbon (4)

This ribbed ribbon is stiff and strong, and available in a range of widths for a variety of uses. Novelty designs are popular, with hearts or flowers, but it comes in plain shades, too.

Uses: To protect the fabric on the inside edge of pants cuffs, or as a waist stay. Decorate edges on the outside of jackets or skirts.

Tip: Machine stitch on the edges or hand sew in place to hold it flat. Prepress grosgrain ribbon to shape it if it is to be used as a decorative finish on a curved edge.

Rickrack braid (5)

Decorative braid and rickrack may be added to embellish the surface of a garment. Many styles and designs are available to suit a whole range of projects.

Uses: Choose luxury braids to embellish jacket edges and cuffs. Rickrack is available in many colors for all kinds of projects.

Tip: Choose braid appropriately and hand sew in place with tiny, invisible stitches. Use silk thread and a small needle. Sew rickrack by machine with a good color-matching thread.

Cords (6)

Decorative and functional cords are available under different names for a variety of purposes. Piping cord (available in a range of diameters) can be covered with bias strips to insert into edges. Rattail is tubular with a satin finish, while mousetail is a slimmer version.

Uses: Covered piping defines an edge when sewn into a seam and adds a decorative detail to all sorts of projects. The satin finish of rattail and mousetail makes them suitable for embellishment for couching, although they can also be used under the surface for textured channel stitching.

Tip: Use a zipper or piping foot to stitch close to the cord.

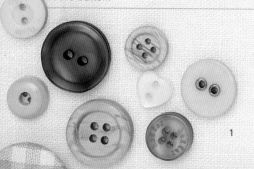

1

Heat-fusible adhesive (7)

This is a dry film of glue that melts when heated with an iron to stick two layers together. It comes as a ¾ in. (1.5 cm) strip on a roll, or as a sheet with a paper backing, for easier application. The backed variety may be bought in pieces or on a roll by the yard.

Uses: Use the strip adhesive for hemming pants and the paper-backed adhesive for appliqué.

Tip: For appliqué, cut a piece and iron it to the back of the additional fabric, then cut out a precise shape to achieve a clean edge.

Bias binding (8)

Bias binding is strips of fabric cut on the bias and folded ready for stitching. It comes in a good range of shades and also in pretty prints, stripes, and novelty versions.

Uses: Cover and neaten raw edges.

Tip: Sew bias binding with good color-matching thread. An adjustable binding foot is a useful tool for sewing on binding.

Twill tape (9)

This narrow tape with a diagonal grain is available in black or white to suit your purpose. Traditionally made from cotton, today it is sometimes made from polyester.

Uses: Stabilize edges and waists to prevent them from stretching.

Tip: Choose 100 percent cotton tape, as there is no give in this tape and it can be preshrunk before being sewn in.

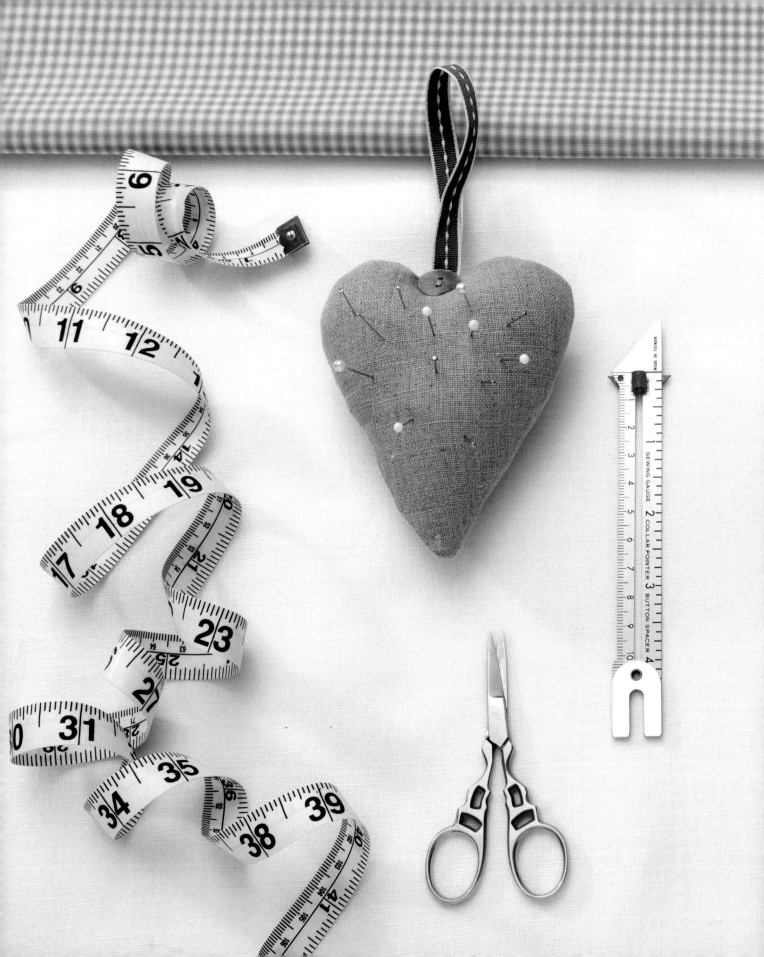

Prep

My school needlework teacher used to say: "To fail to prepare is to prepare to fail." Over the years, I have come to understand the truth of this. No matter how simple or complex a project you are working on, preparation will help you get a much better finished result. It helps to keep all of your sewing tools and equipment in one place. The French have a phrase for this: "mise en place," which means getting everything you need together. I like to write a list, a bit like a shopping list for a particular recipe that includes all of the "ingredients" for a project. This requires thinking in a focused way about what I want to create and achieve. A bit of planning in advance can save a lot of bother later.

Understanding fabrics

Fabrics are the raw material of sewing and often the starting point of a project. Seeing a beautiful array of fabrics in many sumptuous colors and prints in a store can make us feel like children in a candy store—but it can also be a bit confusing at times, too.

Choosing the right fabric for its softness and drape and using it to create a piece of clothing that fits you perfectly is the stuff creative dreams are made of. Visiting a fabric store is a sensory experience and we are often drawn to a particular fabric because of its handle and feel, as well as the pattern and color. If you look through your wardrobe at your favorite items of clothing, I expect the reason you like many of the garments is the choice of fabric. Whether you love that summer dress because of the cool, floaty fabric or those tailored wool pants because they seem to mold to you beautifully, each fabric has been chosen because of the qualities it possesses that make it ideal for that garment.

The language used to describe different fabrics is rather technical. However, it is worth getting to know. Fabrics are made from different fibers that are spun into yarns, which are then woven or knitted to create fabrics. The weave or method of knitting will also dictate the qualities of the fabrics. For example, a closely woven, lightweight wool crepe is completely different to a twill woven wool suiting, even though both use the same fiber.

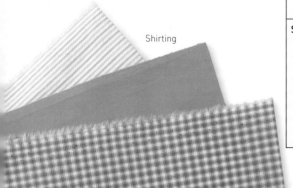
Shirting

Fiber	Source	Description	Properties
Natural fibers	Animal sources (protein), e.g. silk and wool	Wool is a hair and, like human hair, it is covered with small, overlapping scales. It has a crimp to it that allows air to circulate when bundled together.	Wool is soft and warm and is good at absorbing moisture. However, the scales covering the hair can move and contract, causing the wool to shrink. Careful handling is required, so hand washing is recommended.
Natural fibers	Plant sources (cellulose), e.g. linen and cotton	Smooth surface, but the fiber has a twist to it.	Strong and good at absorbing moisture, but can take a long time to dry. Can crease badly, but it can be washed and pressed at high temperatures.
Manmade	Reconstituted cellulose fibers, e.g. viscose (rayon), modal, and acetate	Smooth surface, making them soft to touch. They are often spun in a continuous length.	As it is derived from cellulose, it has similar properties to cotton and linen, but is not very strong when wet, so careful handling when washing is required. It has a lovely, soft drape.
Synthetic	Oil-based products, e.g. polyester, nylon, Lycra, and acrylic	These are spun as a continuous filament and look similar to glass rods. As they are so smooth, they will reflect light and look shiny.	Very strong, lightweight, and good at resisting abrasion. Not very good at absorbing moisture, although they do dry quickly.

Woven

Generally, medium-weight, woven fabrics are easy to handle and are the best choice for beginners. Stiff and bulky fabrics, or those that are fine with little body, are more difficult to sew with.

Denim

Structure: Plain, woven cotton.
Description: Originally designed for workwear, this blue cotton fabric is absorbent, strong, and hardwearing. It is available in medium and heavy weight, and is popular as a fashion fabric for casual wear.
Uses: Choose lightweight denim for shirts or dresses and heavier types for jeans, skirts, and casual jackets.
Tips: Use a strong jeans needle and lengthen the sewing machine stitch to 8 spi (3 mm). Plain and flat-fell seams work well and topstitching in a contrasting thread is a popular finish.

Cotton lawn

Structure: Cotton, plain weave.
Description: A smooth, fine, and lightweight fabric, sometimes plain and often printed.
Uses: Ideal for dresses, shirts, blouses, and lingerie. Can be used on the inside as an underlining to add body or depth to a fashion fabric.
Tips: Use long-bladed, sharp shears for a clean-cut edge and sew with a standard size 9 sewing-machine needle and a stitch length of 12–10 spi (2–2.5 mm). Plain and French seams work well and decorative stitching, with twin or wing needles, creates an attractive decorative finish.

Chiffon

Structure: Plain weave in silk or synthetic fiber.
Description: This transparent cloth is soft and sheer. It was traditionally made from silk but polyester is commonly used today.
Uses: Popular for skirts, blouses, and scarves, chiffon is often used in multiple layers or with a lining below.
Tips: Cut chiffon with long-bladed, sharp scissors and sew with a new standard size 9 sewing-machine needle to avoid snags. Shorten the stitch to 12 spi (2 mm) and use French seams for a tidy finish.

Shirting

Structure: Woven cotton, silk, linen, or polyester-and-cotton mix.
Description: A fine-weight cloth, generally with a smooth finish, either plain, printed, or with a woven stripe or check.
Uses: Shirts, blouses, and dresses.
Tips: Use a standard needle in a fine or medium size (9–11), depending on the weight of the cloth, with a medium stitch length of 10 spi (2.5 mm). Choose plain, flat-fell, and French seams for construction.

Calico

Structure: Closely woven cotton.
Description: This plain-finished, stable, unbleached cotton fabric is available in various weights.
Uses: Use this for test garments, or muslins, when developing a design to check the fit and style. Calico is also popular for craft projects and bag making.
Tips: Use a standard needle in a size to suit the weight of the cloth and choose a 10 spi (2.5 mm) stitch length. Use plain seams to join fabric pieces.

Linen

Structure: Plain-weave natural cloth.
Description: Linen has an obvious plain weave and a tendency to wrinkle unless treated.
Uses: Linen is a classic choice for jackets, pants, skirts, and suits, while lighter weights make good shirts and dresses.
Tips: Cut with sharp scissors to give a good, clean edge. Work quickly, since linen has a tendency to unravel. Consider neatening raw edges before construction. Sew with a standard needle and use a medium stitch length of 10 spi (2.5 mm). Choose plain and flat-fell seams.

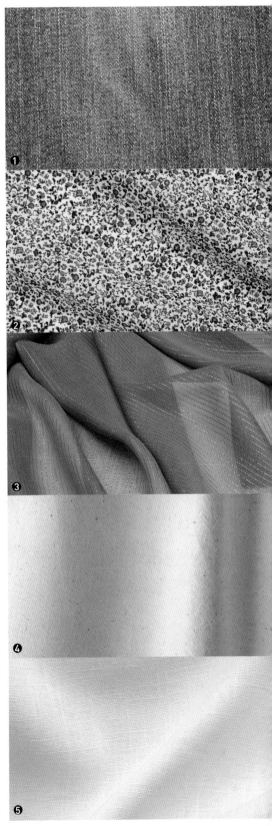

1 Denim 2 Cotton lawn 3 Chiffon 4 Calico 5 Linen

Silks

This natural fiber is made by unraveling and spinning the cocoon of the silkworm into silk threads, which are then woven into fabric.

Silk dupion

Structure: Plain-weave silk.

Description: This is a crisp fabric with an uneven texture because of the slubs in the threads it is woven from. It has a dull sheen.

Uses: Jackets, suits, dresses, and pants, generally for evening or occasion wear.

Tips: As it unravels badly, consider neatening the raw edges before construction. Use a standard size 11 sewing-machine needle and choose silk or polyester thread. Use plain seams to join panels.

Silk organza

Structure: Plain-weave silk.

Description: This transparent fabric is woven from highly spun threads, making it fine, strong, and crisp.

Uses: Use it for evening wear backed with lining. One hundred percent silk organza is a useful underlining, providing support without adding depth or weight to a fashion fabric.

Tips: Sew with a fine size 9 sewing-machine needle and use French or hairline seams for a delicate join. Sew with polyester or silk thread.

Silk satin

Structure: Silk woven into satin (polyester and acetate fibers are also popular).

Description: A satin fabric reflects light because of the many flat threads that lie on the surface, so it has a shiny finish.

Uses: The surface threads are easily damaged, so this makes it a delicate fabric that is more suited to special occasion and evening wear.

Tips: Use a new, sharp Microtex needle to prevent damaging the threads in the weave and sew with a 10 spi (2.5 mm) stitch length. Plain and French seams work well. Sew with silk or polyester thread.

Habotai

Structure: Plain-weave silk (polyester fiber may also be used).

Description: This fine and plain fabric is very soft and lightweight.

Uses: Use habotai silk for lingerie items and blouses. It is also ideal as a lining fabric for coats, jackets, and skirts.

Tips: Cut with long, sharp blades or use a rotary cutter with a self-healing mat (see page 60). Choose a fine size 9 Microtex needle and a small stitch length of 12 spi (2 mm) for seaming. French seams are a good choice. Change the needle frequently to avoid damage to the silk. Use silk or polyester thread.

1 Silk dupion 2 Silk organza 3 Silk satin

(Left to right): Accordion-pleated china silk, Habotai silk, silk organza

Wools and wool mixes

Wool fabrics vary enormously, depending on the breed from which the fibers come, whether they are used alone or mixed with other fibers, and how the fabric is constructed. Woolen fabric can be used for making pants, coats, or chunky knitted sweaters.

Worsted wool

Structure: Plain- or twill-weave wool.
Description: A worsted-wool yarn is produced from long, combed fibers that are highly twisted. It is smooth, strong, and fine.
Uses: Use worsted wool for suits, jackets, skirts, and pants.
Tips: Cut with sharp shears and sew with a standard size 11 needle with good-quality polyester thread. Use a medium stitch length of 10 spi (2.5 mm) and join panels with plain seams pressed open. Take care when pressing, using a pressing cloth to protect the surface and prevent a shine from appearing.

Wool crepe

Structure: Twisted weave.
Description: Crepe fabric can be made from wool but also silk, synthetic fibers, or a mix. Crepe has a pebbly surface and tends not to wrinkle. Although woven, the fabric may have a slight stretch to it.
Uses: Crepe is suitable for dresses, pants, and skirts, and works best for soft, draping styles.
Tips: Preshrink crepe before cutting out and sew with a standard size 11 needle with a 10 spi (2.5 mm) stitch length. Construct garments with plain seams pressed open or use an overlocker.

Bouclé

Structure: Woven or knitted with a textured yarn.
Description: Generally made from wool or a wool-and-synthetic mix of fibers, bouclé has a thick surface textured with curly, twisted loops.
Uses: Bouclé fabric is popular for coats, jackets, and cardigans.
Tips: Cut fabric pieces with sharp shears and sew with a size 12 stretch needle. Choose a longer stitch length of 10–8 spi (2.5–3 mm) and opt for a stretch stitch or narrow zigzag if the fabric is very stretchy.

Loose-weave tweed

Structure: Loosely woven yarns of wool, silk, or synthetic fibers, or a blend.
Description: Loosely woven tweed is generally made from thicker yarns for a luxurious look. Although woven, it may not be stable, and the yarns unravel easily from its cut edges.
Uses: Use any tweed fabric for jackets and coats.
Tips: Consider neatening the edges immediately after cutting and before sewing. Alternatively, cut a lightweight, fusible interfacing and back all pieces to reduce fraying and stabilize panels. Use a size 11 or 12 needle and a 10–8 spi (2.5–3 mm) stitch length. Finish garments with a lining or bind raw edges.

Tartan and checks

Structure: Twill-weave wool or wool-mix fibers.
Description: The pattern within the fabric is created by different-colored yarns woven in a sequence through the cloth. The weave may be tight or loose.
Uses: Tartan is more popular during some seasons than others, and is used for kilts, skirts, pants, jackets, and coats.
Tips: Take care when placing pattern pieces on fabric to account for matching at the seams. Sew with a standard size 11 or 12 needle and use a 10–8 spi (2.5–3 mm) stitch length. Fit a walking foot to the sewing machine to help feed the fabric evenly and make matching seams easier.

Wool coating

Structure: Woven wool or mixed fibers.
Description: A coating is a thick and warm cloth.
Uses: As the name implies, this fabric is used for coats and winter jackets.
Tips: The problems when sewing this cloth occur because of its thickness. When seaming, the upper layer tends to slide over the lower layer, so fit a walking foot to help encourage an even feed. Cut with long-bladed scissors and sew with a large size 14 machine needle. Extend the stitch length to 8 spi (3 mm) because this will work better with the thick fabric.

1 Wool crepe **2** Bouclé
3 Tweed **4** Tartan

Knitted

Knit fabrics are constructed with loops rather than woven warp and weft threads. The fibers used to make the threads/yarns for knit fabric may be natural wool, cotton, or synthetic, or various blends of these, creating a multitude of knit fabrics.

Cotton knit

Structure: Knit.

Description: Light- to medium-weight stretchy cotton. It is very absorbent and stretches as the fabric is pulled. When mixed with Spandex, the stretch-and-recovery properties are even better. The fabric may be dyed a solid color or, as an alternative, it can be surface-printed.

Uses: Most commonly used for T-shirts, but also for dresses, skirts, and underwear.

Tips: Use a stretch needle and choose a stretch stitch if one is available on the sewing machine. If not, set a zigzag to a standard length and narrow width so that the seam line will move if the fabric is pulled. An overlocker is a good tool to use for cotton knit fabric.

Slinky knit

Structure: Knitted viscose/rayon.

Description: Viscose/rayon is a heavy yarn that has a slinky handle. When knitted, it stretches and drapes beautifully.

Uses: As it is available in different weights, use this for dresses, skirts, cardigans, and unstructured jackets intended to drape.

Tips: Place the fabric on a work surface covered with a cotton sheet to prevent the fabric from moving or slipping when cutting. Fit a stretch needle and set to a stretch stitch when using a sewing machine. A walking foot helps to feed the fabric more evenly, too. Sew with an overlocker if one is available.

Sweatshirt fabric

Structure: Knit.

Description: Although more stable than many other knitted fabrics, cotton sweatshirting does stretch and pull. It has a knitted surface with a soft backing.

Uses: Sports clothing and leisure wear. Use this comfortable, warm cloth for loose-fitting pants, sweatshirts, and casual zip-up jackets.

Tips: Choose a stretch or ballpoint needle in a size 12 or 14 and sew with an overlocker or, if using a sewing machine, a stretch stitch and walking foot. Hem with a twin needle to imitate a manufactured stitch.

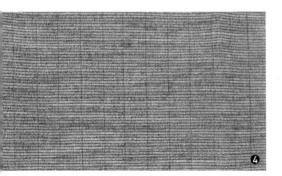

1 Cotton knit 2 Slinky knit
3 Sweatshirt fabric 4 Interfacing

Bonded

Some specially created materials are designed for the internal construction of clothing and are not visible on the outside. These fabrics are essential for producing a perfect finish.

Interfacing

Structure: Matted fibers.

Description: Produced from bonded fibers, this material does not fray or stretch. Interfacing is not intended to be seen, and is used as an internal layer to support collars, cuffs, and facings.

Uses: Use to stiffen collars, cuffs, and facings.

Tips: Choose a suitable weight for the fabric being used and opt for a lighter-weight interfacing if in doubt, as a "too-crisp" finish can sometimes result. Trim away from seam allowances to reduce bulk.

Special-occasion

Occasion wear makes use of the most luxurious and expensive fabrics. Fibers from all sources are constructed in a variety of ways to create special fabrics and garments.

Velvet

Structure: Woven (sometimes knitted) backing with dense pile on surface.

Description: Made from silk, cotton, viscose/rayon, or polyester fibers, velvet varies and this affects its handling. It is a thick material with a luxurious pile held in place by its backing. Velvets on a knitted base drape well.

Uses: Suitable for jackets, skirts, bodices, and special-occasion wear. Velvets that drape well are ideal for skirts and dresses.

Tips: Cut all pieces in the same direction to avoid differences in the way the light catches the pile. Iron with care, using a piece of the same velvet and very delicate pressure to avoid crushing the pile. Use a standard size 12 needle and an 8 spi (3 mm) stitch length. Use plain seams and finger press. If fitting a zipper, insert a concealed version so that there will be no topstitching.

Lace

Structure: Sewn on net, or a knitted or crochet construction. It may be stable or stretchy.

Description: Lace is a delicate, transparent fabric with an intricate pattern or design incorporated. It varies a great deal in quality and price, and is available as all-over lace on the roll or as edging in various widths.

Uses: Use edging lace for trimming skirts, dresses, blouses, and lingerie. All-over lace is perfect for wedding dresses and nightgowns.

Tips: Pin with long, large-headed pins and sew with a fine size 9 machine needle. Lap the seams to retain the design in the pattern and sew with a zigzag, then cut away the excess.

Imitation fabrics

The advent of these fabrics has allowed the look of animal fur and skin to be used without having to harm any animals in the process.

Faux fur

Structure: A knitted base with a dense pile.

Description: Faux fur imitates animal fur of all types and is dyed accordingly. The length of the dense pile and quality of the finish varies.

Uses: Generally, faux fur in fashion is used for coats, waistcoats, hats, and trims.

Tips: Cut through the backing fabric with needlework or embroidery scissors, then tease the pile fibers apart to avoid spreading the fur all over the room. Sew with a stretch needle and use a short, narrow zigzag stitch to sew the backing together when joining panels.

Faux suede

Structure: Knit.

Description: Most modern examples look very realistic, but are much easier to launder and keep clean than real suede.

Uses: Use faux suede for coats, jackets, pants, and bags.

Tips: Place all pattern pieces in the same direction for cutting. Use a Microtex needle to sew with a 10 spi (2.5 mm) straight stitch. Sew with a good-quality polyester thread. Flat-fell seams make a good finish.

1 Velvet **2,3** Lace **4** Faux fur **5** Faux suede

Choosing fabrics

Choosing the right fabric for your project can make or break the finished result. If the fabric is too lightweight, the garment will not hold its shape or structure; if it is too heavy or stiff, the garment will not hang properly. Take note of the suggested fabrics in the pattern as the designer will know which will work best. There are several points to consider when selecting the right fabric for your project.

WHAT IS THE GARMENT FOR?

Consider the occasion and what you will be doing while wearing that particular piece of clothing. Are you making an outfit for a wedding or something to wear to the gym? These projects will require very different fabrics that will need to perform different tasks.

Fiber

Think about the fiber content with regards to the purpose of the garment. A polyester satin fabric may have a beautiful pattern, but will be rather hot and uncomfortable worn next to the skin—a silk crêpe de Chine would be a better choice for that purpose. However, the polyester satin would work well as a jacket lining where it will slide over other clothing worn under the jacket.

Sheen

A satin fabric with a sheen will catch the light, but could also highlight a host of lumps and bumps. A more matte fabric will cover these and give a smooth overall look to the garment.

Drape

The stiffness of a fabric is described as "body." Fabrics with more body will prevent the fabric from draping as much as a fabric with less body. The best way to check this in a store is to unroll the fabric from the bolt and drape and hang it yourself to see the level of drape it has.

PLAIN OR PATTERN

Plain fabrics are easier to work with, but sometimes a pattern is what's called for. Be mindful of how the pattern works on the garment pieces. For example, if you have a large circular pattern, think carefully about where to place the front bodice pattern piece to avoid an embarrassing faux pas. Similarly, a small delicate pattern may get lost if used all over a garment—it might be better used as a contrast or for a collar.

Stripes and checks

When matched perfectly, stripes and checks look great, but wonky stripes do not. Take the time and effort to match stripes up. It will not always be possible to match up all the stripes across the garment, so focus on the ones that are most visible. Stripes can run horizontally across the body and vertically from the bodice down into the skirt.

• Mark on the bodice pattern pieces where you want the stripes to sit.

• Mark on the sleeve pattern where those lines fall on the sleeve head.

• Match up the lines on the pattern pieces with the stripes on the fabric.

Which way up?

Patterns can sometimes have a particular direction. Always check, even if you think it's an allover pattern, otherwise you may find the odd flower or bird that will be sitting on its head. Decide on the top of the pattern and mark it clearly so that you don't forget. I usually pin a note to the edge of the fabric to help.

Nap/Pile

Even when using plain fabrics, there are factors to bear in mind. Some fabrics, such as velvet or corduroy, have a pile or "nap," which need careful consideration. As the pile stands away from the base of the fabric, the light will catch it in various ways. It will also feel different stroked up or down. Decide which is the top and place your pattern pieces accordingly. It is usual to have the nap of a velvet fabric running down the body.

→ 1 Choosing a contrasting fabric can highlight the design details in a garment. The contrast here shows off the button stand and inside collar stand. 2 The structure of a wool tweed is needed to give a jacket its shape, but the lining should be of a much lighter-weight, soft fabric to slip easily over other clothes and not to add bulk. 3 Understanding how a fabric hangs will make all the difference to sewing a successful garment. The soft drape of the jersey shows off the cowl neck on this top.

Interfacing

Interfacing acts as a stabilizer and will support your fabric to help it keep its shape. It can also stiffen and change the feel of a fabric—for example, when used in a shirt collar. There are two basic types of interfacing: fusible and non-fusible (or sew-in). Fusible and non-fusible interfacing can both be made from two different materials: woven and nonwoven (or bonded).

FUSIBLE

Fusible interfacing has a layer of glue on one side that sticks to the fabric. The glue side will have a slight sheen or feel a little bit rougher. Always make sure the glue side is face down on the wrong side of the fabric. It is no fun trying to scrape glue off the plate of your iron. Fusible interfacing is very easy to use as, once it is attached to your fabric, you can use it all as one layer. It comes in different weights, from ultra soft and lightweight to heavy and stiff depending on the level of support and control you want to have.

NON-FUSIBLE (SEW-IN)

Non-fusible interfacing comes in as many varieties and has many of the same features as fusible interfacing, but without glue to adhere it to the fabric.

Therefore, you will need to baste the layers of fabric and interfacing together, usually within the seam allowances to keep them as one layer. Sew-in interfacing can be trickier to work with, as you are having to deal with multiple layers, but it can give a better finished result to the right side of the garment, as it should sit flat against the fabric.

WOVEN

Woven interfacing has a grain line and works just like a regular woven fabric, so it will keep the general feel of your fabric, just make it a bit thicker. It can be harder to find than bonded interfacing and doesn't come in the same range of weights and thicknesses, but it can adhere well to your fabric with no bubbles or creases.

NONWOVEN (BONDED)

Bonded interfacing has no grain line and is made from bonded fibers, like felt. It comes in a large range of weights and thicknesses, from ultrafine to crispy and even bulky. It is more widely available and popular than woven interfacing. Always read the manufacturer's instructions when attaching, as some need steam and some don't, but all bonded interfacing needs to be pressed rather than ironed onto your fabric.

Help!

My fusible interfacing is not adhering properly.

Occasionally fusible interfacing will not work correctly and leave small bubbles or creases where it doesn't adhere properly. To prevent this, press rather than iron the interfacing and leave it to cool completely before lifting if off the ironing board.

Attaching interfacing to the facing will ensure it holds its shape and supports the curve of the neckline.

Fabric preparation

Once you have the pattern cut out to the correct size, with any alterations made, you are ready to prepare the fabric to be cut.

Your pattern will tell you the type and amount of fabric needed for your garment. Now you need to check for flaws and preshrink it in preparation for cutting. Many factors influence how to prepare the fabric, such as fiber content, construction, and the type of outfit being made.

PREWASHING

Whatever the fabric you are using, it is always a good idea to prewash. This removes any residual "dressing" left in the fabric from the manufacturing process and anticipates any shrinkage that may occur in the initial wash. Launder the fabric according to the manufacturer's guidelines or, if you cannot obtain that information, just wash the fabric as you would the garment. Let the fabric air dry, as tumble drying can cause problems with further shrinkage and may even damage the fabric.
If using a fabric that will require dry cleaning after construction, use a steam iron and iron all over with plenty of steam to help preshrink the fabric.

CHECK FOR FLAWS

After the fabric has dried, press it all over and check for flaws. Although it is unlikely you will find anything, for peace of mind it is better to check before cutting out than to realize afterward that there is a big mark or flaw in a visible place. If you do find anything, you can try and work around it.

SQUARING UP

Sometimes, if a fabric has been doubled over and wound onto a bolt, it can get twisted and the grain lines distorted slightly so it sits in a diamond shape rather than a straight rectangle. To counteract this, pull the fabric along the opposite diagonal to make it square again. Press the fabric and let it lie flat to cool.

RIGHT SIDE? WRONG SIDE?

With a plain or textured fabric it can be difficult to tell the right side from the wrong side, because they can look very similar. Often there are small pin-prick marks along the selvage of the fabric (this is where the fabric was supported during processing on tentering hooks). If you run your fingers over the marks, one side should feel rough and the other should feel smooth—the rough side is the right side.

Useful fabric terms

Selvage This is the narrow, heavier band that runs down both sides of a length of fabric. It is where the weft (filling) threads have wrapped around the edge of the warp (lengthwise) threads and returned to be woven in the opposite direction.

Warp These are the lengthwise threads that are placed on the loom first to form the basis of the fabric.

Weft These are the filling threads that weave up and down through the warp threads to create the cloth.

Grain The grain of a fabric follows the length and is parallel to the selvage edges. When placing pattern pieces on fabric, the grain arrows must lie parallel to the selvage for the garment to hang properly.

Bias The true bias or true cross lies at 45 degrees to the warp and weft. The fabric is unstable when pulled in this direction, as it does not follow the grain. However, this can be an advantage if a draping effect is required, because clothes hang softly when cut this way. Bias binding is cut on the bias to prevent crinkles and unsightly tucks when covering a shaped edge.

 ## Try this

To cut a length of fabric across the grain and achieve a perfectly straight line, pull out one thread from the weft, i.e. the threads across the length and not parallel to the selvage. As you pull out a single thread, the fabric will crinkle and, if it pulls free without breaking, a line will be obvious through the fabric. Cut along this line.

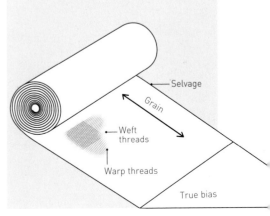

Selvage

Grain

Weft threads

Warp threads

True bias

Pattern envelope information

You will find the essential information you need on the outside of the pattern envelope (before opening it up and fighting with the tissue paper that never seems to go back in the envelope quite the same way again!). The pattern information includes advice on the type and quantity of fabric to choose, and on any other extras you need to buy to complete the piece of clothing illustrated, as well as how to choose the correct size.

PATTERN ENVELOPE FRONT

The front of the pattern envelope displays the initial vital information to help you select the right pattern for your shape and size.

Pattern number (1)

This identifies each pattern, making it easy to order your selection.

Photograph or illustration (2 and 3)

The front of the pattern envelope usually shows a photograph or sketch of each item of clothing, complete with variations. This might be a skirt in two or three lengths, or a shirt with a choice of collar styles, but all views will be shown, usually from the front. A photograph gives a more realistic idea of how the finished garment will look, while an illustration may use a certain amount of artistic licence by elongating the model. Always remember your own shape when choosing a pattern and do not be fooled by the elegant model in the illustration, whether a photograph or a sketch.

Size (4)

The size or sizes included in your envelope are stated on the front, and a chart is often printed on the flap of the envelope, though sometimes this information is contained inside the envelope. Generally, there will be a range of at least three sizes offered by the pattern, but some multisize patterns may include 10 or 12 options. Make sure to buy the pattern in the size range that best covers your measurements.

Sizes (4) shown in more detail on back of pattern

Pattern number (1)

Photograph (2)

Illustration (3)

Sizes (4)

PATTERN ENVELOPE BACK

On the back of the pattern envelope you will find detailed information about your pattern.

Silhouette key (5)

Some companies suggest the figure types a garment style is suitable for by using a very simple key of triangles and rectangles. This supports the knowledge you have of your own figure (see pages 46–47) and helps with pattern selection.

Description (6)

A short written description of each item of clothing is given, with details such as how it should fit, whether a lining is included, and information about fastenings. This, in addition to the outline view and main illustration, will give a complete vision of the finished garments.

Notions/Haberdashery (7)

This is where the extra requirements needed to complete each garment are included—for example, the length and type of zipper, or the number and size of buttons required. Lining and underlining requirements are also listed.

Fabric (8)

Information about suitable fabrics is always included to help you to choose appropriately. This will suggest the weight or stretch required for a good fit. You may already have a fabric in mind and this will confirm its suitability, or make you aware of other aspects of the design you had not considered.

Diagrams showing garment detail (9)

The front and back views of each item included in the pattern envelope are illustrated, showing seam and dart positions and fastenings. This adds to the visual information given in the photograph or sketch on the envelope front.

Fabric quantity guide (10)

As well as offering suggestions for choosing suitable fabric, charts are also included to show how much you need to buy for each view and size. Since fabric can be bought in a range of widths, following this chart will help you avoid buying too little or too much material.

Garment measurement details (11)

Measurements of the completed garments are included to help you to visualize how the finished item will look. For example, the skirt length, or the hem circumference on a pair of pants. These details are not always evident from the outline diagrams or illustrations, and this allows you to choose or reject a particular pattern, or be aware that alterations will be required to achieve the look you want.

The pattern envelope
The back of the envelope carries a lot of essential information, including how to calculate the amount of fabric you will need. This one has dual languages.

Labels pointing to the envelope:
- Silhouette key (5)
- Description (6)
- Notions/haberdashery (7)
- Fabric (8)
- Diagrams showing garment detail (9)
- Fabric quantity guide (10)
- Garment measurement details (11)

INSIDE THE PATTERN ENVELOPE Inside the pattern envelope, you will find information pages to guide you through the construction of your new garment. Sheets of tissue paper with the pattern pieces printed on one side are included and will need to be prepared before you use them.

Downloadable patterns

There are more and more independent pattern companies who provide downloadable patterns as well as printed versions. Downloadable patterns can be printed off at home and used as a master copy so you can trace off the specific size you need.

PATTERN INSTRUCTIONS

Having chosen suitable fabric and notions, the next step is to read the information pages to gain an overview of the steps to creating your new garment. It is a good idea to check over all the stages of construction before cutting into your fabric. The instructions show how to lay out the pattern pieces and cut out the fabric both economically and to give the best finish. After this, step-by-step instructions advise on the order of construction and the techniques involved in combining the fabric pieces. When you are satisfied with the information gleaned from the pattern, it is time to get started.

Line drawings (1)
Line drawings show details of the finished items included in the pattern with a number or letter to indicate the view you plan to follow. The pattern pieces may look similar to each other, so this helps you to differentiate between them; for example, a knee-length or a calf-length skirt.

Pattern pieces (2)
All the pattern pieces are listed or shown as small-scale diagrams and are numbered to make it easy to identify them when cutting and selecting the tissue pieces.

Measurement chart (3)
This is often included on the instruction sheet, but may be printed on the tissue itself. It helps to identify the correct size you need to cut out. (See pages 48–49 for advice on selecting the most appropriate size.) Some indicate how and where to take your body measurements.

Fabric cutting layouts (4)
Various layout options are given as a guide to how to best fit the pattern pieces on the fabric, depending on the width of the cloth and the view you've chosen. This may also include interfacing, underlining, and lining.

Information key (5)
A key is also included to make sense of the layout guide, indicating the right and wrong sides of the fabric and whether lining or interfacing have to be cut out, too.

Step-by-step guide (6)
Brief instructions, along with diagrams, provide the information you need to make each step clear and comprehensive. Some basic sewing knowledge is required, but these instructions are all that is needed to construct the garment, provided they are followed carefully and in order.

Different pattern manufacturers display information in slightly different formats.

Step-by-step guide (6)

Line drawings (1)

Measurement chart (3)

Fabric cutting layouts (4)

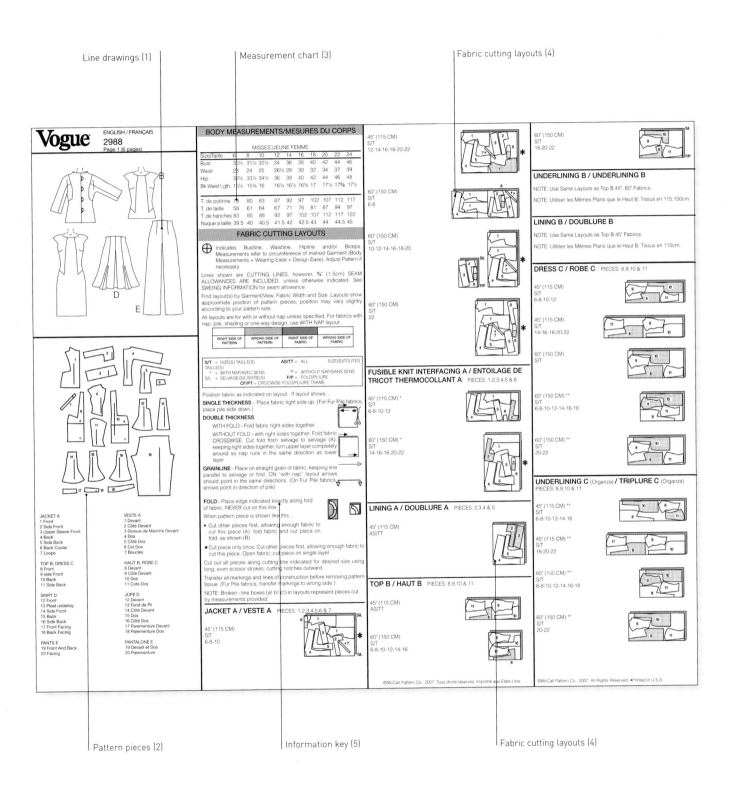

Pattern pieces (2)

Information key (5)

Fabric cutting layouts (4)

Understanding pattern symbols

The symbols printed on the pattern pieces may seem like an elaborate code, but this shorthand is easy to follow when you know how to decipher the shapes and marks.

WHAT IT ALL MEANS

Commercial pattern companies tend to use the same symbols, and so it should only take a short time to learn what the information means and how to use it. Once you can recognize the message given by each printed shape or mark and how to use it, you can sew with any pattern easily. Some of these symbols help in laying out the pattern on the fabric, while others need to be transferred to the fabric to accurately match pieces later in the construction.

Pattern number or name (1)

Each pattern piece shows the company that produced it and includes a number or name identifying it from all other patterns.

Part number and description (2)

Each piece will be named and have a number indicating its part in the finished garment; for example, front, collar, sleeve, pocket, etc.

Number of pieces (3)

The pattern will state how many pieces you should cut out in fabric, lining, and/or interfacing.

Seam allowance (4)

This is the name given to the border added to the edge of a pattern, between the cutting line and the sewing line so that the fabric pieces can be sewn together and the edges folded and finished.

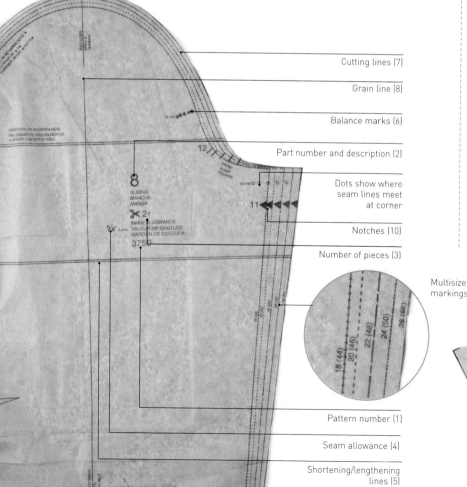

Cutting lines (7)

Grain line (8)

Balance marks (6)

Part number and description (2)

Dots show where seam lines meet at corner

Notches (10)

Number of pieces (3)

Multisize markings

Pattern number (1)

Seam allowance (4)

Shortening/lengthening lines (5)

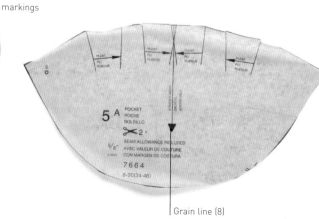

Grain line (8)

Shortening/lengthening lines (5)

A double line drawn horizontally through a pattern piece shows where it is best to shorten or lengthen a garment to achieve an appropriate length.

Balance marks (6)

Dots and spots printed on a paper pattern are important in helping to place the fabric panels together. These are often used for marking dart or tuck positions and should be transferred with tailor's tacks (see page 62).

Cutting lines (7)

Traditionally, patterns were produced for individual sizes and the cutting line was indicated with a solid line and the sewing line by a dotted line. On most patterns today, where several size options are included, a range of lines is used to identify different sizes and the sewing line is assumed to be a seam allowance width inside this. Work out which line is used for your size (dots, dashes, solid, etc.), then cut along these lines for each pattern piece.

Grain line (8)

This is a line with an arrow at each end; it tells you where to place the pattern piece on the fabric. Unless the pattern specifically tells you otherwise, the grain line will always run parallel to the selvage. This will ensure that the garment hangs correctly and doesn't twist or warp when it is worn.

Fold arrows (9)

A line with arrows that point in to the edge of the pattern piece indicates that the pattern piece should be placed on the fold of the fabric. The pattern should be placed exactly onto the edge of the fold to ensure no extra fabric is included through the middle of that pattern piece.

Notches (10)

These marks vary between pattern manufacturers (they can be triangles or T-shapes), but they all show how to line up the fabric pieces so that the garment fits together correctly. This ensures that panels are put together correctly and longer, shaped seams can be eased together in the right place. Similarly, when sewing a sleeve into an armhole, single (front) and double (back) notches are used so that the arms are inserted in the correct armholes.

Button placement (11)

This is shown with a circle with a cross in it.

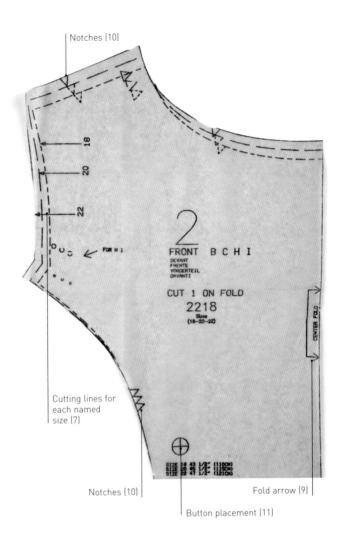

Notches (10)

Cutting lines for each named size (7)

Notches (10)

Fold arrow (9)

Button placement (11)

Using notches

To mark the notches, you can either cut around them or you can make a small snip into the seam allowance, which is quicker and just as effective.

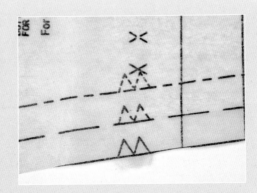

Matching up notches

Make sure to link up double notches with the corresponding double notch; likewise with single notches.

Measuring

The beauty of creating your own clothes is that you can make them to fit your individual figure and shape. Although commercial pattern companies, like clothing manufacturers, work on averages when creating their size ranges, the clothes you create from dressmaking patterns can be altered to give a much better fit before making them up in your chosen fabrics.

GENERAL MEASURING RULES

When using a standard pattern, you must have accurate body measurements so that you can choose the size closest to your own silhouette. Follow the rules below for easy and precise measuring:

- Get a friend to help you take your measurements. It is hard to reach certain areas and to make sure the tape measure is level where you cannot see it. This also makes the process more enjoyable and less of a chore.

- Use a full-length mirror to check that you are placing the tape measure in the correct places and between the right points. Even if you have a friend to help, a mirror is helpful for you both.

- Wear well-fitting undergarments when taking measurements and do not take your measurements over clothing. You need to have complete access to every limb and body part to find out its length and circumference.

- Stand tall, with your feet together, and do not breathe in. You need to have truthful figures to work from.

- Measure accurately, making sure the tape is flat and starts and finishes at the proper points. Use the fitting guide opposite to help you to know how to take each measurement.

- Place the tape firmly (but not too tightly) around the body and do not leave any slack. Ease is built into the pattern for comfort and style, so there is no need to add any more.

BODY LANDMARKS

Horizontal:

Bust (1) Hold the tape level and measure the fullest part of the bust. A well-fitting bra is essential in achieving this.

Waist (2) Tie a length of soft elastic lightly around your middle and it will automatically fall into the waist position. Measure at this point.

Hip (3) This is the fullest part of the bottom, and its position varies from one person to another.

Chest (4) Measure across the center front, just above the bust, from armhole to armhole, approximately 3 in. (7.5 cm) below the neck level.

Back width (5) Measure across the center back between the armholes, approximately 6 in. (15 cm) below the prominent neck bone.

Shoulder (6) Take this measurement from the neck edge to the shoulder bone.

Upper arm (7) Place the tape measure around the bicep, while the arm is slightly bent, with your hand on your waist or hip.

Wrist (8) Measure the wrist with a small amount of ease.

Vertical:

Height (9) Mark your height against a wall, without shoes and with your feet together, with your heels to the wall.

Nape to waist (10) Measure from the prominent bone in your neck to the waist, using the elastic method to highlight your waist position.

Shoulder to front waist (11) Measure from the shoulder, over the bust point, to the waist.

Arm length (12) With your hand on your hip, measure from the shoulder bone to the wrist, following the bend of the elbow.

Waist to hip (13) Measure from waist level to the hip. This is often a standard measurement, but knowing how you compare to the standard is important for making appropriate alterations.

Waist to floor (14) Measure from waist level to the floor, following the contour of the hip.

Waist to knee (15) Measure from waist level to mid-knee.

Size charts and measurements

Selecting the right size for your body measurements is vital to achieving a good fit.

PHOTOCOPY THIS

Write all your measurements down and remember to re-measure if your body changes shape over time.

Measurement chart		
Landmark	Standard measurements	Personal measurements
1 Bust		
2 Waist		
3 Hip		
4 Chest		
5 Back width		
6 Shoulder		
7 Upper arm		
8 Wrist		
9 Height		
10 Nape to waist		
11 Shoulder to front waist		
12 Arm length		
13 Waist to hip		
14 Waist to floor		
15 Waist to knee		
16 Crotch depth		

MEASURE ACCURATELY

Stand in front of a full-length mirror while you, or a friend, take your body measurements. Keep the tape measure parallel to the floor for horizontal measurements and make sure the tape is flat with no twists. Keep the tape measure snug but not tight, and remember to breathe normally.

RECORD YOUR MEASUREMENTS

Photocopy the chart provided here and write down all your measurements in the right-hand column. Use the diagrams on pages 46–47 to help you know where to take your body measurements. Compare your measurements with those given by the pattern company. These can be found on the outside of the envelope, but they are sometimes printed on the tissue paper inside. Decide the size you are closest to and write those measurements down in

Multisize patterns

Patterns normally offer a choice of sizes, making it easier to create a well-fitting garment for a variety of figures. This may be three or four sizes, although some multi-patterns offer a much larger range.

The advantage of such a large size range is that it makes it possible to buy just one pattern and to choose the cutting lines to achieve a good fit. Since most of us are of a nonstandard size, we can use the pattern lines to create an individual fit from a commercial paper pattern.

the central column. Highlight any anomalies (for example, bust measurement or back length) and be aware of these when cutting out and adapting your paper pattern.

MEASURE THE PATTERN PIECES

Check your measurements against the actual pattern before deciding which size to cut out. To do this, select the relevant pattern pieces and measure the actual size of the pattern without seam allowances and darts. Ease will be included, so bear this in mind and compare pattern size with your measurement.

CUT OUT THE PAPER PATTERN

Make a decision about the size that best suits you and cut out the tissue paper. If you need to adapt the pattern, do this now (see pages 64–67).

As a general rule, choose skirts and pants using your hip measurement, and tops and jackets with your bust measurement in mind. However, this is not always the case and it is important to have a feeling for your general build. For example, if you have a small frame yet a large bust, using this measurement will result in a garment that may fit at the bust but will be too big elsewhere. Here, use the measurements based on your shoulders, back, and chest, and make a bust enlargement to the pattern.

Measure the pattern pieces

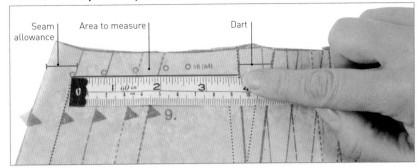

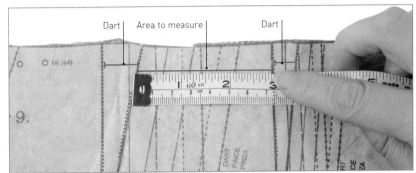

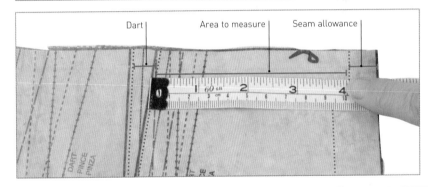

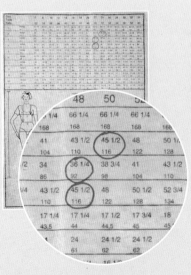

1 Mark your own measurements onto the size chart and take note of where they lie in relation to the standard measurements. Make a decision on the size or sizes required. If one of the measurements appears as an anomaly, the pattern will need to be adjusted separately in this area.

2 Find the relevant pattern pieces and lay them out flat, noting the cutting line key for the size or sizes needed (see pages 44–45).

3 Go over the cutting lines required with a colored pen or pencil and draw new lines to join or merge between sizes, creating a smooth line. Where seams join, make sure the lines on both pattern pieces follow the same angle. A French curve is a useful tool for this task (see page 14). When the lines are completed, cut out the pattern pieces and continue with the construction.

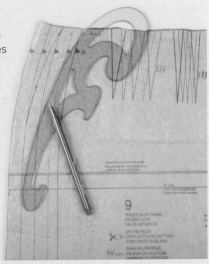

Making and fitting a muslin

Once you have measured accurately, but before you cut into your expensive fabric, you may decide to make a muslin. A muslin is a fabric prototype—an initial shell of the pattern made in an inexpensive fabric such as calico. It is the best way to test the fit of your pattern.

However, if your pattern is pretty simple you may not need to go to this extra effort. Sometimes just adding extra seam allowances can be enough to adjust the fit as you try the garment on during the sewing process.

PREPARATION

Fold the calico in half with the grain. Place the pattern pieces on the calico parallel to the grain line, and trace around them with a pencil. Mark on the center front (CF) and center back (CB), and draw in the bust lines, waistlines, the biceps line, and the elbow line. Mark in the hip line on a skirt and all the grain lines. It is important to mark these out on the calico so that, once you have made up the garment, you can see if the lines are balanced and in alignment with the body.

SEWING YOUR MUSLIN TOGETHER

Sew your muslin together, beginning with the darts while the pieces are flat. Press the front darts toward the side seam. Next, sew the front and back bodice shoulder seams and side seams together and press them open. Sew up the underarms of both sleeves and then set the sleeves into the finished armholes (see pages 148–149). Do not press the sleeve caps or you will flatten out the ease. For a skirt, stitch the darts first before sewing up the side seams.

METHODICAL WORKING

When you are pattern cutting, it is good practice to work in a methodical manner. Create a history of how your pattern was drafted and all the stages that this involves. When a mistake becomes apparent, it is then easier to retrace your steps and identify where the mistake happened. Many mistakes are made by sewing pieces together the wrong way up. Working in a step-by-step way helps to keep mistakes and inaccuracies to a minimum. Never be tempted to ignore a problem. Chopping pieces off your patterns or muslins will usually show up on the finished article. So sorting out problems at the paper pattern stage will save valuable time and money later on.

TRY ON YOUR MUSLIN

Before trying on your muslin for the first time, tie some elastic around your waist—this will mark the natural waistline—and mark the fullest part of the bust and low hip on your

Tips for working methodically

Working methodically allows you more scope to be creative once you have learned the basic principles.

- Label everything thoroughly, with the name and date of the pattern piece, i.e. Left Skirt Front (cut 1), Cuff (cut 4), Cut on Fold, and so on. Mark on the CB and CF lines, grain lines, balance lines, notches, and size of seam allowance. This will help to avoid confusion at every stage.

- Trace off the pattern pieces at every stage of pattern manipulation, and keep and label the stages.

- Always write on your pieces the right way up and on the correct side—if necessary mark "Right Side Up" (RSU) on pieces that can't be turned over.

- Notches are vital for matching up pattern pieces, for checking them at the pattern stage, and for sewing up—don't forget to put them on, as it will save you a great deal of time later (see page 45).

- Cut one pattern piece at a time, and check all the pattern pieces to ensure that they fit together where necessary.

- Mark on all the darts and details on your fabric pieces with tailor's tacks or chalk (see page 62).

- When sewing your muslin together, always sew to the seam allowances. If you are inaccurate by even a fraction of an inch, the size of your muslin will be altered considerably.

- Any alterations that you make on your muslin should be copied to your pattern immediately, before you forget what or where they were. Don't forget to add seam allowances back on where you have chopped parts off your pattern.

Plumb line

To find the true CF, make a plumb line by tying a string loosely around your neck. Thread another length of string loosely through it and tie a slightly weighted object on the end. Arrange the plumb line at the CF neck and let it hang down. Mark the exact CF line with sticky tape on your undergarments or leotard, and repeat the process for the CB.

undergarments or a leotard with sticky tape to check that these points on your body line up with the relevant points on your muslin.

WHAT IS BALANCE IN A GARMENT?

Perfect balance is when a garment's CF, CB, waistline, and hip line are aligned with the corresponding points on the body. It is important to balance your muslin correctly, because all other garments will be produced from this base. Getting this right will remove the need to correct all subsequent garments that you produce using this pattern.

Using a dress form
If you have invested in a dress form, you can fit your muslin to a dress form padded out to your own personal measurements.

ASSESSING THE FIT OF YOUR MUSLIN

When you try on your muslin, stand back and look at your garment in a long mirror. Assess the fit and note the position of the balance lines on the muslin. Check that the CF, CB, waist, bust, and hip lines align to your body. It is important to stand straight and look forward. Ask someone to help you with this stage, as it can be difficult, particularly when you are trying to see the back. Looking down or twisting will render the assessment of fit inaccurate.

Be aware of how the garment feels on the body—the bodice should be fitted, but not tight. Note any excess loose fabric or pulling across the garment. The armhole must not feel restricted, and you should be able to move your arm freely. Remember to look at the side seams and check that they are on your sides and not drifting forward or backward.

Taking your time to properly assess and alter the muslin at this stage will be worthwhile. A perfectly fitted muslin will ensure that the designs you produce subsequently will fit beautifully.

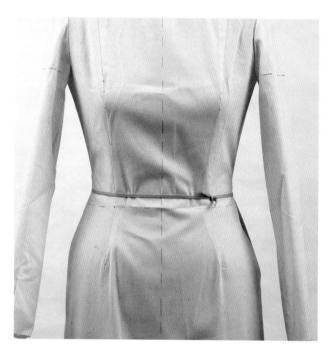

1 Tie a cord or length of elastic around your natural waist. Compare the tied line to the waistline marked on the muslin. If, as shown here, the two lines are not the same, the waistline will need to be adjusted on the pattern.

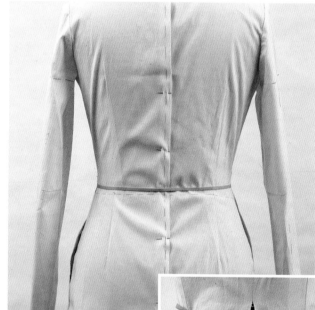

2 Here, two alterations are needed. The bodice is too long and the waist is too small. To correct this, measure the difference between the elastic and the pencil line; this will give you the amount to shorten the bodice pattern by. The tightness at the waist is best adjusted by opening the side seams. Measure the amount of extra room required and add it to the pattern.

FITTING THE SLEEVE

You can assess the sleeve fit when it is on the stand or on the body. The center grain running down the sleeve should line up slightly in front of the skirt or pants side seam. Look at the sleeve on the arm to see that the wrist is central within the sleeve hem, and check that the sleeve is not dragging up against the arm at the front or back. If dragging is present, take the sleeve out and readjust the sleeve cap by moving it either forward or backward around the armhole. This may be only a very slight adjustment, no more than ¼ in. (6 mm).

Incorrect sleeve alignment
This alignment would cause the sleeve to drift toward the back.

Correct sleeve alignment
The central sleeve grain should start ⅜ in. (1 cm) behind the bodice shoulder line. The biceps line should be horizontal and the central grain should continue down slightly in front of the garment side seam.

Help!

My muslin is too big.

Pinch out any obvious excess fabric through the seams and darts of your muslin, making sure that the balance lines remain straight. Mark the adjustments with a pencil, and transfer them to your pattern.

My muslin is too small.

Unpick the restricted area, releasing the tension. Measure the gap that is created, and add in the amounts needed where necessary.

My muslin needs major adjustments.

You will need to permanently alter your muslin if any adjustments are major, and perhaps even make another. Always ensure you make the corresponding adjustments to your pattern. The muslin is an important part of making your own patterns, and often several are needed before the fit is completely right.

Laying out the paper pattern

Once you have your pattern altered and ready to make up, the next job is working out how to best lay out and cut the pattern pieces. Luckily, the pattern designer will have done this for you, so all you need to do is follow the diagram for the layplans included in your pattern instructions.

What pattern pieces do you need?

Often a pattern comes with different options or "views" that might involve different sleeves or necklines. The pattern information will let you know which pieces you will need to make up that specific version of the pattern. There will usually be a pattern inventory listing all the pattern pieces by name and number. Use this to check the pieces that you need and tick them off as you collect them together.

One of the wonderful things about making your own clothes is that you can tweak things to get what you actually want to wear. So you may wish to combine elements from the different "views" of a pattern to create the garment you really want—taking the neckline from one but the sleeves from another, for example. It is important to know which pattern pieces correspond to which view so you can make these decisions.

Different options

A Dress front
B Dress back
C Sleeve version 1
D Sleeve version 2
E Sleeve version 3
F Pocket
G Neck binding
H Sleeve binding version 1
I Sleeve binding version 3
J Pocket binding

Pattern inventory

How to follow a layplan

A layplan is basically a map of how to lay out the fabric and pattern pieces in the least wasteful and most practical way. There are several points to consider before putting blade to fabric and it is better to check twice and cut once when it comes to laying and marking out your pattern.

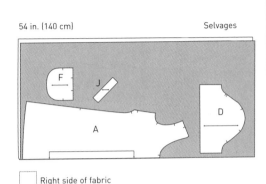

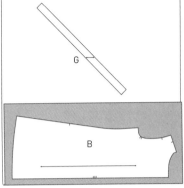

☐ Right side of fabric

▨ Wrong side of fabric

DIFFERENT WIDTH FABRICS

Most dressmaking fabrics will come in either a narrower width, 45 in. (114 cm) or a wider width, either 54 in. (140 cm) or 60 in. (150 cm). This often means that different layplans will be required, as sometimes less fabric is needed for a wider width fabric. Also, as garment sizes increase, more fabric may be required to make up larger sizes, so an additional layplan may be required to show this.

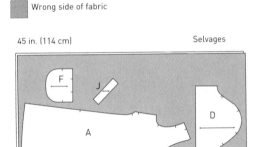

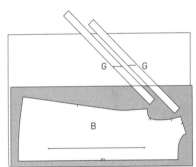

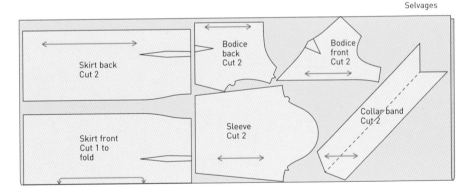

WITH OR WITHOUT NAP

A fabric with a "nap" can either have a one-way pattern on it or a pile to it like velvet or corduroy, which means that the pattern pieces should all be laid out in the same direction. Sometimes this can mean you need to allow for extra fabric, but it is worth following as you could easily end up with a beautiful garment in which one pattern piece has motifs or the pile of the fabric placed upside down, creating a shadow on the incorrect pattern piece.

Fabric with a pile or nap
If a fabric has a pile or a one-way pattern, all of the pieces must be laid in the same direction; otherwise, some panels may appear different when the garment is finished.

Plain fabric
On plain fabric with no pile, nap, or pattern direction, pieces can be dovetailed to make best use of the fabric, provided that the grain arrows are followed.

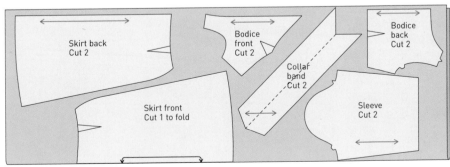

HOW TO FOLD THE FABRIC

In domestic sewing, the fabric is usually cut in a double layer. This saves time and requires fewer pattern pieces, as the majority of garments are symmetrical and one pattern piece can be used to cut both left and right sides of the garment. Usually the fabric is folded in half along the length, bringing the two selvages together.

For larger pattern pieces, the fabric is often folded across its width—when cutting a circular skirt, for example.

Sometimes the pattern calls for both the front and back pieces to be cut on the fold. This can mean that both selvages should be folded in to meet in the middle, creating two fold lines.

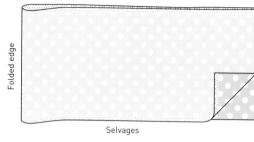

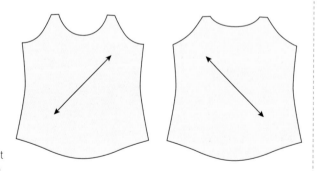

FOLLOWING THE GRAIN LINE

1 The grain line on the pattern shows you how to place the pattern pieces on the fabric. Grain lines always run parallel to the selvage. To check they are parallel, first place the pattern piece on the fabric.

2 Measure from one end of the grain line to the selvage, then measure from the other end of the grain line to the selvage. When both measurements are equal, the pattern is on the straight grain. It is very important to follow the grain lines to make sure that the garment hangs straight and true and will not twist and warp when worn.

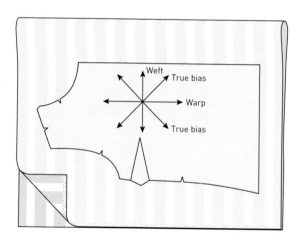

RIGHT OR WRONG SIDE UP?

This is a question that comes up frequently in our workshops: Should you cut the fabric with the right side up or the wrong side up? There are benefits to both. With the right side up, you can see the pattern for better pattern placement. But with the wrong side up, you can transfer the pattern marking directly on to the wrong side of the fabric. So it really comes down to your own personal preference.

CUTTING ON THE BIAS

When cutting on the bias grain of the fabric, the fabric should be laid out in a single layer and a whole pattern piece used to cut and mark the fabric. If the fabric is folded, the bias grain will run in different directions on the two halves of the pattern.

Remember to flip the pattern over once it has been cut to make sure that you get a "mirror pair" of pattern pieces and not two singles.

Working with patterned fabrics

Having a pattern that runs smoothly both down and around the body can lift your sewing to a new level of professionalism. It shows that care and consideration have been taken in the making of that garment, and it isn't difficult to do—it just takes a little more thought and preparation. Having said that, it is not possible to pattern match throughout the whole garment, as seams are angled and pattern pieces can be an odd shape. The main lines to consider are the true vertical and horizontal lines through the garment.

PATTERN REPEAT

One of the first things to consider is the size of the pattern repeat—that is, the distance from the start of the pattern to where it repeats itself. For example, in a multicolored stripe, you might measure from the top of one color of stripe to where that color features again, while in a floral pattern you would measure from one focal point of the pattern to where it next occurs. The measurement is usually taken along the selvage, as it is easier to see the straight line between pattern repeats here.

The repeat can vary in size from 1–1½ in. (3 or 4 cm) up to 12 or 16 in. (30 or 40 cm) if the pattern is a large floral design.

IS THE PATTERN EVEN OR UNEVEN?

Also check to see if the pattern is even or uneven. A striped or checked fabric can have evenly symmetrical stripes or checks, but can also have a design that is not symmetrical.

You can do the right-angle check to test this:
Fold the fabric in half widthwise, and then fold back the top corner so that it sits at right angles to the edge of the selvage. Have a look at the pattern. If it's even, the pattern should match up along the folded edge of the top layer. If it's uneven, the pattern will be different and won't line up.

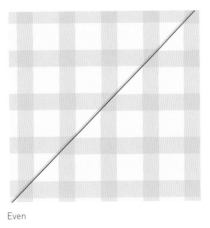

Even

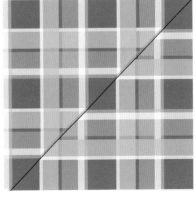

Uneven

PATTERN PLACEMENT

It is much easier to start pattern matching the most visible seams first. People's focus will usually be around your face, so the upper center seams will be the most prominent. Also think about where the focal point of a pattern will be. If a pattern has very specific focal points, it might be best to offset the pattern around the bust area so that the focal point avoids the apex of the bust. Prominent stripes also look much better in a poker-straight line down the center front.

You might want to consider how the sleeves within the bodice relate to the pattern. If your pattern has a strong horizontal element, running the pattern across the chest and on to the sleeve will give a truly professional touch. Just line up the underarm point on the sleeve with the bottom of the armhole on the bodice and the pattern will run across both.

The next most obvious place to consider the pattern is down the center back. But remember: As with all the pattern pieces you are matching the pattern on the sewing line, not on the cutting line, so take into account the center back seam allowance if there is one.

The side seams are not so much of a consideration because they are not as visible. However, running the pattern around the bodice under the bust dart is far more appealing to the eye.

It is also worth pattern matching from the bodice onto the bottom half of the garment. A stripe or check looks much better if it flows down the body across the waist seam.

1 The vertical stripes have been placed in the center of the dress. **2** The strong geometric print has been carefully positioned to work with the proportions of the body. **3** Here the check does not align in order to create a more casual, rebellious look. **4** The pattern aligns neatly down the center back. **5** The direction of the stripes changes to create different effects in different segments of the garment. **6** The tunic and pants work together with the pattern following the center-front line.

HOW TO MATCH THE PATTERN

Having decided you need to match the pattern and checks, there are several ways to do this. The type of patterned fabric will help you to determine which one is the best for the project you're working on. It is best to decide where you want the pattern matching to focus and mark out those pattern pieces first. You may also need to consider purchasing extra fabric to match an awkward pattern more accurately.

Cutting double

If you have a nice, even pattern (see page 57), you may be able to line up the two layers of fabric on top of each other with the pattern matching. You may have to roll back the first layer to make sure that the pattern matches the bottom layer. You can then use the pattern notches to mark where the paper pattern piece sits in relation to the pattern on the fabric.

Cutting one piece first

If you have an uneven patterned fabric you may find it easier to cut your pattern pieces out in a single layer. This way you can make sure that the pattern is running "true" across the fabric. Cut out one piece first, then remove the paper

pattern. Lay the cut-out fabric piece onto the flat fabric matching up the pattern. This can then be used as a template to cut out the second piece. BUT remember to flip the first cut-out piece so that you get a PAIR.

Drawing the fabric pattern onto the paper pattern

This method is ideal if you want to make sure the pattern on the fabric runs across the body and onto the sleeves to give a truly professional finish. Lay the first pattern piece on the fabric and draw on the lines to show where the fabric pattern runs. You can then use these markings to make sure that the pattern flows across onto the sleeve head, or around the body of the garment.

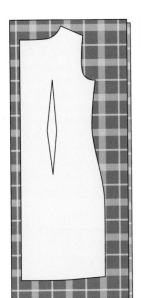

Cut double.

Cut one piece first.

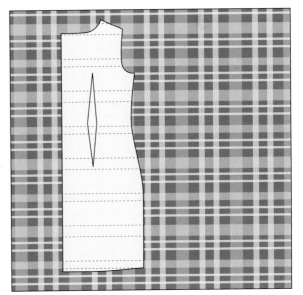

Draw the fabric pattern on the paper pattern.

Pinning and cutting fabric

There are two basic methods of marking out the pattern pieces you wish to cut. I use both, depending on the type of fabric and how much of a rush I'm in. However, it is always best to place the pattern pieces that need to be cut on the fold on the fabric first, as they have to be positioned in a specific place. Then you can fit the rest of the pieces in around them.

PINNING

In our workshops, we often find that people either use too many pins or not enough. The rule of thumb is to pin the corners first, then go on to the curved sections, and finally the long straight edges. A stable fabric will not need a lot of pinning. Remember that the job of the pin is to keep the pattern flat to the fabric. Too many pins will buckle and lift the pattern and fabric, making it tricky to cut accurately.

Another rule of thumb I use is to pin roughly a hand's width apart. This keeps the pins evenly spaced and will not distort the pattern too much.

WEIGHTS AND CHALK

The second method is to weight down the pattern pieces and draw around them with tailor's chalk or fabric marker. This can be quicker than pinning, but it is very important when cutting out the shapes to cut off the chalk line. If parts of the line remain, it means that the pattern has not been cut accurately to the correct size and this could alter the fit of the garment.

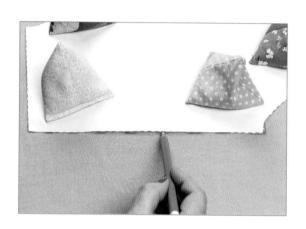

SCISSORS OR ROTARY CUTTER?

We have a number of quilters attending our dressmaking workshops and most of them are rather deft with a rotary cutting wheel. This can be a quick way to cut out your pattern pieces, but a word of caution: You must use a self-healing mat underneath where you are cutting and move the mat with you as you cut. It can also be tricky to get a rotary cutter into tight corners and it is much better used with a steel ruler for straight edges.

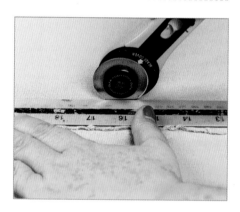

Personally, I prefer to use a good pair of dressmaking scissors. Always cut the full length of the blade where you can. If you are right-handed, cut clockwise around your pattern pieces or, if left-handed, using a pair of left-handed scissors, counterclockwise. This ensures that the bottom blade sits just under the pattern and the top blade should slice down exactly on the edge of the paper pattern.

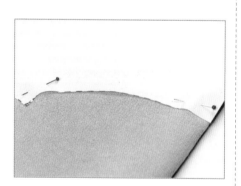

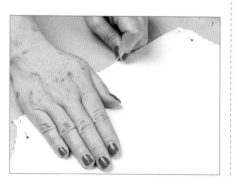

If you are not lucky enough to have a proper cutting table you will probably need to use the dining room table, so make sure to stand up and stretch periodically to save your back when bending over to cut out your fabric.

Marking fabric

Once the pattern pieces have been cut out, you need to transfer the information about how to construct the garment from the pattern to the fabric. There are many tools and gadgets on the market to help you with this, but sometimes the more traditional methods work just as well.

BALANCE MARKS AND NOTCHES

These are usually marked on the pattern by a small triangle or T on the cutting line. You can mark them with chalk (but remember to mark both layers if you are cutting double) or with a very small snip. Always use only the tip of the scissors for this, as it is easy to cut too far and leave a hole in the seam allowance when the garment is sewn up.

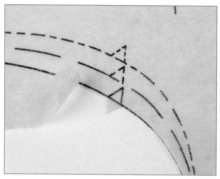

Cutting around a notch Cut notches "out" rather than "in" to prevent weakening the seam.

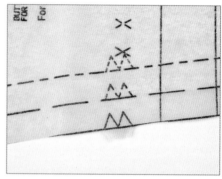

Matching up notches Make sure that you link up double notches with the corresponding double notch, and likewise with single notches.

TRADITIONAL TAILOR'S TACKS

These can take time, but they can be the best method to use on very delicate fabrics or ones that can mark easily.

1 Thread a needle, but don't knot it at the end. Sew a small stitch at the point that needs to be marked, leaving the thread tail.

2 Sew another stitch but do not pull it tight; instead, leave a loop of thread and another tail before snipping off the thread.

3 When you pull apart the layers of fabric, snip the threads in between.

4 This will leave little thread tails in both sides of the fabric.

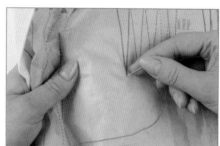

1

2

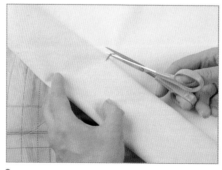

3

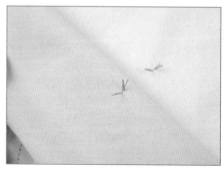

4

TAILOR'S CHALK AND CHALK PENS

Traditional triangular tailor's chalk should have the edges kept nice and sharp. A quick way of doing this is to use an old pair of scissors (not your beautiful dressmaking ones) to sharpen the chalk. Partly open the scissors and draw the edge of the chalk between the blades. Make sure to do this over a trash can.

There are also many products that use traditional chalk in a pen form, which can be more user-friendly.

MARKER PENS

These can be water soluble or air erasable. They can work very well on plain or light-colored fabrics, but can get a bit lost on dark or highly patterned fabrics. Always remember to put the lid back on straight after using, as they will dry out very quickly.

> ## Try this

To mark dots or points in your pattern, make a small hole in the pattern at the dot or point and rub the chalk over the hole. The chalk will go through the hole in the paper and leave a really accurate mark on your fabric.

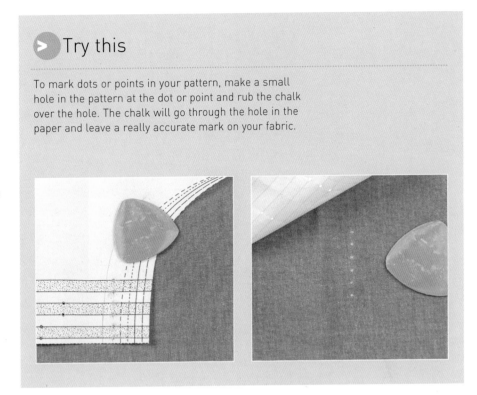

DOUBLE PINNING

This is a bit of a cheat and works in a similar way to traditional tailor's tacks.

1 Place a pin through the pattern at the point to be marked and gently wiggle it through the paper.

2 Then flip over the fabric. Where the pin is poking though, push another pin back through to the pattern side.

3 When the two layers of fabric are separated, each will have a pin in it. Just make sure that the pins don't fall out!

4 Reposition the pins so that they sit securely in the fabric to indicate the positions of the markings until required.

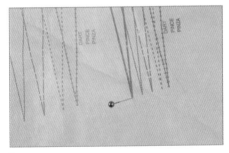

1

2

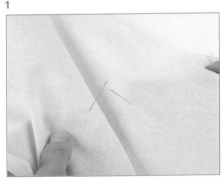

3

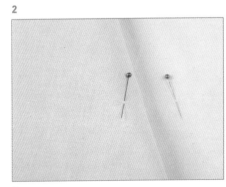

4

Adapting a pattern

Commercial patterns are based on standard measurements, but very few people correspond exactly to these, so it is often necessary to make small alterations to improve the fit.

For best results, make any changes to the paper pattern and then construct a muslin in calico (see pages 50–53) in order to check the fit. Transfer any further alterations back onto the paper pattern before cutting out and making the garment.

LENGTH

Changing the length of pattern pieces is relatively easy to do. Simply take the relevant measurement (waist to hem, or nape of the neck to waist, for example) on the person for whom the garment is being made, compare this with the actual pattern size, and then adjust the pattern as shown on the right.

ADAPTING PANTS LEG LENGTH

Measure the length of the side seam from the waist to the hem and alter the pants paper pattern accordingly. Fold up excess length to shorten, or cut and move the pattern pieces apart before inserting paper pieces to lengthen them.

Horizontal parallel lines through a pattern suggest the best place to lengthen or shorten a garment. To lengthen a pattern, simply cut along the line, move the pieces apart by the required distance, and stick a piece of paper behind them to cover the gap. To shorten a pattern, fold up the excess length. You will normally need to finish the adjustment by redrawing the sides of the pattern at the point of adjustment in a smooth line. Be aware that sometimes it is better to make smaller length adjustments in more than one place than one large alteration.

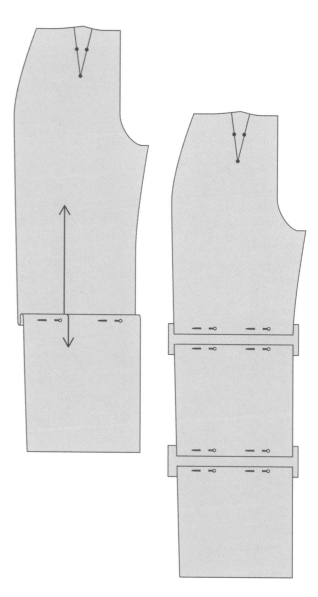

WAIST

The most obvious solution to altering a waist is to alter the size of the darts. More, or less, fabric can be pinched away at the waist and, if necessary, the darts can be lengthened or shortened to improve the shaping.

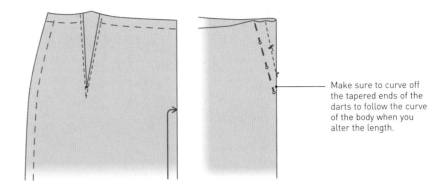

Make sure to curve off the tapered ends of the darts to follow the curve of the body when you alter the length.

LARGER STOMACH

To adjust a pattern to create more room in the stomach area, cut into the paper pattern both horizontally, at the widest part, and vertically through a dart. Pivot this at the side seam—to retain the length of the side seam and enlarge the dart. Redraw the side seam in a smooth line and reshape the dart.

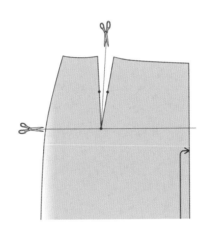
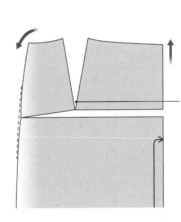

Snip into the seam allowance up to the stitching line to allow the pattern to pivot from the correct point on the stitching line.

SMALLER STOMACH

If there is excess fabric in the stomach area, this can be removed by cutting into the pattern, as above. In this case, fold the pattern in on itself to remove excess fabric and reduce the size of the dart. Redraw the side seam in a smooth line and reshape the dart.

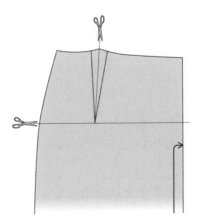
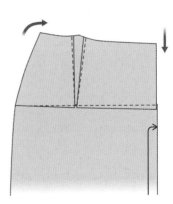

LARGER SEAT

More fabric can be built into the seat of a skirt or dress by cutting into the paper pattern. Cut horizontally at the largest part of the hip and also vertically through the dart. Pivot this at the side seam to enlarge the dart and create more fabric for the seat. Redraw the side seam in a smooth line and reshape the dart.

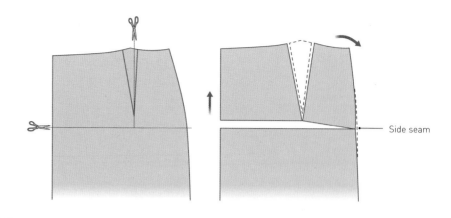

Side seam

SMALLER SEAT

To reduce excess fabric in the seat, cut horizontally through the paper pattern in the problem area and vertically through a dart. Fold the pattern in on itself and redraw the side seam in a smooth line and reshape the dart.

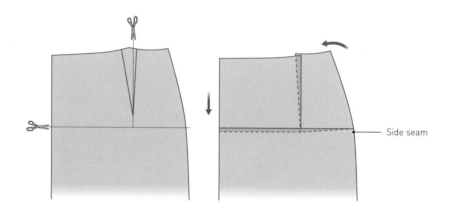

Side seam

BACK ADJUSTMENTS

Accommodate a broad or narrow back by cutting into the back armhole area. Make a horizontal and a vertical cut in the shoulder and armhole.

• To allow more fabric for a broad-backed and wide-shouldered figure, move the cut pattern piece out and reshape the shoulder and armhole.
• For a broad back but narrow shoulders, pivot on the shoulder seam and reshape.
• For wide shoulders but narrow back, pivot on the armhole and reshape.
• For a narrow back and shoulders, move the cut pattern piece into the pattern.

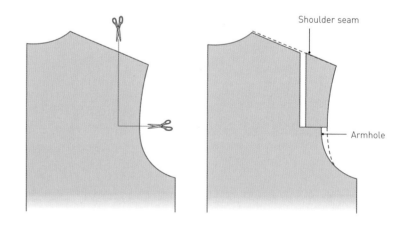

Shoulder seam

Armhole

LARGER BUST

First, choose a pattern with waist and armhole darts or a princess seam, which will allow adjustments to be made.

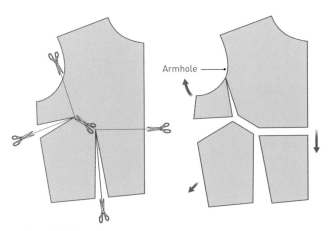

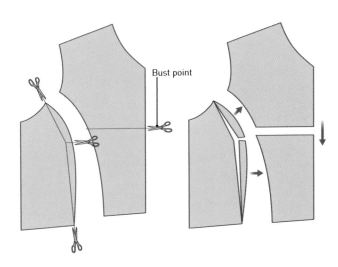

Bodice with darts

Cut the pattern through the darts, the center front, and the armhole. Pull the pattern pieces apart to create more space for the bust, pivoting at the armhole. Reshape the darts.

Princess line bodice

Cut horizontally through the bust point and lengthen to add space for the bust. Cut and move the side front pattern piece, as shown, to allow more fabric and to retain the seam shaping.

SMALLER BUST

Start with a pattern close to the body measurements to minimize alterations.

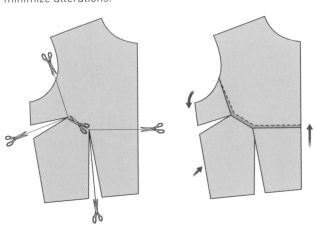

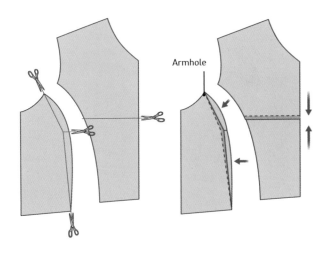

Bodice with darts

Cut into the darts and overlap the pattern pieces, taking care not to alter the seam lengths. Reshape the darts.

Princess line bodice

Cut horizontally through the bust point and overlap the pattern pieces. This will take up the excess fabric in the length. Pivot at the armhole to avoid disturbing the armhole measurement.

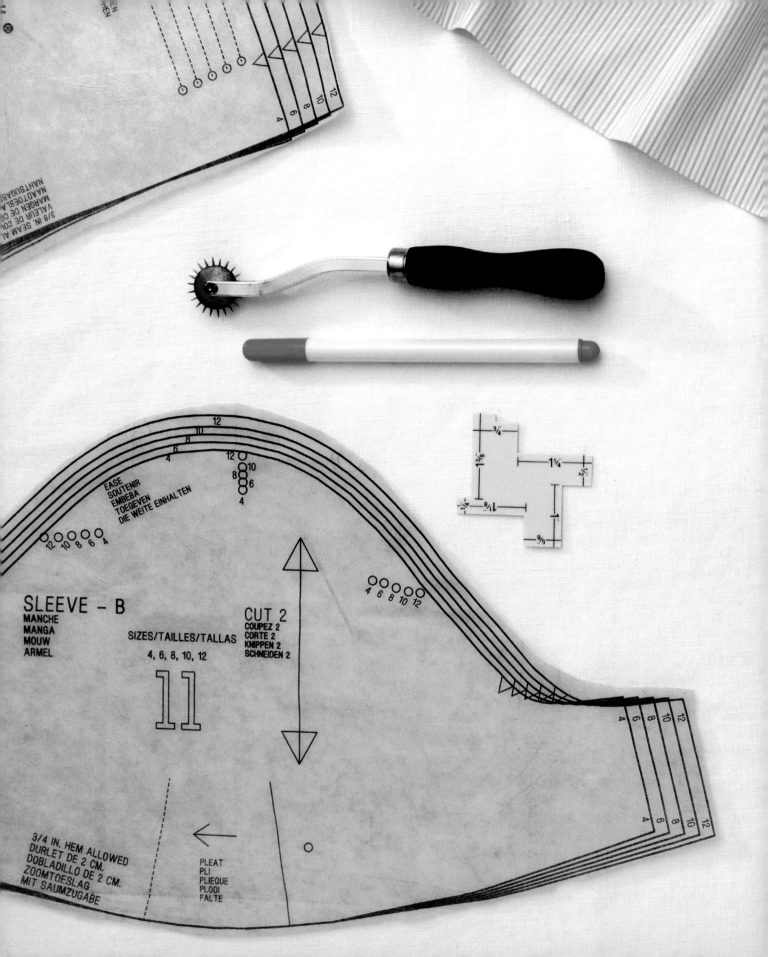

Construction

Once you have prepared and assembled the components for your project you can sew it all together. Bear in mind the sequence of techniques you need to use to construct your garments. If you have made your own pattern, it is worth writing an order of work. This will help to keep you on track so that you can construct your new garment effectively and successfully.

Pressing matters

This may at first appear to be an incidental topic in a compendium of dressmaking processes and techniques. However, I believe it to be one of the most important. It is the act—or rather, art—of pressing your garment throughout the sewing process, as well as the final press, that will set your clothes to the highest standards.

By paying close attention to the pressing of your garment at every stage of each seam, pocket, placket, or collar, you set the stitches into the fabric, which allows them to perform their job of holding several pieces of fabric together much better.

Please don't confuse pressing with ironing: they are entirely separate. Pressing requires you to use the iron as a precision tool, lifting and pressing it down rather than sweeping it across the fabric, to flatten, shape, or crease very specific areas on a garment.

Pressing also requires a light touch. A heavy hand can result in over-pressing, which knocks the stuffing out of a fabric, leaving it lifeless and without its natural bounce. It can also distort the raw edges of a fabric, so both the fabric and the garment need to be handled very carefully.

As you make your garment, specific areas will require pressing in order to enable the next step or process to be sewn more accurately. For example, it is much easier to sew across a seam that has already been pressed. Make sure you remove all basting or pins before pressing, as these will either indent into your fabric or scratch the bottom of your iron.

Also, if you are using steam, be sure to allow the fabric to cool in position. This ensures that the fabric is set in place.

Particular parts of the iron perform different jobs when pressing

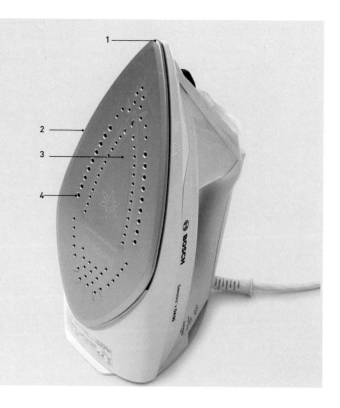

1 The pointed toe of the iron is the part that is most useful, as it allows you to get into specific areas of the garment for very targeted pressing. It can be particularly helpful over a curved seam or a shaped dart, where using the whole iron would flatten and distort the three-dimensional form of the garment.

2 The sides of the iron can be used to press a closed seam from the right side of the fabric by gently nudging the fabric away from the seam line.

3 The flat bed of the iron is excellent for getting your weight behind the pressing of hems, flat seams, and the body of the garment.

4 The jets of steam from the flat bed of the iron can hover over a woolen or knit fabric to delicately ease it.

There are several items of equipment that will really help with the pressing of your garments.

Iron

Make sure it is good quality. It should be reasonably heavy to have some weight behind the press, as well as a function to vary and turn off the steam. You could invest in a tank iron, which holds a large reservoir of water that is converted to boosts of steam when needed. The power of the steam is greater than that of an ordinary iron and it does not require refilling so frequently.

Ironing board

Try and get an ironing board that comes up to waist height. It should also be well padded. If the padding is a bit scant or on the old side, you can always add more in the form of quilting batting and make another cover to fit over the board.

Pressing cloth

This is invaluable, as it separates the direct source of heat from your garment, giving it a little bit of protection and preventing shine and scorch marks. A damp pressing cloth can also impart moisture to help achieve perfectly flat seams. Your pressing cloth doesn't need to be anything special (a piece of linen or calico is fine), but it should be washed first. When working with fine fabrics, use a square of silk organza. Not only will it allow you to see through to the fabric beneath, but it is also robust enough to protect the fine material it covers.

Tailor's ham

This is a large, egg- or ham-shaped bolster that features different curves to enable garments to be pressed on it without flattening out the three-dimensional form. Tailor's hams are traditionally made from calico on one side and a wool fabric on the other. Usually they are stuffed with sawdust, as this absorbs the steam when pressing.

Sleeve roll

This does a similar job to a tailor's ham, but it allows you to press smaller and more difficult areas, such as sleeves. Both items are easy to make.

Sleeve board

This looks like a miniature ironing board. It makes pressing those small and awkward places a lot easier. Good-quality sleeve boards have the stand at the far end, which enables you to press along the whole length of a sleeve.

Clapper

This is a piece of old tailoring equipment and makes pressing creases a lot easier. It is a flat piece of wood, usually with a handle that can be shaped to a point. When you are pressing a heavier fabric such as denim, steam the area and then press down firmly with the clapper over the area to press. The clapper pushes the steam down through the fabric and helps to set the press. It is great for pressing the hems on jeans.

Your fingers and hands

Touch is one of the most important ways of assessing the amount of pressing required. Use your fingers to press out seams on delicate fabrics and your hands to hold seams flat after steaming—but be careful not to burn yourself.

Tailor's ham

Tank iron

Sleeve roll

Sleeve board

Clapper

Ironing board

Creating shape

This is where the alchemy of sewing starts. Taking a flat, two-dimensional piece of fabric and transforming it into a three-dimensional garment to cover the curves, angles, and contours of the body means working the fabric into the shapes we desire. This involves manipulating and managing the excess fabric to create the desired shape—a process known as suppression. Suppression covers a range of features: darts, gathers, pleats, tucks, and shirring. These are some of the most useful.

Darts

A dart is a very structured way to change the form of a flat piece of fabric. Darts are wedge-shaped sections of fabric that are folded out and stitched together to remove excess fabric and create a three-dimensional shape.

Darts can also be used to create a more personalized fit to a garment by altering and adapting the darts within the pattern itself.

Think of the way we fold out a section of flat paper to make a cone. The center of the "cone" is usually the apex of the curve the fabric needs to be shaped over. On a garment, this could be the bust point on a bodice, over the buttocks, or even across the shoulder blades.

Although the pivot point of a dart may be the apex of a curve, the dart point will always be away from this to allow for a flatter area at the apex to create a softer, more dome-like shape.

Darts can be moved around the pivot point to create different effects or features.

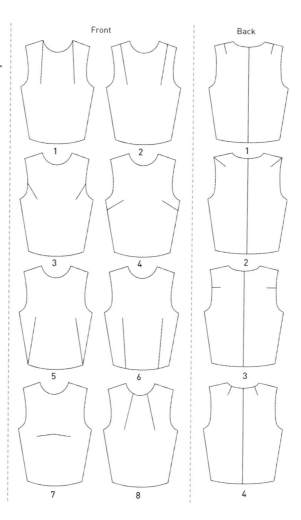

Darts can be placed in a number of positions to shape the garment in different ways and create the perfect fit.

FRONT DART POSITIONS

1 Neck point A dart in this position can provide a good fit across the chest, as it follows the slightly curved hollow of the body.

2 Center shoulder A dart here, used in conjunction with a waist dart, can be changed into a princess seam to achieve a smooth shape.

3 Armhole This placement is often used; again, it can be used with a waist dart and changed into a curved princess seam to achieve a smooth shape.

4 Side seam Positioning the dart here means that it is kept out of the way and is very discreet.

5 French dart These darts are placed at an acute angle on the waist, up to the bust. These darts look great on vintage-style garments.

6 Waist darts These darts work well on very fitted shapes and can be matched up with darts on a skirt to give a neat and structured look.

7 Center front darts Darts here can be changed into gathers to create an interesting detail at the front.

8 Neck darts Darts in this position can be changed into soft pleats to add detail to the neckline.

BACK DART POSITIONS

1 Shoulder darts Including a dart here provides a good fit for slightly rounded shoulders.

2 Shoulder point darts A better fit for prominent shoulder blades can be achieved by placing darts here.

3 Armhole darts These can be used to create a better fit for a sleeveless bodice.

4 Back neck darts Darts here can provide a better fit at the top of a center back opening if it gapes slightly.

BASIC DART

This is the simplest way to add shape
to a garment. The basic dart runs
from the edge of a pattern piece in
toward the fuller parts of the body,
such as the bust, shoulder blades,
curve of the stomach, or buttocks.
It is comprised of two legs that
converge on a point.

Darts sewn in heavy or thicker
fabrics can be trimmed down to
reduce bulk in the dart. They can also
be slashed open along the fold and
pressed open. In both cases the dart
should not be trimmed or cut up to
the point, as this will weaken the
dart point.

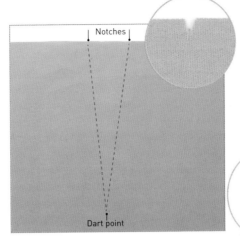
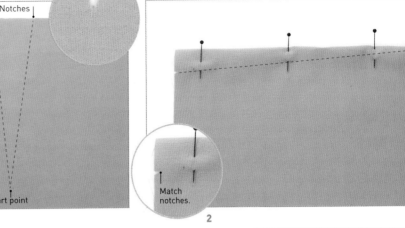

1

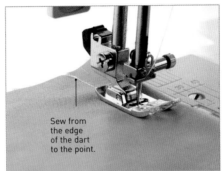

Sew from
the edge
of the dart
to the point.

3

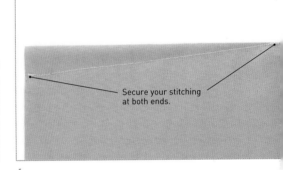

Secure your stitching
at both ends.

4

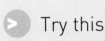

Try this

To get a nice, straight line of sewing,
pull out the threads on the sewing
machine so they are quite long. Start
your sewing, then pull the extra-long
threads around to the front and hold
them to the point of the dart. Use the
long threads as a sewing guide to keep
your stitching straight. If you catch the
long threads, just carefully pull them
out with a pin after sewing.

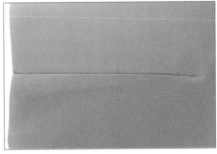

The finished basic dart: inside

The finished basic dart: outside

1 Mark out the dart on the wrong side of
the fabric.

2 Fold the fabric right sides together,
matching the notches. To ensure that the
two sides of the dart match up, insert a
pin through the marked dot on one side
of the dart and bring it out through the
corresponding dot on the other side.
Repeat along the dart line, then pin along
the sewing line.

3 Sew from the notches on the edge in
toward the point of the dart.

4 Secure your stitching at the start and
finish by reversing or tying off the threads.

Tip: To get a super-smooth shape to your
dart, aim to finish your stitching about
⅜ in. (1 cm) short of the dart point along
the fold of the dart, then curve your
stitching to meet the point. It may be
helpful to think of cresting over the brow
of a hill. This will smooth off the point of
the dart and prevent pointy dart dimples.

FISHTAIL DART

Also known as diamond darts or contour darts, these are for contouring over the curves of the figure throughout the main body of a garment. The points and the width of the dart are marked on the pattern. As with all darts, sewing should begin at the widest part—so these darts are sewn in two halves.

1 Mark out the dart on the wrong side of the fabric with tailor's tacks (see page 62).

2 Starting at the widest part of the dart, sew a small, flat, straight section in the center of the dart line and then up toward the point.

3 Curve off your sewing as you reach the point. Secure your stitching as for the basic dart (see page 73).

4 Go back to the beginning and overlap your first line of stitches. Sew up toward the other point of the dart.

You should have a row of sewing that starts at the top of the hill, dips down into a valley, and comes back up to the crest of another hill. You should end up with smooth lines of sewing that echo the curves of the body.

Tailor's tacks

1

2

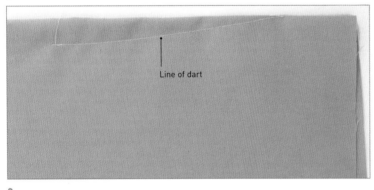

Line of dart

3

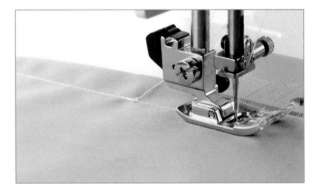

4

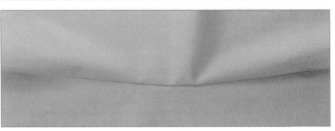

The finished fishtail dart: inside

The finished fishtail dart: outside

1

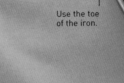

Use the toe
of the iron.

2

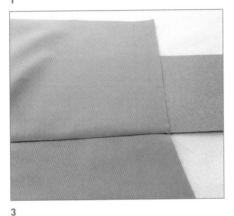

3

4

PRESSING DARTS

1 Press the dart as it's been sewn; this sets the stitches into the fabric.

2 To prevent accidental pleats on the right side of the fabric, always press from the right side, using the toe of the iron to gently push and ease the fabric flat and away from the seam.

3 You can also slide a thin piece of cardstock under the dart to prevent the line of the dart from being pressed through to the right side.

4 You may want to use a tailor's ham to give shape and a pressing cloth to prevent shining the fabric. For more information, see Pressing Matters (page 71).

Help!

My fabric has bunched up at the start of sewing.
Make sure to start your sewing about ⅜ in. (1 cm) in from the edge of the fabric. Reverse to the edge of the fabric and continue forward.

The fabric has bunched up when I reversed at the end of the dart.
As you get to the point of the dart, drop the needle down into the fabric, lift up the presser foot, turn your sewing around, and sew back up the line of stitching for about ⅜ in. (1 cm) to secure your sewing.

Gathering

Gathering is a very simple way of dealing with excess fabric. It involves sewing rows of even running stitch by hand or machine and then drawing the threads up to create a series of small pleats and tucks in the fabric. It can be used in a variety of ways to create interest and detail in a garment.

GATHERING BY HAND

Thread a sharp hand-sewing needle with a length of thread slightly longer than the piece of fabric you want to gather. Secure the end of the thread with a big knot.

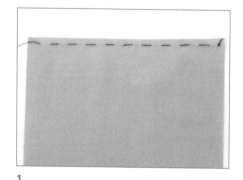

1

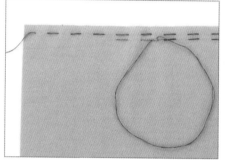

2

3

4

1 Sew a row of even running stitch ¼ in. (6 mm) away from the raw edge. Leave this row unfinished and slide the needle off the thread.

2 Sew a second row of running stitch, securing the end as before, ¼ in. (6 mm) away from the first row and slide the needle off the thread.

3 Gently pull up both threads and ease the fabric along, creating the gathers.

4 When you have gathered the fabric to the length you require, fasten off the long gathering threads (see below).

 Try this

How to tie a big knot
Thread the needle and then bring the tail of the thread back up and trap it between the tip of the needle and your middle finger.

Still holding the tail end of the thread, wrap it around the needle four or five times.

Using your index finger to catch the wrapped knot, slide it down the needle and onto the thread.

Pull the wrapped knot down the rest of the thread to the end, where it will knot itself.

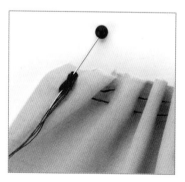

Fastening off gathering threads
The quickest way of fastening off gathering threads is to begin by placing a pin vertically at the end of the gathering stitches. When the threads have been pulled up, wind them in a figure eight around the pin to hold them securely. If you want to adjust the gathers before fastening off, just pull out the pin and move the gathers.

MACHINE GATHERING

This works in a similar way to hand gathering, but provides a smaller, more even gather.

1 Turn the stitch length up to the longest length.

2 Sew a row of stitches ¼ in. (6 mm) from the raw edge, leaving both the start and end of the row unsecured. Sew a second row ¼ in. (6 mm) from the first in exactly the same way.

3 Pull up the bobbin threads from both ends of the gathering (the bobbin threads are less likely to break). You can pull them through to the top to make it easier.

4 Ease the fabric along the threads to create the gathers. When you have gathered the fabric to the length you require, secure the threads as before.

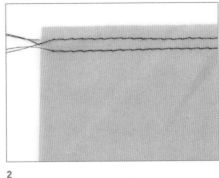
1

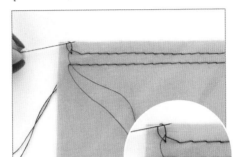

2

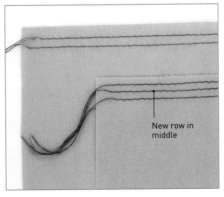
3

4

TWO ROWS VERSUS THREE ROWS OF GATHERING STITCHES

If you want to create a more evenly distributed gather, especially on light- or medium-weight fabrics such as cotton lawn or linen, an extra row of gathering threads will help.

Two rows

When sewing a gathered piece of fabric onto a flat piece, the usual two rows of gathering thread can be sufficient, but the gathers can be spaced farther apart and have a more "bouncy" look to them.

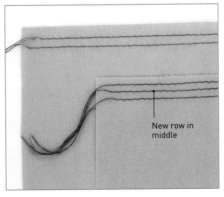

New row in middle

Three rows

1 Working a third row of gathering stitches below the seam allowance gives you more control over the gathers. Sew the seam in between the second and third rows of gathering stitches.

2 Carefully remove the third row of gathering stitches. This may not be suitable for fabrics that will mark easily, such as chiffon or silk habotai, as pinholes may be left in the fabric after removing the stitching. So with these fabrics it's best to try and keep all the rows of gathering stitches inside the seam allowance.

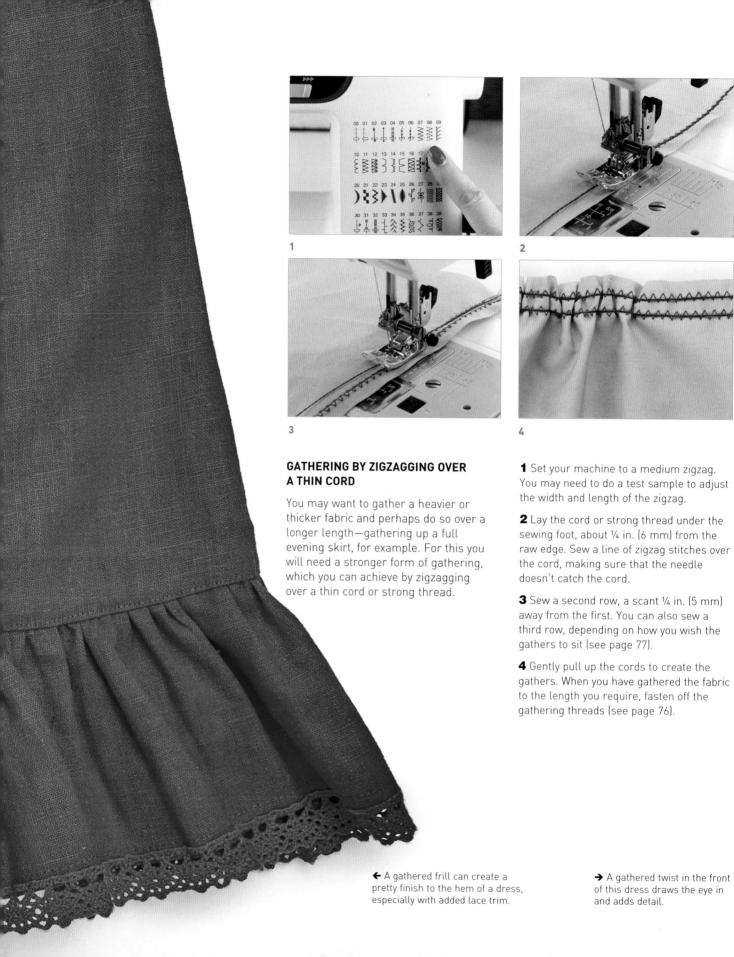

GATHERING BY ZIGZAGGING OVER A THIN CORD

You may want to gather a heavier or thicker fabric and perhaps do so over a longer length—gathering up a full evening skirt, for example. For this you will need a stronger form of gathering, which you can achieve by zigzagging over a thin cord or strong thread.

1 Set your machine to a medium zigzag. You may need to do a test sample to adjust the width and length of the zigzag.

2 Lay the cord or strong thread under the sewing foot, about ¼ in. (6 mm) from the raw edge. Sew a line of zigzag stitches over the cord, making sure that the needle doesn't catch the cord.

3 Sew a second row, a scant ¼ in. (5 mm) away from the first. You can also sew a third row, depending on how you wish the gathers to sit (see page 77).

4 Gently pull up the cords to create the gathers. When you have gathered the fabric to the length you require, fasten off the gathering threads (see page 76).

← A gathered frill can create a pretty finish to the hem of a dress, especially with added lace trim.

→ A gathered twist in the front of this dress draws the eye in and adds detail.

Pleats and tucks

Pleats and tucks are like the origami of the sewing world. They are folds and creases that can be a more controlled way of dealing with excess fabric. They provide a flatter finish and a more tailored look to your garments, as well as being a beautiful way to add decoration to your clothes.

There is debate on the actual difference between a pleat and a tuck, as the terms are almost interchangeable these days. Strictly speaking, a pleat is a fold in the fabric and is used to create shape and deal with excess fabric.

A tuck, on the other hand, is a folded-out section of fabric that is sewn in place and folds flat to the garment. It can also be used both vertically and horizontally for decoration.

Unpressed or open pleats can create shape and form but still give a soft silhouette, while sharply pressed pleats and tucks give a sense of structure and precision to your clothes.

The size and quantity of pleats and tucks can also depend on the type of fabric you are using. A heavier or thicker woolen fabric, for example, will require wider and perhaps fewer pleats or tucks to avoid additional bulk in the folding of the fabric, whereas light cotton voile can cope with lots of smaller, compact pleats or tucks.

In their simplest form, pleats and tucks are just pinches of fabric caught and pushed over to one side. To be truly effective, however, they must be marked out with precision so that they can be sewn accurately.

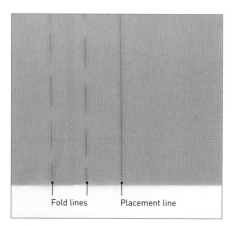

Fold and placement lines

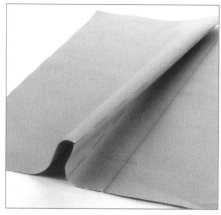

As the "mountain" crease is pulled over to the placement line a "valley" crease is created along the second fold line.

MARKING OUT PLEATS

All pleats have two types of lines to help them sit correctly:

The fold line This is where the fabric is creased and folded back to create the pleat; it is usually drawn with a dashed line.

The placement line This is where the folded edge of the pleat sits; it is usually marked with a solid line.

These lines can also be marked by a very small snip at the edge of the fabric.

Deciding whether to mark the pleats on the right or wrong side of the fabric depends on the type of fabric that you're using. Using pen or chalk on the right side may not be appropriate for very delicate fabrics; instead, it's best to mark the fold and placement lines on the wrong side of the fabric and use basting stitches to transfer the lines to the right side, making it easier to see where the pleats need to sit.

The width of the pleat and the spacing between pleats can create some interesting effects within a garment, so it's very important to make sure the fold and placement lines are marked clearly.

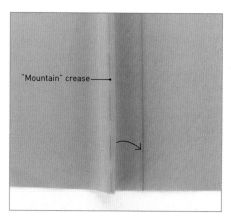

Make a "mountain" crease in the fabric on the fold line.

The "mountain" crease in the fabric now lays along the placement line.

Help!

My pleated panel is now too small/too large to fit into the rest of the garment.

Go back and check the marking out for the pleats. Inaccurate marking and pressing—even if only by ⅛ in. (2–3 mm)—can, over a series of pleats, create a large discrepancy in the finished size of your pleating.

Pressing out already pressed-in pleats can be tricky. Fabrics made from natural fibers will mostly respond to steam and moisture to reset them, but synthetic fibers can be very difficult to unpress, even with the use of steam and moisture. So accuracy in the first instance is essential.

> Try this

It is always worth playing around a little bit and getting the pleats right in paper first. You can highlight the contrasting underlay with a colored pen and open up the pleat to make sure it works correctly.

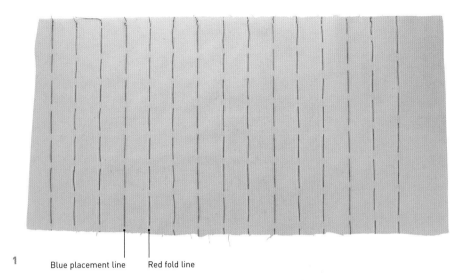

1

Blue placement line   Red fold line

KNIFE PLEATS

These are regular, even pleats all facing in the same direction and can be used in groups to create a stunning effect. They are the most common type of pleat and are the basis of most other pleats, too.

1 Mark the pleats on either the right or the wrong side of the fabric, depending on your fabric, with a basting stitch (I have used blue for the placement lines and red for the fold lines.)

2 Pinch along the second red fold line so that the crease of the pleat folds over toward the blue placement line. Fold the pleat over toward the blue placement line. Gradually fold each pleat and pin in place as you go. It is the bottom, or inside, fold line that will act as a guide to keep the pleats even in size.

3 Transfer your fabric to the ironing board and press each pleat in place. Make sure to remove the pins and any basting threads before you press, as they will leave indents in the fabric.

4 Secure the pleats in place by sewing a long row of hand basting (or machine basting) stitches across the top edge of the pleated piece of fabric, or along both raw edges if it's a pleated panel.

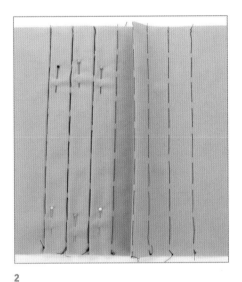

2

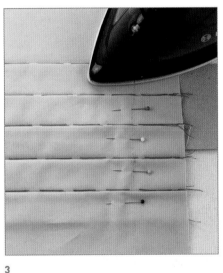

3

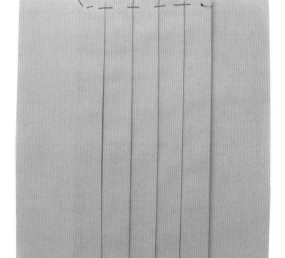

4

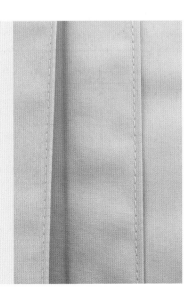

> Try this

Pleats on lighter-weight fabrics, such as linen cotton or even some lightweight wools, can be edge-stitched down the length of the pleat. This gives a very sharp, crisp look, instead of allowing the pleats to just become folds in the fabric. Do this before securing the pleats along the top edge.

BOX PLEATS

These are pleats that face away from each other. The pleats should be of equal width and they usually meet at the back, although they don't have to.

Like knife pleats, box pleats also require two lines to accurately create the pleat—the dotted fold line and the solid placement line. Mark these in different colors to make it easier to see what goes where. Here, the red thread shows the fold lines and the blue thread is the placement line.

1 From the wrong side of the fabric, carefully pinch the fabric along the dotted fold line, making sure to keep the crease along the marked line. Bring the fold line over to meet the placement line and pin it in place.

2 Crease along the second fold line and bring that over to the opposite side of the placement line. There should be two folds meeting each other along the placement line. Pin these in place.

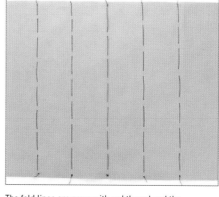

The fold lines are sewn with red thread and the placement line with blue thread.

3 Move everything over to the ironing board and press the pleats in place, using a pressing cloth or piece of cardstock to prevent the pleats from marking through to the right side of the fabric.

4 Secure the pleats in place by sewing a line of basting stitches across the top.

Inverted box pleats

This really couldn't be simpler: An inverted box pleat is just a box pleat the other way around. The same process applies for marking and stitching, but an entirely different effect is achieved. The only difference is that you begin the box pleats sequence from the right side, rather than the wrong side.

INVERTED BOX PLEAT PARTIALLY STITCHED

1 Fold the fabric with the right sides together, so that the two fold lines (basted in red) are directly on top of each other. Pin in place.

2 Sew from the top of the pleat down the marked fold line for the desired length, or to where the pattern dictates.

3 Open out the garment and the now stitched pleat so that the sewn line sits on the placement line of the pleat. Carefully pinch along the fold lines, continuing from the stitched section along the remaining part of the pleat and bring them into the center along the placement line. Pin everything in place.

4 Secure the pleats in place by sewing a line of basting stitches across the top.

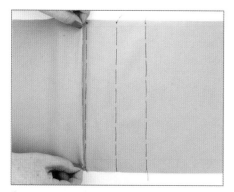

1

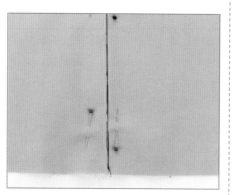

2

3

4 Wrong side

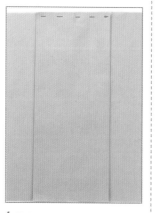

4 Right side

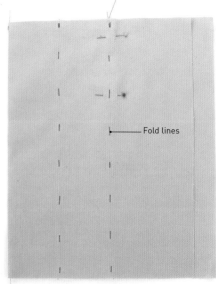

Fold lines

1

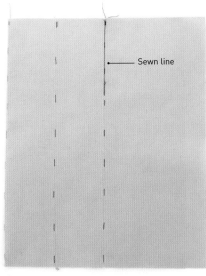

2

Sewn line

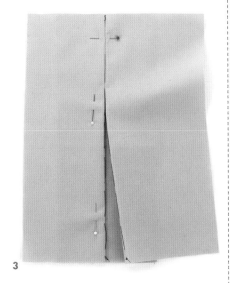

3

4

INVERTED BOX PLEAT WITH AN UNDERLAY

In addition, a contrasting fabric underlay can be added to further enhance the inverted box pleat. The fabric is sewn to either side of the pleat first. Accuracy is key here, as the seams will form one of the folds of the pleats. Most of the markings for this type of process will be on any commercial pattern, but if you are adding one to a project, a bit of thought is required to get the sums right in calculating the widths of the pleats and underlay.

In our sample we have used a pleat width of 2 in. (5 cm). This means the underlay will be double that—4 in. (10 cm) in width, plus the seam allowance required to sew it together on either side—⅝ in. (1.5 cm) x 2. So the total width of the underlay will be 5¼ in. (13 cm).

1 With right sides together, pin one side of the pleat to the underlay and sew down the seam. Press the seam flat—not open—and neaten the seam allowance.

2 Now do the same to the other side of the pleat and underlay.

3 Fold over ¾ in. (2 cm) from both seam lines and bring them into the center of the underlay. Pin in place.

4 Transfer to the ironing board and press, using a cloth or piece of cardstock to prevent marking. Sew a row of basting stitches across the top of the pleats.

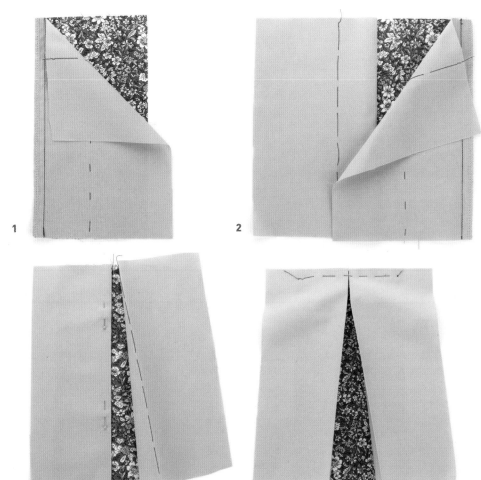

1

2

3

4

Spaced tucks

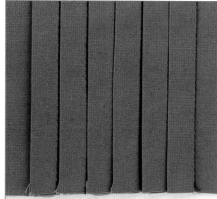

Blind tucks

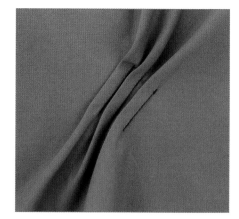

Released tucks

SPACED TUCKS

These are tucks that have a gap between the next and subsequent tucks, creating a more open feel. They are marked out in the same way as pleats.

BLIND TUCKS

These tucks sit close to each other, with the fold of one tuck sitting along the stitching line of the next and subsequent tucks. This creates a definite texture to the fabric.

RELEASED TUCKS

These often featured in vintage-style clothing and are an excellent way of manipulating excess fabric and creating shape to define the contours of the body. They are marked in a similar way to pleats and other tucks, but quite often they are not folded out along a straight line, so dots or small circles are used to mark out the folds instead.

They are not stitched completely along the length of the fold, but only secure a section of the fold; this allows the excess fabric to be nipped in to create the desired shape and then released again.

They are very effective at helping to secure drapes of fabric across the body.

Pin tucks

These are much smaller than usual tucks and it is generally only the fold line that is marked.

Method 1

Pin tucks can be sewn very accurately with a quilter's quarter-inch foot. The fold of the tuck runs along the blade of the foot, making it very easy to sew accurately.

Method 2

Pin tucks can also be sewn using a twin needle. If the top tension is tightened slightly, this will cause a ridge in the fabric between the two rows of sewing. This type of tuck looks very pretty on a lightweight fabric such as a cotton lawn.

Sometimes—if there is a large number of pin tucks or the pattern piece is quite small, for example—it can be much easier to sew the pin tucks in place before cutting out the pattern piece. Place the pattern on top of the pin-tucked fabric and then cut out the pattern piece.

Pin tucks

Method 1

Method 2

Pin tucks can create a focal point at the neckline of a dress or tunic.

Shirring

Traditionally, shirring was done by hand and looked very similar to smocking. Since the advent of the mechanical sewing machine, however, all manner of once laborious tasks have become a lot quicker and easier.

The basic premise of shirring is to use a thin elastic thread instead of the bobbin thread. As this thin elastic passes through the bobbin tension mechanism, it is stretched slightly when it creates the stitch with the normal top thread. The elastic contracts once the stitch has been created, thus drawing the fabric up into gathers.

It is a very gentle technique, so is best suited to lightweight fabrics such as cotton lawn or poplin, although it can be used on ordinary craft cotton with very pleasing results.

Shirring is most commonly seen used in rows to mimic traditional smocking. Used in a free-motion style, however, it can create a very beautiful effect on a light or sheer fabric.

All machines are different and may require a different setting to deal with the elastic thread. Always carry out a test sample to make sure you get the desired results on your garment. No one likes unpicking shirring!

Too loosely wound   Perfectly wound   Too tightly wound

 ## Try this

You need to have a light amount of tension while hand winding to make sure that the elastic doesn't become too loose and sit untidily on the bobbin.

 ## Try this

As you are shirring the fabric, it is most likely that the bobbin will run out of elastic. To minimize this inconvenience, wind three or four bobbins before you begin shirring, so that all you have to do is switch bobbins and carry on. Do try not to run out of thread mid row, though!

Help!

My shirring doesn't seem to be working—the elastic is either too loose or too tight.

You may need to alter the bobbin tension slightly to allow the elastic to pass through at the correct tension, but only do this as a last resort. Always alter the tension by small increments—a quarter turn of the tension screw is usually enough. That way you can keep a check on how much you've altered it by and easily return it to your normal setting.

Here is a brief ticklist if you encounter any problems:

- Make sure that the bobbin isn't over wound with elastic.

- Make sure that the elastic hasn't popped out of part of the bobbin tension mechanism.

- Don't sew through layers of fabric; it will be too thick for the elastic to pull up the fabric.

- Try increasing the stitch length.

1

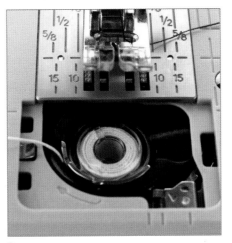

2

3

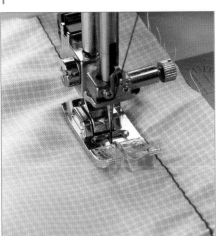

4

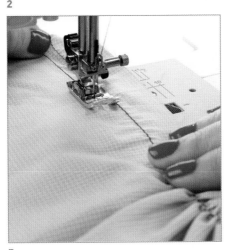

5

6

HOW TO SHIRR

1 Hand wind the thin elastic thread onto the bobbin.

2 Insert the bobbin into your machine, making sure that the elastic passes all the way through the tension mechanism, following the path that the normal thread would take.

3 Bring the elastic up to the top plate as you would do normally, so that both top thread and elastic are sitting on the plate, tucked under the presser foot.

4 Set your stitch length to longer than normal (your machine may work better with a very long stitch—sew a test sample to make sure). Start sewing a row and backstitch as usual to secure your sewing.

Carry on to the end of the fabric and backstitch again to secure the stitches.

5 Sew the second and subsequent rows, making sure they are evenly spaced. You can use the right-hand side of the presser foot as a guide to run along the previous row of sewing. The first row will not shrink up the fabric as much as you might expect, but each subsequent row of shirring will contract the fabric a little further.

Tip: Always have the fabric flat as you are sewing. Have one hand behind and one hand in front of the needle to keep the fabric flat as you sew.

6 You may be happy with the amount of gathered fabric once all the lines of shirring have been sewn—but if you want to shrink the fabric a little further, gently steam the shirring with the iron. This will contract the elastic a bit more and firm up the shirring.

Seams

Seams can be as beautiful as they are practical. Whether they are completely hidden or a visible feature, they perform a vital role—that of holding two or more pieces of fabric together securely.

There are many different types of seam. Each has its own merits and is best sewn in a particular type of fabric or to perform a specific job.

At first glance, sewing an accurate seam appears to be such a basic skill that it might be overlooked. In fact, it can be the downfall of the simplest of projects unless it is completely mastered. Flat, even seams can make even the most rudimentary of garments look professionally made.

The most typical seam allowance used in dressmaking is ⅝ in. (1.5 cm). This allows for plenty of fabric in the seam allowance so that it can be altered if necessary and should also take the strain placed on it by the wearer.

Seams are most commonly sewn with the seam allowance hidden on the inside of the garment. But, as with most rules, there are times when it just works to break them and seam allowances on the outside can be classed as a "design feature."

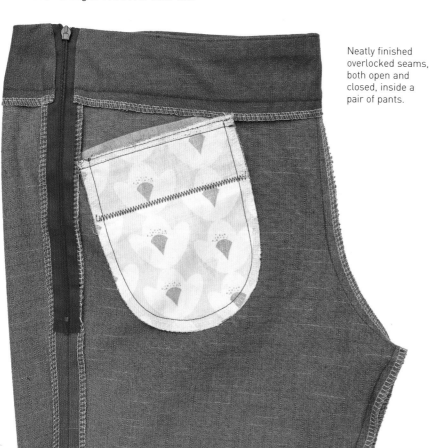

Neatly finished overlocked seams, both open and closed, inside a pair of pants.

> Try this

To help you sew in a straight and even line, most modern sewing machines have different marks on the sewing plate to indicate the different seam allowance widths. Place the edge of the fabric against a specific line to sew a perfectly straight seam.

If your machine doesn't have these marks already, a handy tip is to place colored washi tape on the sewing plate at the correct distance.

Help!

Small pleats have appeared on the right side of my fabric when I press the seam allowance to one side.

To prevent this from happening, press from the right side, using a pressing cloth and the toe of the iron to gently nudge the fabric into place.

BASIC SEAM—OPEN AND CLOSED

This is the most fundamental of seams and the basis for all others.

1 Place the two pieces of fabric to be joined with the right sides of the fabric together. Pin together to hold in place.

2 Lay the pieces of fabric under the presser foot, with the edge of the fabric running along the correct seam allowance guide and the back edge of the fabric overhanging by about ⅜ in. (1 cm). Drop the needle down into the fabric.

3 Backstitch to the end of the fabric, continue forward to the end of the seam, and then backstitch again for about ⅜ in. (1 cm) at the end. Backstitching secures the end of the seam, preventing the stitches from pulling apart. It essentially performs the job of tying a knot in the threads.

4 Press the seam flat, just as it's been sewn. This not only keeps the fabric nice and flat, but also sets the stitches into the fabric so that the row of sewing doesn't create a ridge. This is especially important when working with fine or sheer fabrics. Once the seam has been sewn, it can become either an open or a closed seam.

5 An open seam After the first press to set the stitches, open the seam allowance up and flatten it out like a book. Carefully press, using the toe of the iron along the seam line to keep the seam allowance flat. The edges of the seam allowance may be neatened. This type of seam is fairly generic, but works very well with thicker or heavier fabrics.

6 A closed seam Once the first press to set the stitches in place has been done, flip the seam allowance over to one side and press it in place.

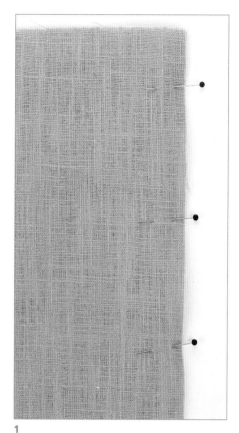
1

2

Backstitch to secure the end.
3

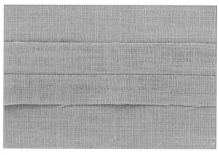
5

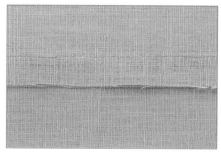
6

This line marks where to turn on a ⅝ in. (1.5 cm) seam allowance.

1

2a

Drop the needle down into the fabric and pivot.

2b

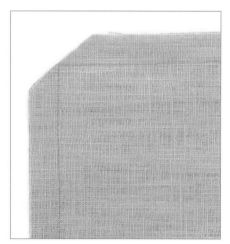

3

4

TURNING A CORNER

Turning a corner is a very straightforward process, but there are a few techniques that will give a beautifully crisp finish.

1 A lot of modern sewing machines have a whole series of marks and lines on the metal sewing plate. Sometimes there will be a horizontal one that marks the ⅝-in. (1.5 cm) distance. As you approach the end of the fabric, line up the front edge of the fabric with this mark and it will give you the point to pivot on.

2 To get a nice, sharp corner, drop the needle down into the fabric at the point of the corner. This will act as a "book mark" for the fabric and prevent you from losing the sewing line. Lift the presser foot and pivot the fabric around the needle until the edge of the fabric is back on the seam allowance guide **(a)**. Drop the presser foot and carry on sewing **(b)**.

Once you have sewn the seam, you will need to deal with the seam allowance to allow the corner to sit perfectly. The way you do this depends on whether the corner is external or internal.

3 An external corner Trim off the corner of the seam allowance diagonally to allow the rest of the seam allowance to sit inside the space in the corner.

4 An internal corner Snip the seam allowance into the corner. This releases the seam allowance and allows it to be folded back, creating an open V-shape at the corner.

 Try this

If you want a super-crisp corner on a slightly heavier fabric, stop immediately before you come up to the corner point and sew one stitch diagonally across the corner instead of stopping directly on the point. This sounds counterintuitive—but leaving that very slightly flattened-off corner allows the seam allowance more room to sit nicely inside the corner, making it appear sharper.

CURVED SEAM

This is sewn in the same way as the basic seam—but once it is stitched, it is dealt with slightly differently.

The edges of the fabric will be different in length from the stitching line—imagine concentric circles. So, for a concave or "sad" curve, the edge of the fabric will be shorter. Snip into the seam allowance at regular intervals to release the tension in the curve and allow the seam allowance to fold back and sit flat.

With a convex or "happy" curve, the edge of the fabric is longer than the stitching line, meaning that the seam allowance will pleat up and overlap, creating bulk when the seam is folded back. Snip small V-shapes out of the seam allowance, leaving it free to lie flat.

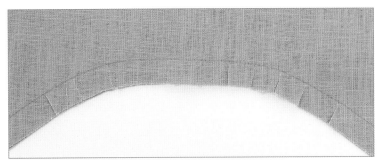

Concave curve

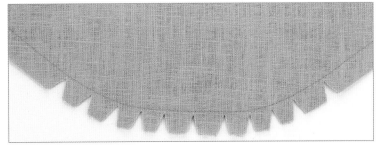

Convex curve

LAYERING A SEAM

Seams can sometimes be rather bulky and unsightly when seen from the right side. To avoid this, layer the seam allowance.

Once you have stitched the seam and pressed it flat, trim one side of the seam allowance down to about half its width. Keep the seam allowance next to the outside of the garment untrimmed to ensure that it looks smooth from the right side.

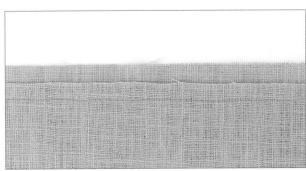

A layered seam allowance

FRENCH SEAM

This is a nice, neat seam that is sewn twice to enclose all the raw edges, so it works perfectly for sheer or very lightweight fabrics. It is not really suited to heavier fabrics, as the folded-over seam creates bulk.

1 Place the fabrics with the wrong sides together and sew a ⅜ in. (1 cm) seam. Trim both sides of the seam allowance back to ¼ in. (6 mm).

2 Press the seam as it's been sewn to set the stitches, then press the seam open and flat.

3 Fold the fabric back on itself so that the right sides are together, enclosing the raw edges of the seam allowance. Crease along the seam line, press, and pin in place.

4 Sew a second seam just under ¼ in. (6 mm) wide, encasing the seam allowance within the seam. Press the seam allowance to one side.

1 Wrong sides together

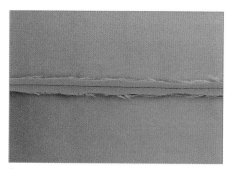
2

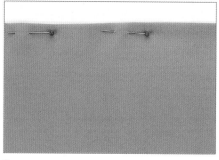
3 Right sides together

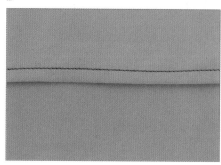
4

HAIRLINE SEAM

A hairline seam is a variation on the French seam. It is best used on sheer fabrics such as chiffon or organza that will have no stress put upon the seam. Joining the panels of a sheer overskirt with a separate lining is a good example.

1 As with the French seam, place the wrong sides of the fabric together. Sew a seam just over ⅜ in. (1 cm) wide, then sew a second row as close as possible to the first. Press the seam as it's been sewn.

2 Trim the seam allowances as close to the rows of stitching as possible.

3 Fold back either side of the seam and crease along the stitching line. Pin so that the raw edges are enclosed.

4 Set the machine to a narrow zigzag and a shorter stitch. Zigzag over the edge of the seam, making sure to catch and cover the raw edges inside the seam. You may need to do a test piece to assess the width and length of the zigzag to get the best results.

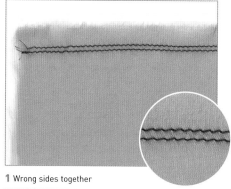
1 Wrong sides together

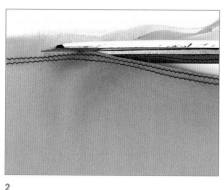
2

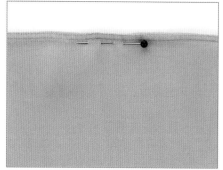
3 Right sides together

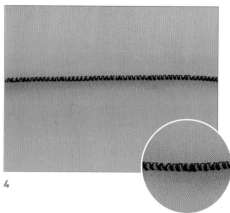
4

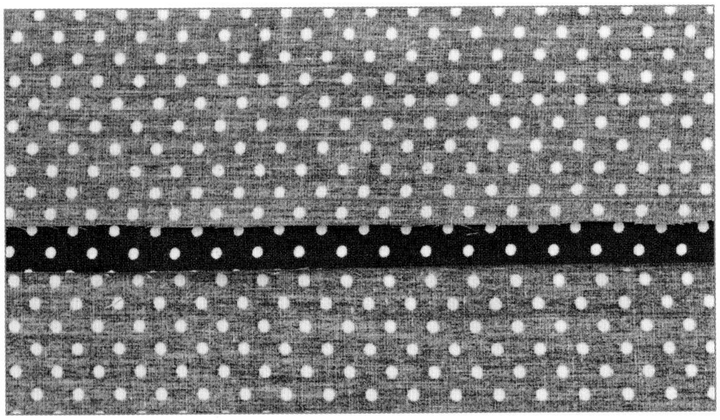

1

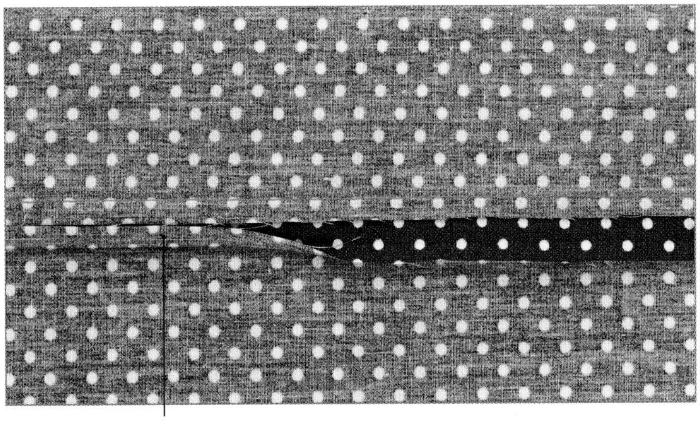

2 Folded-over seam allowance

Keep pins horizontal.

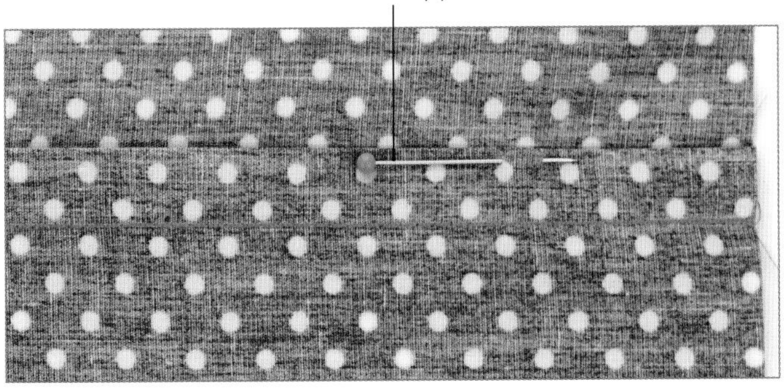

3

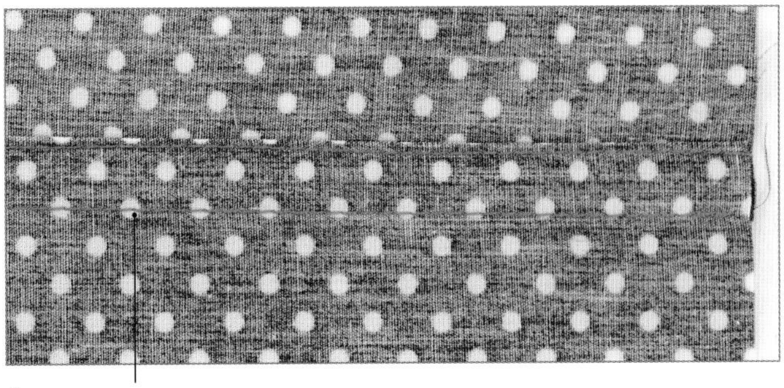

4 Keep edge stitching close to edge of seam.

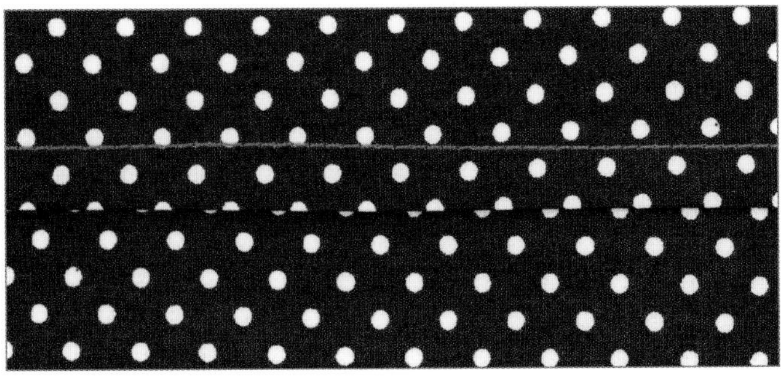

Finished flat-felled seam

Right side

Wrong side

FLAT-FELLED SEAM

Flat-felled seams are strong and usually used on tailored shirts or pants. These seams can withstand quite a bit of strain placed on them, but will still lie flat against the body. Jeans are a good example of this.

There are several different ways to create a flat-felled seam, but I have found this to be the simplest.

1 Place the fabrics with the right sides together and sew a normal ⅝-in. (1.5 cm) seam. Press the seam flat as it's been sewn and then press it to one side. Trim down one side of the seam allowance to just ¼ in. (6 mm).

2 Fold the other side of the seam allowance down over the trimmed one, so that the raw edge sits along the sewing line. Press this in place.

3 Fold the whole seam over along the stitching line, so that all of the raw edges are underneath the seam. Pin in place.

4 Edge stitch down the seam allowance.

Finishing seams

The seams in a garment perform the vital job of holding everything together, but to help them do this and also to make everything look beautiful, the raw edges of the seam need to be finished or neatened in a way that is appropriate both to the fabric and to the usage of the seam.

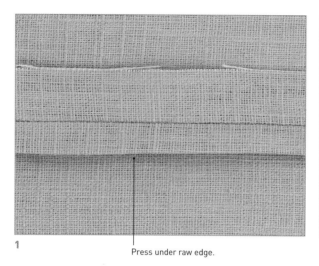

1

Press under raw edge.

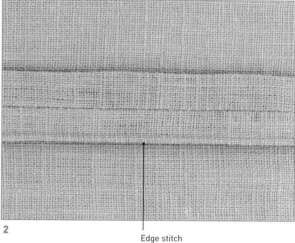

2

Edge stitch

3

A CLEAN FINISH

This is an excellent way to finish a seam if you do not possess an overlocker and are using a fairly lightweight fabric.

1 Stitch the seam and press it open. Press under the raw edge of one seam allowance by ⅛ in. (3 mm). Remember to use a pressing cloth or piece of cardstock under the seam allowance to prevent the seam from marking through to the right side of the garment.

2 Edge stitch the fold to hold it in place.

3 Repeat this for the other side of the seam allowance.

ZIGZAGGED SEAM

Zigzagging gives a good finish on more stable fabrics such as cotton poplin or linen. It also tends to give a better finish on closed seams, as the double layer of fabric stabilizes the zigzag stitch.

Sew the seam and press it flat as it's been sewn.

1 Set the machine to a medium width and stitch length. You may wish to do some test samples to gauge the correct setting for your machine.

2 Line up the seam allowance under the presser foot so that the right-hand side of the zigzag sews about ⅛ in. (3 mm) away from the edge of the seam allowance. Sew down the length of the seam.

3 Trim back the seam allowance to the line of zigzag stitching.

4 Press the seam to one side.

1

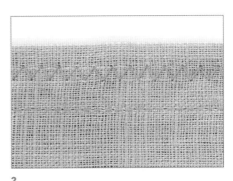
2

3

4

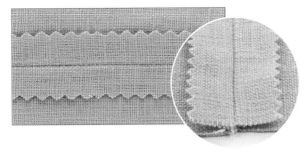

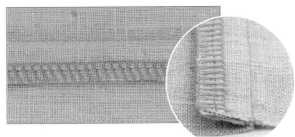

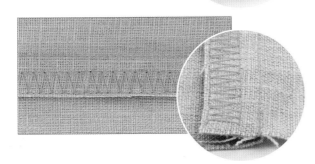

PINKED SEAM

Pinked seams are very easy to create—you just need a pair of pinking shears. Sew the seam and then press it flat as it's been stitched.

Using the pinking shears, trim off about ⅛ in. (3 mm) of the seam allowance to create a neat, zigzagged edge to the seam. The seam can then be pressed open or to one side, as your pattern dictates.

OVERLOCKED SEAM

This is the quickest and most convenient way of finishing a seam. We will cover overlocking in more detail in Chapter 4 (see page 212).

After sewing the seam, overlock the seam allowance, trimming off just enough fabric to get a clean finish to the edge. The seam allowances can be overlocked separately, but this can be a bit tricky after the seam has been sewn, so more often they are finished closed.

MOCK OVERLOCKED SEAM

A mock overlock is more of an elaborate zigzag stitch sewn on an ordinary sewing machine. Most modern sewing machines have a function for doing this. It gives the impression of an overlocked seam, but will not trim any fabric off. It can also be used in place of overlocking when sewing with jersey; we will cover this in more detail in Chapter 4 (see page 212).

As with a normal zigzag, the best finish is obtained by sewing the mock overlock entirely on the seam allowance and trimming back the excess fabric close to the stitching.

HONG KONG FINISH

This traditional method of finishing seam allowances with a binding is known as the Hong Kong finish. It is labor-intensive and therefore usually reserved for high-end garments. For this technique, the wrong side of the fabric is exposed in the seam allowances, so use a reversible fabric or one with a wrong side that you like. This finish is not suitable for curved seams for which the allowances need to be clipped to lie flat.

1–2

1 Cut enough 1½ in. (3.75 cm)-wide bias strips to bind the edges of all the seam allowances that you wish to finish. Because the joins in pieced strips would be glaring, make sure that you have enough fabric to make long, unpieced strips. The extra width of the strips makes the process easier and can be trimmed away later.

2 Stretch press the strips.

3 Place a garment section wrong side up. Lay a bias strip, right side down, along the edge to be bound. Sew in place, stitching ¼ in. (6 mm) from the edge (the width of your presser foot).

TIP The binding is applied to the seam allowances before the garment is constructed, so it is imperative to make a fitting muslin (see pages 50–53) and correct your pattern as needed before beginning. Seams finished in this manner should not be altered.

4 Using a pressing cloth, press the work as sewn to embed the stitches, then press the seam allowance and the bias strip away from the garment section.

5 Fold the bias over the seam allowance edge onto the right side of the garment piece. Pin, placing the pins in the ditch of the seam.

6 With the garment wrong side up, stitch in the ditch to secure the binding.

7 Turn the piece over. Trim the bias strip about ⅛ in. (3 mm) from the stitching.

8 Refer to your pattern directions for the construction sequence. For each seam, place the garment pieces wrong sides together, aligning the bound edges. Pin and then stitch each seam.

9 Press the work as sewn to embed the stitches, then press the seam allowances open. On each allowance, stitch in the ditch over previous stitching through all thicknesses.

10 Follow your pattern directions to complete the garment.

Placing the seam allowances on the outside of the garment is a nice way to emphasize line and add texture.

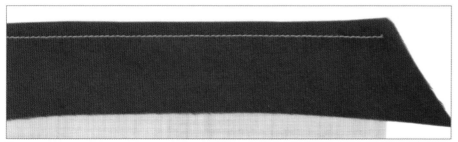

3

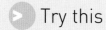

> Try this

Try using prints, checks, or bold
colors for the binding fabric.
Have fun!

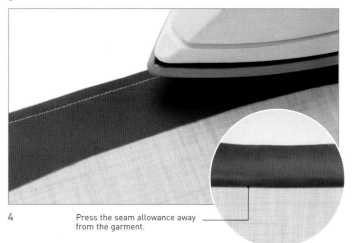

4 Press the seam allowance away
from the garment.

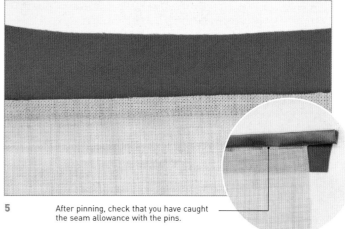

5 After pinning, check that you have caught
the seam allowance with the pins.

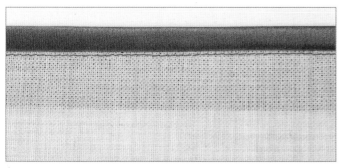

6

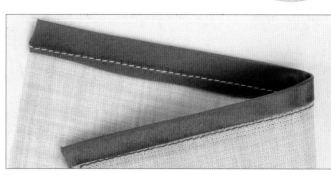

7

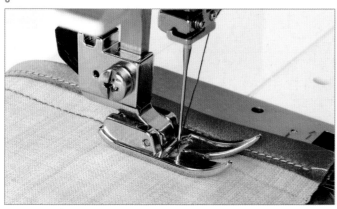

8

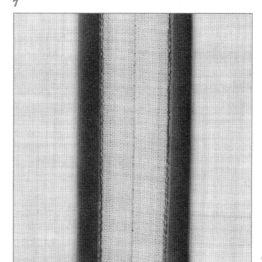

9

Pockets

Pockets are one thing I find an absolute must in most of the clothes I make. Not only are they useful, but they are also the perfect opportunity to add detail and interest to your garments.

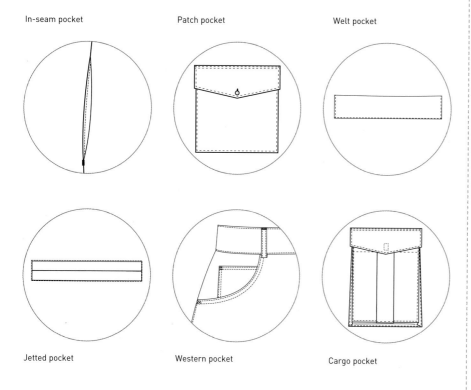

In-seam pocket

Patch pocket

Welt pocket

Jetted pocket

Western pocket

Cargo pocket

In-seam pocket These are usually in a side seam of a garment, but they can be placed in any seam where a pocket would be useful.

Patch pocket This is another piece of fabric sewn onto the garment, and can be of almost any shape and size.

Welt pocket These are most commonly found on jackets, and can be sewn with a flap as well.

Jetted pocket These are used on jackets and also as the back pockets on tailored pants.

Western pocket These are synonymous with jeans and work very well on close-fitting pants.

Cargo pocket Similar to a patch pocket, but more three-dimensional.

In-seam pocket

This pocket can be inserted into most seams, both horizontal and vertical. The pocket bag can also be topstitched around to show on the right side of the garment to add extra detail.

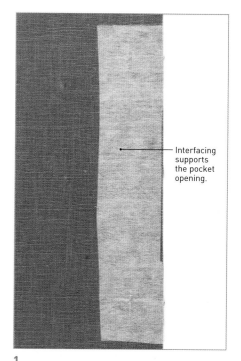

Interfacing supports the pocket opening.

1

Help!

My pocket opening is sagging.

Sometimes—if the fabric is lightweight, for example—the stitching of the pocket opening will need to be reinforced to create a crisp opening. Fix a thin strip of iron-on interfacing to the wrong side of the pocket opening on both sides of the seam allowances where the pocket will be stitched.

1 Mark the pocket opening on the right side of the garment with tailor's chalk or a fabric marker pen.

2 Lay the pocket bag right side down on the right side of the front of the garment. Taking a ⅜-in. (1 cm) seam allowance, sew the pockets in place. Repeat the process, laying the pocket bag on the back of the garment.

3 Press the pocket bags and the seams away from the body of the garment, and understitch (see page 232) the pockets to the seam allowance to prevent the pocket bags from rolling back.

4 Place the front and back garment pieces and pocket bags right sides together. Pin together around the garment and pocket bags, making sure that the pocket opening marks are lined up.

5 Taking a ⅝-in. (1.5 cm) seam allowance, sew from the top of the seam down to the top pocket opening point. Pivot at this mark, sew around the pocket bag as far as the bottom pocket opening mark, pivot again, and continue down the rest of the seam.

6 Neaten the seam using your chosen method (see pages 94–96).

7 Flip the pocket toward the front of the garment and press carefully, making sure to keep the seam allowances flat.

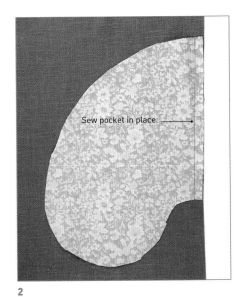

Sew pocket in place.

2

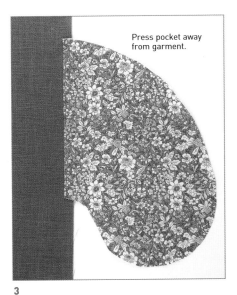

Press pocket away from garment.

3

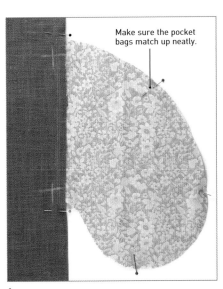

Make sure the pocket bags match up neatly.

4

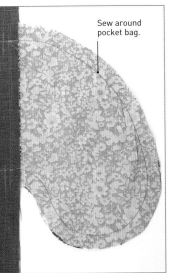

Sew around pocket bag.

5

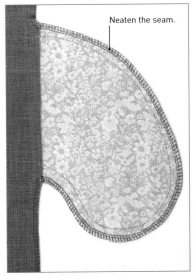

Neaten the seam.

6

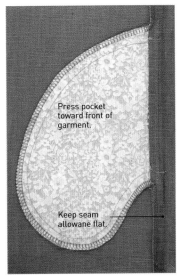

Press pocket toward front of garment.

Keep seam allowane flat.

7

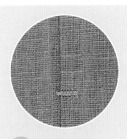

> **Try this**

Sew a reinforcing bar of satin stitch at the base of the pocket opening. This could serve as a decorative bit of sewing, too.

Patch pocket

↑ A perfectly stitched patch pocket is a thing of beauty. The contrast piping adds definition to the geometric shape.

Patch pockets are one of the most versatile of all pockets and lend themselves to infinite variations and applications. They can be used on the backs of pants, as breast pockets on shirts, or as feature pockets on skirts—in fact, anywhere you think you might need a pocket.

This sample shows a curved patch pocket, but they can be any shape you choose. Most patch pockets have an extended pocket facing, which is folded over to neaten the top edge of the pocket. Sometimes a separate contrast pocket facing can be used.

1 Mark the fold line for the facing using your preferred method (see page 80).

2 On the garment, mark the placement line for the pocket with basting stitches.

3 Press under ⅜ in. (1 cm) across the top of the pocket edge.

4 Fold the pocket facing down onto the right side of the pocket along the fold line. Using a ⅜ in. (1 cm) seam allowance, sew from the fold down to the bottom of the pocket facing on each side.

5 Bag out the pocket facing and turn the right way round. Poke out the corners of the facing and press the pocket flat. Topstitch across the bottom of the pocket

facing for decoration and to keep the facing flat.

6 Sew a row of easing stitches around the curved base of the pocket inside the seam allowance.

7 Gently draw up the easing threads to create the curved shape at the base of the pocket. Press around the folded curved edge to keep the shape.

8 Line the top edge of the pocket up along the pocket placement marks on the garment and pin it in place.

9 Edge stitch around the pocket, making sure to reverse at the start and finish to lock in the stitches. Gently press.

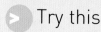 Try this

To reinforce and strengthen the corners of the pocket, add a decorative rectangle or triangle of stitching—this is practical as well as beautiful.

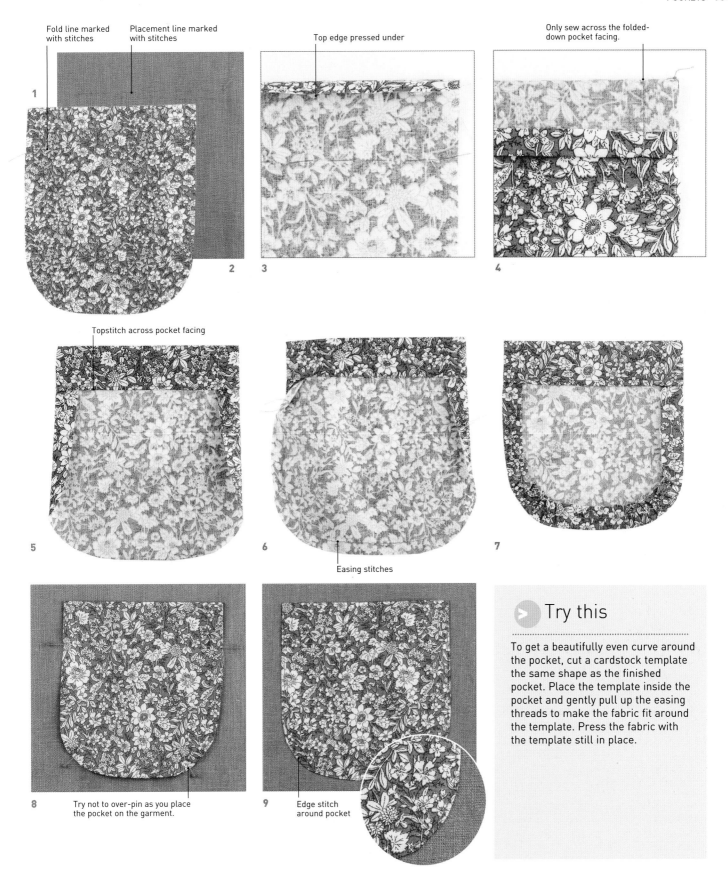

1 Fold line marked with stitches

Placement line marked with stitches

2

3 Top edge pressed under

4 Only sew across the folded-down pocket facing.

5 Topstitch across pocket facing

6

Easing stitches

7

8 Try not to over-pin as you place the pocket on the garment.

9 Edge stitch around pocket

> ## Try this

To get a beautifully even curve around the pocket, cut a cardstock template the same shape as the finished pocket. Place the template inside the pocket and gently pull up the easing threads to make the fabric fit around the template. Press the fabric with the template still in place.

Welt pocket

Welt pockets look wonderful as a detail on a jacket and are very straightforward to sew. Just be accurate with your marking and stitching. If you have a fabric that has a loose weave, make your stitch length a bit shorter to keep all those threads in place.

The "welt" of the pocket is a folded-over bar of fabric that sits just inside the bottom edge of the pocket. When the pocket is open, the back of the pocket will be seen, so you need to take this into consideration. If you want to use a contrast lining and allow this to be seen, that's fine. But if you would prefer the visible "back of the pocket" to be the same as the main garment, you will need a pocket facing as well as the pocket lining. (Of course, the facing could be in a completely different fabric again.)

A rough rule of thumb is that the pocket facing should be approximately half the depth of the back pocket.

1 Apply interfacing to the wrong side of the pocket opening **(a)** and mark out the pocket placement on both the right and the wrong sides of the garment **(b).**

2 With right sides together, fold the welt piece in half lengthwise, and sew across the short edges, taking a ⅜-in. (1 cm) seam allowance.

3 Trim the corners and turn the welt right side out. Use a point turner to help push out the corners. Press the welt flat. Machine baste across the open side of the welt.

4 Place the welt between the bottom placement marks, so that the sewing line is between the two placement lines. Pin in place and sew between the placement marks, making sure that your sewing does not go over the welt onto the garment.

5 With both pieces right side up, lay the pocket facing over the pocket back, aligning the top edges. Zigzag stitch across the bottom of the pocket facing to attach it to the pocket back. Machine baste the top edges together, ¼ in. (6 mm) from the edge.

6 Place the pocket back right side down along the top pocket placement line, with the raw edges toward the welt and the sewing line in line with the placement marks. Pin and sew in place along the top pocket placement line, making sure that the ends of your sewing start and finish about ⅛ in. (3 mm) inside the sewing line for the welt. This ensures that the welt sits over the pocket opening and there will be no gaps.

7 From the wrong side, carefully cut along the center line, making sure to cut through the garment layer only. Stop ⅜ in. (1 cm) from the end and snip into the corners to create a Y-shape. Make sure not to snip through your sewing, but get as close as you can.

8 Pull the pocket back through the opening to the wrong side of the garment and adjust it so that it sits flat.

9 Fold the pocket back down so the bottom edge lines up with the welt seam allowance **(a)**. Pin **(b)** and sew **(c)** along the seam line directly on top of the first row of sewing.

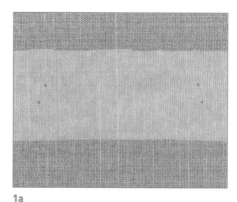

1a

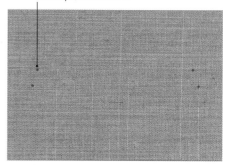

Pocket placement marks

1b

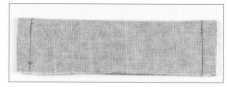

2

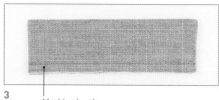

3

Machine basting

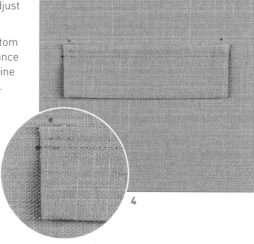

4

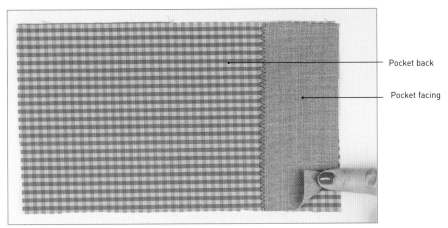

Pocket back

Pocket facing

5

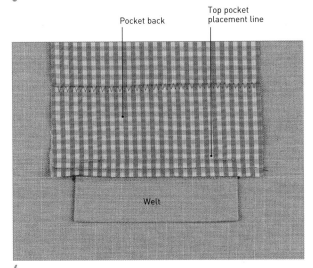

Pocket back

Top pocket placement line

Welt

6

Line up back pocket with welt seam allowance.

9a

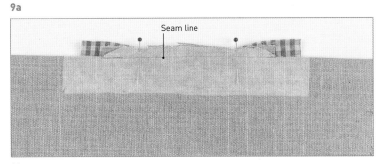

Seam line

9b

8 Wrong side

9c

10 Fold the pocket back down **(a)** and this will flip up the welt so that it sits flat on the right side of the garment **(b)**.

11 Fold the garment over sideways to reveal the small triangles at the sides of the pocket opening. Sew across the triangles between the ends of the placement lines, reverse stitching a couple of times to ensure the stitching is secure, and then sew down the side of the pocket bag.

12 You can neaten the edges of the pocket if the pocket is going to be visible inside the garment.

13 Finally, catch the sides of the welt down, either by hand or by machine sewing across the welt.

Try this

If the pocket is to be enclosed in a lining, the edges can be pinked to keep things neat or even bound if the pocket is going to be visible on the inside of the garment.

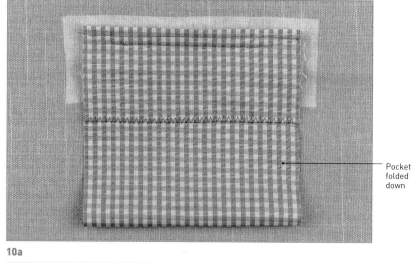

10a

Pocket folded down

10b

Welt flipped up

11

Triangles

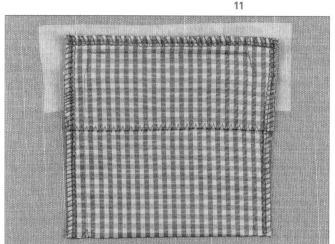

12

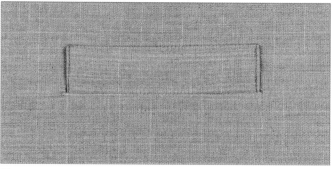

13

Jetted pocket

Jetted pockets are all about precision and, when they are sewn accurately, they can look amazingly professional. They are sometimes called "double welt" pockets, but this isn't strictly correct: A welt pocket is sewn with the welt as a finished component added into the process, whereas a jetted pocket has the welts created as part of the sewing process.

As with the welt pocket, you need to consider the back of the jetted pocket and use a facing—unless you want the lining to be seen.

1 Attach interfacing to the wrong side of the garment over the pocket area.

2 Transfer the pocket markings to the right side of the garment and to the wrong side of the pocket jets. Draw in a box on the jet to make sewing parallel lines easier.

3 Place the jet on top of the garment with the right sides together, matching up the markings on the jet so that they sit directly over the markings on the garment pieces, and pin in place.

4 Sew along the long sides of the box on the pocket jet, making sure that both rows of stitching are parallel and the same length. This is very important for accurate jets!

5 Cut down the middle in between the parallel lines of sewing on the pocket jet, stopping short by ⅜ in. (1 cm). Snip in to meet the ends of the sewing lines, cutting right up to the end of the last stitch, but don't cut through the stitching itself. Then flip the garment over and do the same through the garment layer.

> **Try this**
>
> ....
>
> Turn the fly wheel by hand to get the stitches accurately to the ends of the box.

1

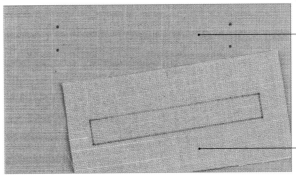

2

Right side of garment

Wrong side of pocket jets

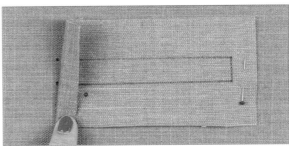

3

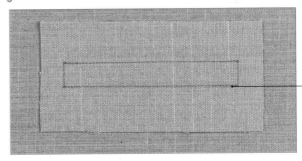

4

Stitching should be equal and parallel.

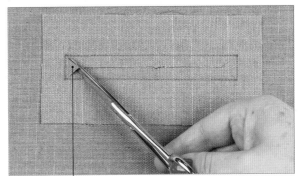

5

Do not cut through stitching.

6 Pull the pocket jet through the gap to the wrong side of the garment. Carefully press the bottom jet seam open and continue to press out from the seam to either end of the jet. Do the same for the top jet seam.

7 Poke the little triangles back to the wrong side too.

8 Fold the pocket jet down over the seam allowance to create the first lip of the pocket. Do the same with the other side of the jet. From the right side adjust the jets so that the lips of the pocket are even. Press and lightly steam in place.

9 Baste the jet lips of the pocket together so it holds its shape while you complete the rest of the pocket.

10 Fold the garment back to reveal the little triangles left at the short sides of the pocket opening. Stitch across the base of the triangle so your stitching starts and finishes at the end of the jet seam. Make sure to reverse at the start and end of your sewing to secure the stitching.

11 Lay the front pocket lining with the right side down so the top edge of the pocket is level with the bottom jet seam allowance. Pin in place **(a)**. Flip the garment over, then fold the garment back to reveal the jet seam allowance **(b)**. Sew through the jet seam allowance and the front pocket lining, sewing directly on top of the seam line **(c)**. Fold down the pocket and press flat away from the jetted opening **(d)**.

12 Place the pocket facing over the top edge of the back pocket lining so both pieces have the right side uppermost and the raw edges are flush. Zigzag across the bottom edge of the pocket facing and baste across the top to keep both layers together.

13 Lay the back pocket, and its facing, with the right side down onto the wrong side of the pocket so the top edge of the pocket is level with the top jet seam allowance. Pin in place. Flip the garment over and fold it back to reveal the seam allowance. Sew through the jet seam allowance and back pocket lining, sewing directly on top of the seam line.

14 Line up the back pocket lining so it sits flat over the front pocket lining. Sew down the sides and across the bottom of the pocket bag **(a).** Neaten and finish the seam allowances **(b).**

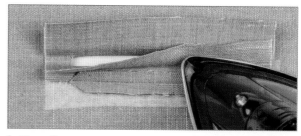

6 Wrong side

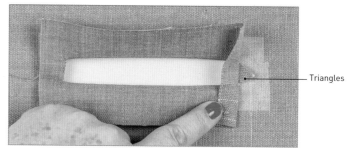

Triangles

7

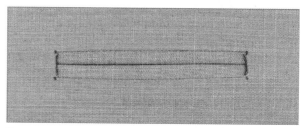

8 Right side

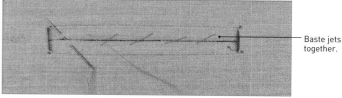

Baste jets together.

9

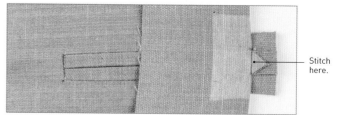

Stitch here.

10

> ## Try this

From the right side, herringbone stitch across the welts to hold them in place. This prevents the pocket from bagging and stretching while the rest of the garment construction process takes place.

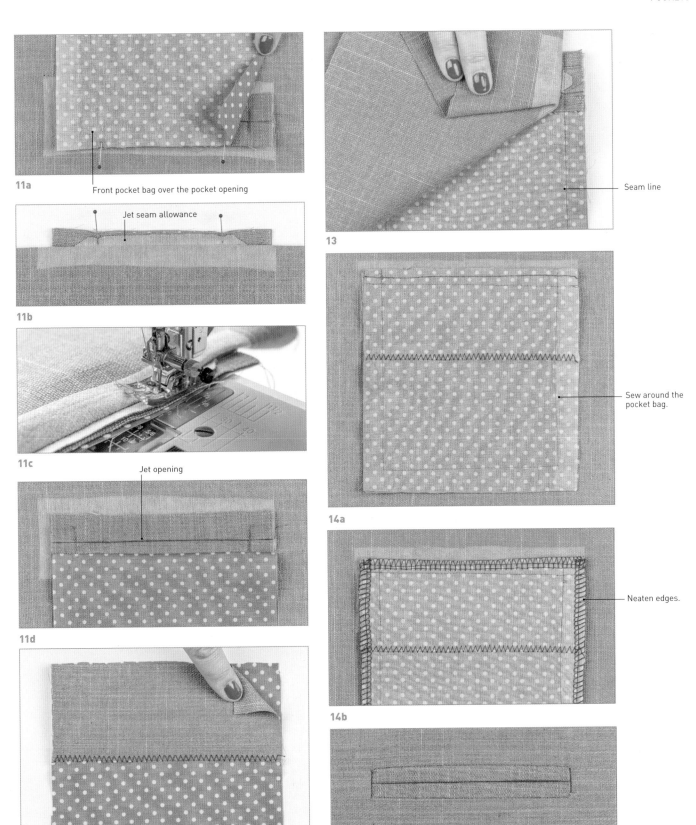

11a Front pocket bag over the pocket opening

11b Jet seam allowance

11c

11d Jet opening

12

13 Seam line

14a Sew around the pocket bag.

14b Neaten edges.

Finished jetted pocket

Western-style pocket

A Western-style pocket is one with a cut-away front section. Another name for this type of pocket is the jeans pocket or "J" pocket, as this is the shape of pocket used most frequently in jeans. The high, curved shape of the pocket allows you to slide your hand into the pocket very easily in a close-fitting pair of pants such as jeans. Although the cut-away shape is usually curved, it can be angled to give a more contemporary feel.

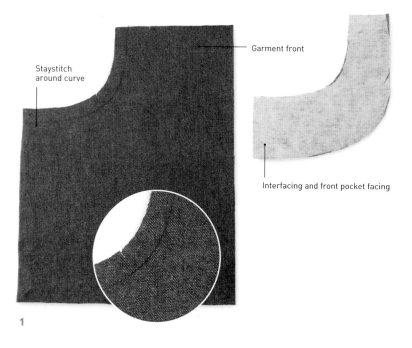

Staystitch around curve

Garment front

Interfacing and front pocket facing

1

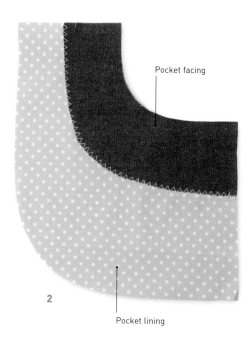

Pocket facing

Pocket lining

2

The front of the pocket is cut away, which will reveal the back of the pocket, so this will require a facing; a facing is also needed to neaten the front curved edge of the pocket. Both of these facings can be in decorative or contrast fabrics if you choose. This leaves the pocket bag, which should be of a lighter-weight fabric than the garment to avoid adding extra bulk to the inside of your garment.

1 Apply interfacing to the wrong side of the front pocket facing and staystitch around the curve of the pocket opening on the garment front.

2 Lay the wrong side of the front pocket facing onto the right side of the front pocket bag. Make sure that the curves of the pocket openings match up. Sew around the bottom edge of the front pocket facing

with a zigzag to keep it all flat. Make up the rest of the pocket using both layers of the front pocket and front pocket facing as one.

3 With right sides together, place the pocket front facing on the garment front. Pin and sew around the curved pocket opening.

4 Layer the seam (see page 91) and snip into the remaining curved seam allowance.

5 Flip the facing back to the right side and understitch (see page 232) the facing to the seam allowance, but not to the garment.

6 Fold the facing back to the wrong side and press in place, rolling the facing to the underside. Edge stitch around the curved pocket opening through all layers.

7 With the wrong side of the facing against the right side of the pocket bag, lay the pocket back facing over the back pocket bag. Line up the top edges and machine baste together. Zigzag over the bottom edge of the pocket back facing to attach it to the pocket bag. This reduces the bulk; if you are using lighter-weight fabrics, you can use a seam here instead.

8 With right sides together, lay the back pocket over the front pocket. Match up the raw edges of the pocket bag and sew the front and back pocket bags together around the curved bottom edge. Make sure to keep the main garment out of the way. Neaten the seam allowance.

9 Machine baste the pocket bag flat to the side seam of the garment.

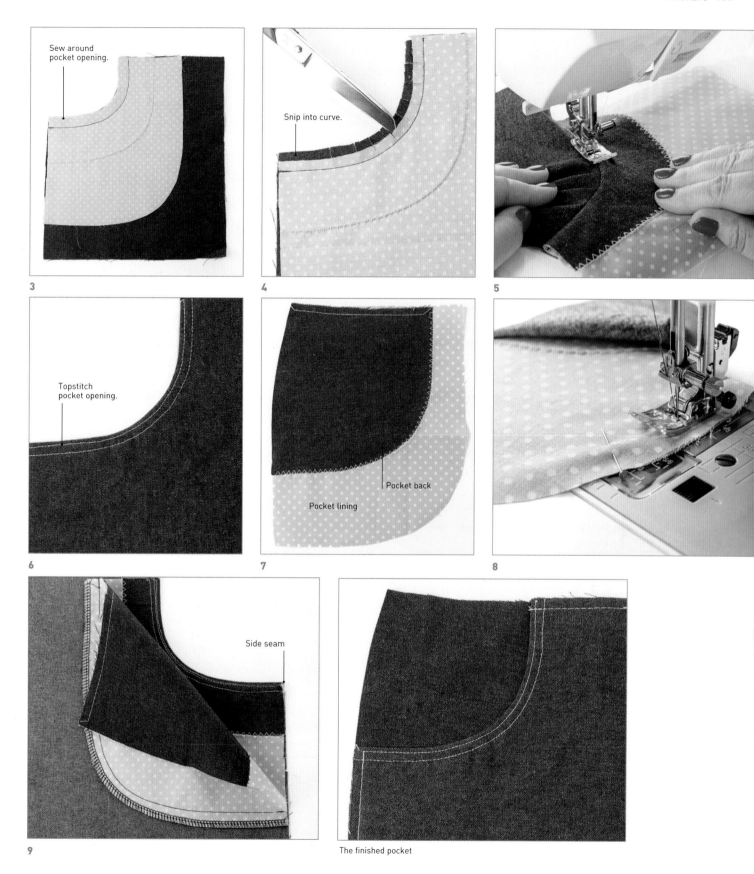

3 Sew around pocket opening.

4 Snip into curve.

5

6 Topstitch pocket opening.

7 Pocket back

Pocket lining

8

9 Side seam

The finished pocket

Cargo pocket

Cargo pockets are chunky, solid-looking, utilitarian pockets. Similar to patch pockets, there are a whole range of variations that can be achieved. Although best suited to more robust fabrics such as cotton drill or even heavy-weight linen, the contrast of a chunky pocket made up with a more delicate fabric such as washed silk georgette can be very effective.

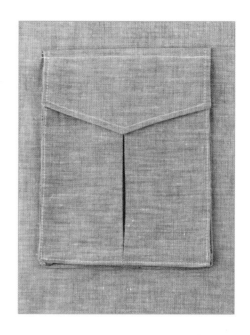

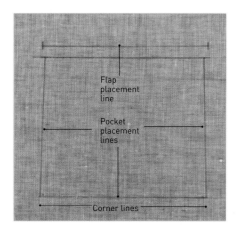

1

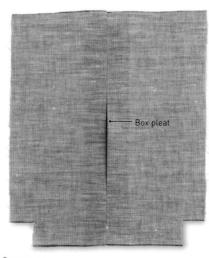

2 Right side

Fold and topstitch in place.

3

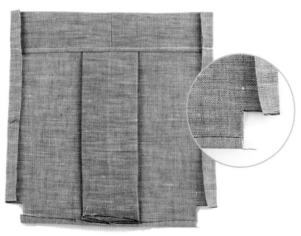

4 Wrong side

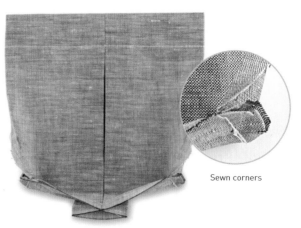

Sewn corners

5 Right side

This sample uses a pleated pocket with a flap. It is generally a good idea to make the pocket flap about ¼ in. (6 mm) wider than the pocket, so that the flap will sit neatly over the pocket and the pocket will not be visible along the sides of the flap.

1 Mark out the pocket placement lines on the right side of the garment.

2 Create a box pleat down the center of the pocket piece (see page 82). Finish the pleat by sewing a small distance along the pleat fold line at the top and bottom of the pleat. Press the pleat flat.

3 Fold under ⅜ in. (1 cm) across the top edge of the pocket, then fold the top edge under again along the fold line; this creates the pocket facing. Topstitch along the bottom of the facing to secure it in place.

4 Press under the seam allowance along the three remaining sides of the pocket. This will act as a guide later.

5 Fold the pocket with the right sides together to pinch together the bottom corners. Sew across the corners.

6 Trim off the excess fabric from the corners and turn the right way around.

7 Fold the seam allowance under the sides and base of the pocket and press in place to create a crease that runs around the front of the pocket.

8 Edge stitch along each of these creases, stopping at the corners and starting again once the corner has been turned.

9 Place the top of the pocket at the top placement line, line up the base of the pocket at the bottom points, and pin in place. Make sure that the four corners of the pocket base are directly under the four corners of the front of the pocket.

10 Edge stitch around the pocket base, pivoting at each corner before continuing.

11 A small rectangle or triangle can be sewn at the top corners of the pocket to reinforce the pocket opening (see page 100).

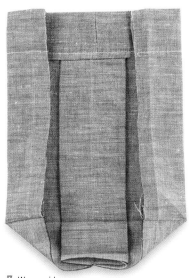

7 Wrong side

7 Right side

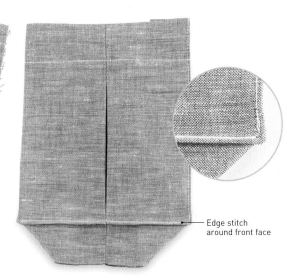

Edge stitch around front face

8

9

10–11

Pocket flap and interfacing

Pocket flap and lining

12

13

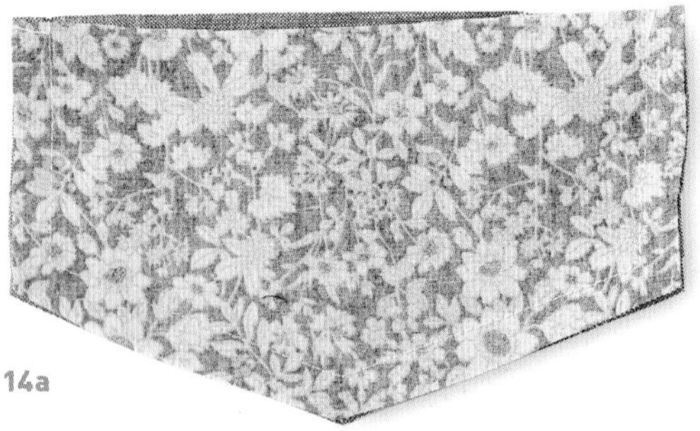

14a

14b

Keep corners sharp.

If the fabric is rather heavy you can sew one stitch across the corner to keep a sharp point.

15

18

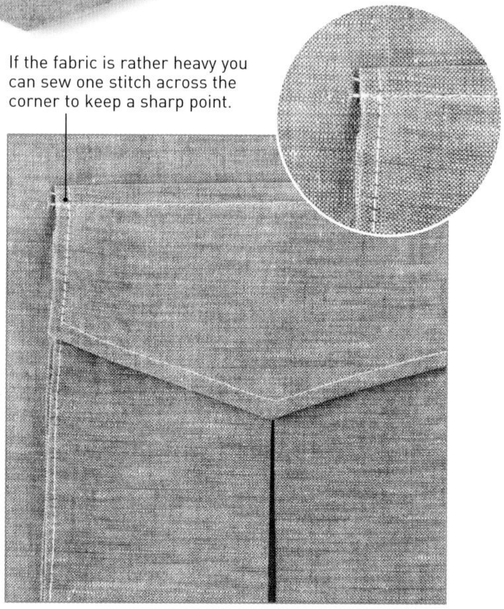

19

12 Apply interfacing to the wrong side of the pocket flap.

13 The pocket flap lining should be just a fraction smaller than the pocket flap. This allows the lining to be eased onto the flap and ensures that the pocket flap has to roll under very slightly, keeping the lining hidden.

14 Pin the flap and the lining right sides together. Ease the lining so that it will fit the flap and all the raw edges are sitting flush **(a)**. Sew around the side and bottom edges of the flap, pivoting at the corners to keep them nice and sharp **(b)**.

15 Clip the excess fabric off the corners and turn the flap right side out. Poke out the corners and press flat, making sure that the lining is not visible from the right side. Topstitch around the sides and point of the flap.

16 Baste the open edge together through all the layers.

17 Place the pocket flap right side down on the right side of the garment along the placement line.

18 Stitch in place along the placement line, and trim the seam allowance back by ¼ in. (6 mm).

19 Fold the pocket flap back down, press in place, and topstitch the pocket flap down, enclosing the trimmed seam allowance.

This horseshoe-shaped patch pocket is given a three-dimensional quality by adding in an inverted box pleat.

Openings and closures

One of the joys of a handmade wardrobe is that you can give a much better finish to your clothes. The openings and closures of your garments are one of those areas you can pay special attention to, ensuring that the way you get in and out of your garments remains secure. There is nothing more frustrating than a zipper that comes apart from the dress or a buttonhole that unravels.

Openings and closures are also a way for you to add your own personal style to your clothes; after all, the devil is in the detail. Just having a flash of a contrasting fabric on a bound opening makes a shirt that bit more unusual and special. It is these well-considered details that really set a handmade garment apart from mass-produced items of apparel.

Placket opening   Placket opening

1

Placket opening

A placket opening is the traditional opening used on men's shirt sleeves. Quite often it has a point at the top of the placket and is then known as a tower placket. It also works well as a front opening on shirts and blouses, as all the raw edges are enclosed, giving a nice, neat finish.

This technique can seem quite complicated, but is actually quite straightforward. A bit of accurate pressing to start will definitely help. Using a contrast fabric can add interest, too, although it is best to avoid a very fine fabric as the seam allowances will be visible through the fabric.

1 Start by marking the placket opening on the wrong sides of both the sleeve and the placket.

2 On the placket, press under the long sides by ³⁄₁₆ in. (5 mm), then press under the edges of the tower so that the point remains in the center.

3 Place the placket opening line directly over the sleeve opening line and then pin in place.

Tip: To get the placement lines lined up beautifully, put a pin through the top of the placement line on the placket and then poke the same pin through the top of the placement line on the sleeve. This will ensure that the placket stays vertical.

4 Sew along the placket opening lines, making sure to pivot accurately at the corners.

5 Cut through the center of the placket opening, stopping ³⁄₈ in. (1 cm) short of each end. Snip a Y-shape into the corners, taking care to get in nice and tight but not to cut through the stitching line.

6 Gently press the placket away from the garment.

2

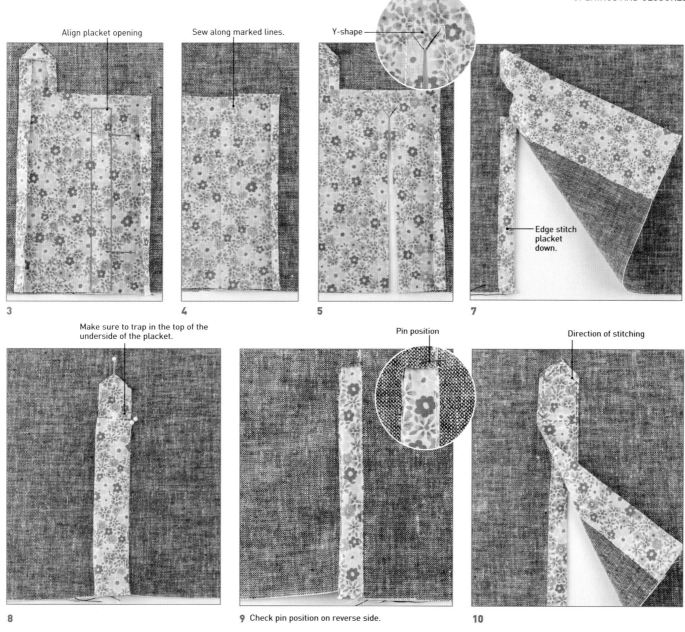

Align placket opening

Sew along marked lines.

Y-shape

Edge stitch
placket
down.

3

4

5

7

Make sure to trap in the top of the
underside of the placket.

Pin position

Direction of stitching

8

9 Check pin position on reverse side.

10

7 Pull the placket through the opening to
the right side. On the side without the tower
point, fold the placket over the seam
allowance so that the folded-under edge
of the placket sits just over the row of
stitching. Pin in place. Edge stitch the
placket down, sewing from the hem to the
top of the opening.

8 Fold over the other pointed side of the
placket so that the folded edge sits just
over the line of sewing. As you pressed the
placket earlier, it should all fall into place.
Pin in place.

Tip: To keep it all sitting beautifully,
before folding over the pointed side of the
placket, carefully press the top seam of
the opening with the toe of the iron. This
will help the sides of the placket to sit
accurately and flat under the pointed
section of the placket.

9 Check to see where the end of the
opening is and mark with a pin. You will
need to sew across this later.

10 Starting at the hem of the placket, edge
stitch up the long side and pivot around the
corners of the pointed tower shape. When
you reach the pin marking the end of the
opening, pivot and sew across the placket.
Sew back up the placket for four stitches,
and then sew back across the placket again.

Continuous-bound opening

A continuous-bound opening is a beautiful way to neaten an opening. It works well as both a sleeve opening and at the back neckline. It is a more delicate method than the traditional placket opening, and so more suited to finer fabrics such as a cotton lawn or silk crêpe de Chine.

1 Start by marking the opening placement line on the right side of the garment.

2 Using a shorter than usual stitch length, sew a line ⅛ in. (3 mm) from the placement line up one side, pivot at the end of the placement line, sew across the top of the placement line, and pivot ⅛ in. (3 mm) away from the line to sew back down the other side.

3 Using sharp scissors, very carefully cut through the placement line, stopping just short of each end. Snip a Y-shape into the corners of the rectangle, taking care to get in nice and tight, but not to cut through the stitching line.

4 Press under a scant ¼ in. (5 mm) along one long edge of the binding.

5 Place the right side of the unpressed edge of the binding to the wrong side of the cut opening. Open the cut gap and lay along the length of the binding. The center of the opening will sit away from the edge of the binding, but that's fine. Pin it in place.

6 With the cut opening on the top so that you can check that everything is caught in place, sew along the binding, ¼ in. (6 mm) from the edge.

7 Carefully press the binding toward the seam allowance.

8 Fold over the binding to the right side of the garment, bringing the folded edge of the binding so that it sits just over the line of stitching. Pin in place.

9 Edge stitch the binding down so that it covers the previous row of sewing. Press the binding flat.

10 To finish, fold the binding together and sew diagonally across the top of the binding. This holds everything neatly in place.

 Try this

If you want to hand finish the binding, make sure to sew the binding to the right side of the opening first. You can then hand catch the binding to the wrong side of the garment.

Tip: Usually the right sides are sewn together, but here the binding is attached to the wrong side first. This means that the topstitching is done from the right side, making it easier to sew close to the edge while still catching everything down.

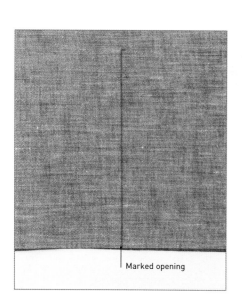

Marked opening

1

Stitch around opening.

2

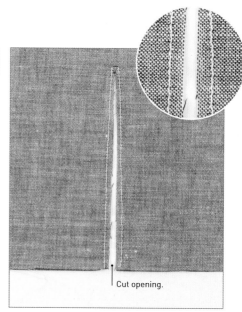

Cut opening.

3

4

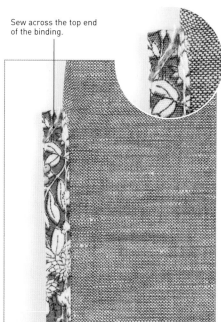

Sew across the top end of the binding.

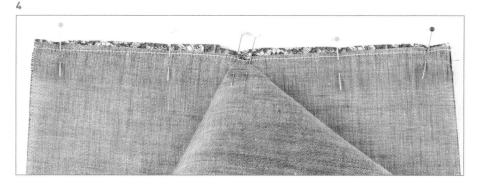

5

10

Sew across the end of the opening split.

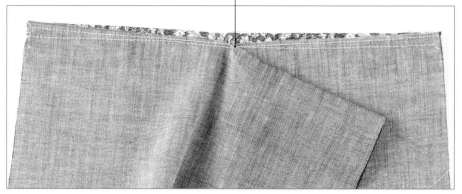

6

8

Finished continuous-bound opening

Center-back vent

A center-back vent is an opening at the base of a seam, which allows for ease of movement within a garment. It is often used in straight or pencil skirts, and also on the back of a jacket.

A center-back vent is created by extending the lower part of the seam allowance out by the desired width of the vent facing.

The left side will usually overlap the right side when the vent is in the center back. Occasionally, there can be two vents in the back of a garment—on a jacket, for example. In this case, the vents will overlap away from the center back seam.

1 Apply interfacing to stabilize the back vent area. The interfaced area needs to extend from ¾ in. (2 cm) above the start of the vent down to the hem and along the hemline so that the interfaced area is just over double the width of the hem.

2 Begin by marking the hemlines and the center back lines on the wrong sides of the garment.

3 Neaten the hemlines of the left and right backs, using your preferred method (see pages 234–241). On the underlap (the right back, as worn), fold the hem back to the right side and sew down the leading edge of the vent extension.

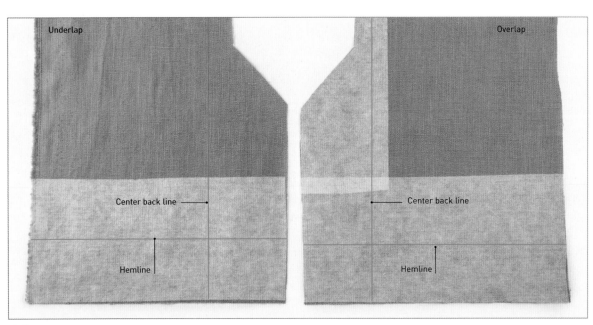

Underlap   Overlap

Center back line   Center back line

Hemline   Hemline

1–2

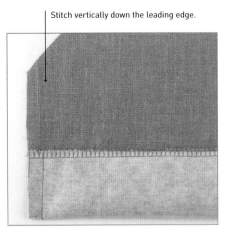

Stitch vertically down the leading edge.

3

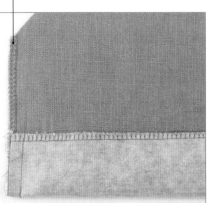

Neaten leading edge

4

Hand stitch the hem on the leading edge.

5 Wrong side

4 Neaten the leading edge of the vent extension to just past the start of the stitching.

5 Turn the hem back to the wrong side, and use a point turner on the corner. Press under the leading edge of the vent extension so that it sits in line with the seam. Hand stitch the seam allowance down.

6 On the overlap (the left back, as worn), neaten the leading edge of the vent extension and fold the extension back to the right side. Sew horizontally across the vent extension along the hemline.

7 Trim away the excess fabric on the extension only. Turn back the right way and use a point turner on the corner.

8 Sew down the center back seam, pivoting at the top of the vent, and then continue sewing along the diagonal edge of the back vent.

9 From the wrong side of the garment, the underlapped extension should be uppermost and the overlapped extension underneath. Clip the center back seam allowance just above the pivot point of the stitching. Press the center back seam open.

10 On the right side of the garment, press the overlapped vent in place and topstitch across the diagonal top edge of the vent from the edge of the vent to the center back seam. Make sure to reverse stitch at the start and finish to secure the sewing.

11 Continue to blind stitch (see page 237) the hem in place.

 Try this

I like to add a strip of interfacing to the inside of the hemline so that it just protrudes over the hem. When hand sewing the hem, the blind hem stitches will then go through the interfacing, not the fabric, keeping everything invisible from the right side. But make sure the interfacing is properly adhered to the fabric.

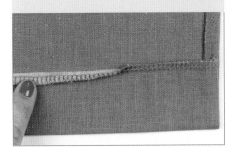

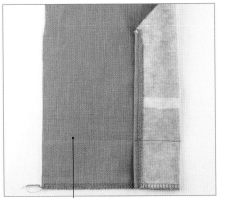

6   Sew horizontally along the hemline.

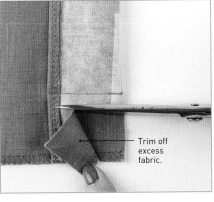

7   Trim off excess fabric.

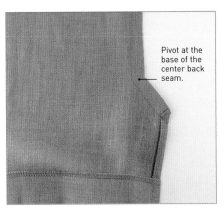

Pivot at the base of the center back seam.

8

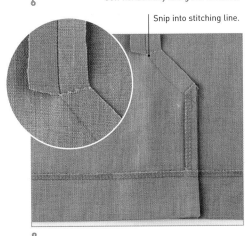

Snip into stitching line.

9

10   Finished vent

11

Buttons and buttonholes

The right kind of buttons can really finish off a garment, so do take this into consideration when making an item for your handmade wardrobe.

The different colors and designs of buttons are infinite but they fall into two basic categories: buttons with holes and buttons with shanks. Buttons with holes are usually of the two-hole or four-hole variety. As they will lie completely flat against the fabric when sewn on, there is little space between the button and the garment to allow an additional layer of fabric to sit between when the button is fastened and passed through the buttonhole.

This is why a thread shank is required. It lifts the button slightly above the garment it is sewn to, allowing the other side of the garment with the buttonhole to sit neatly underneath the button once it has been buttoned up. As you are sewing on the button, slide a matchstick underneath it. This prevents you from pulling the threads too tight and not leaving enough loose thread to create the shank.

 Try this

When sewing on a button, use approx. 1 yard (1 m) of thread. Double up the thread and pass the looped end through the eye of the needle. Make all the ends level and then tie a knot. This means that you will be sewing with four strands of thread, making each stitch stronger—so you will need fewer of them.

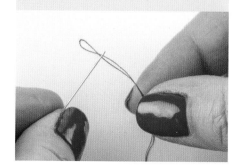

1

2

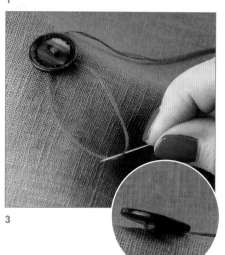

3

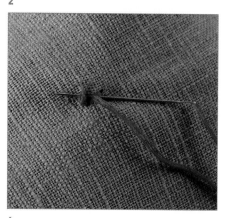

4

HOW TO SEW ON A BUTTON

1 Tie a good knot in the end of the thread, one that will not pull through the fabric, or sew a few locking stitches into the fabric first.

2 Pass the needle from the back to the front of the garment and through the first hole of the button. Slide a matchstick under the button, then thread the needle back down through the other hole of the button.

3 After several stitches have been made through the button, pass the needle so that it comes through the fabric under the button and remove the matchstick. Wind the thread around the button shank three or four times in order to strengthen the button shank.

4 Pass the needle through to the underside and sew a few locking stitches through the visible threads.

BUTTON WITH A SHANK

1 Tie a good knot in the end of the thread or sew a few locking stitches into the fabric first.

2 Sew a stitch through the fabric and, with the needle still in the fabric, thread on the shank of the button.

3 Pull the needle through to complete the stitch.

4 Hold the button and press it slightly so that, as you pass the needle through the fabric to sew a stitch, the needle passes through the button shank as well.

5 Sew several stitches in this way and then sew a few locking stitches through the visible threads.

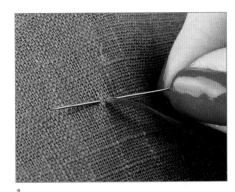
1

2

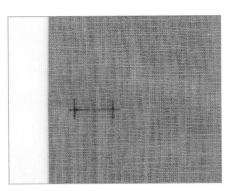
4

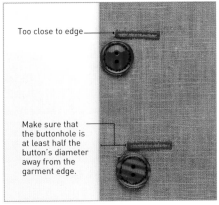
5

MEASURING FOR A MACHINE-STITCHED BUTTONHOLE

Most modern sewing machines have some form of automatic or semi-automatic buttonhole stitch already preprogrammed. This makes sewing regular-sized buttonholes a lot easier.

However, they still need to be marked out accurately. A general rule of thumb is that the end of the buttonhole should be no less than half the button's diameter away from the edge of the garment. This is because the button will usually pull to the farthest end of the buttonhole and, if it's too close to the edge of the garment, the button could hang over the edge.

Buttonholes should be marked with a fabric pen or chalk to show the length of the buttonhole. If they are being marked to be hand sewn, a placement line should be shown as well.

After stitching, the buttonhole needs to be opened. The easiest method is to use a really sharp seam ripper.

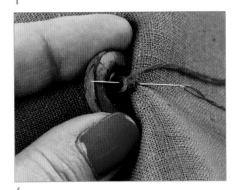
Marking the buttonhole

Too close to edge

Make sure that the buttonhole is at least half the button's diameter away from the garment edge.

Correct position for buttonhole

Try this

To avoid accidentally cutting through the end of the buttonhole, place a pin up and over the end of the buttonhole just in front of the end bar. The pin will stop the seam ripper from going too far.

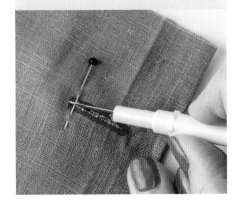

BOUND BUTTONHOLE

Bound buttonholes can look very pleasing on coats and jackets, and also work well if sewn in a contrasting fabric. They are a little more involved, but really worth the effort for a fine finish to a garment.

If the buttonholes are sewn onto a jacket, you will need to create holes in the corresponding facing. The buttonhole positions can be marked out on both the garment and the facing at the same time, ensuring that everything lines up. To make the facing, see page 124.

Help!

....

My buttonholes don't align.

If you are sewing several bound buttonholes—down the front of a coat, for example—it can make life much easier to cut yourself a cardstock template to the correct dimensions of the buttonhole. That way you can just draw around the template to mark out the position of the buttonholes.

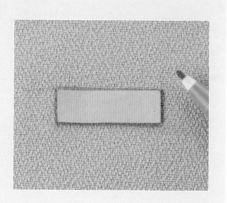

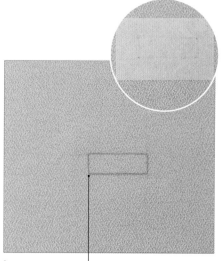

1   Buttonhole position

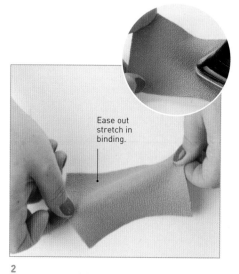

Ease out stretch in binding.

2

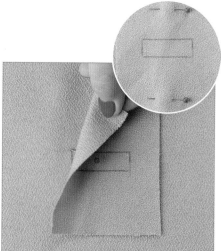

3   Wrong side

4

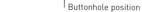
Snip into corners.

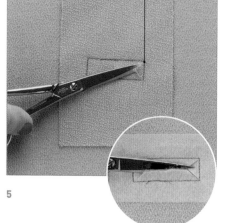

5

6

1 Mark out buttonhole position. Apply interfacing to the reverse of the buttonhole areas on the garment to support the fabric.

2 Cut a rectangle of fabric on the bias, at least 1¼ in. (3 cm) longer and 2 in. (5 cm) wider than the finished buttonhole. (The reason for cutting it on the bias is to allow a bit of ease to let the button pass through the opening.) Press and steam this as you try and pull out the stretch in the fabric. This will flatten out slightly thicker fabrics and make them sit better once in position.

3 Draw out the buttonhole on the wrong side of the bias-cut rectangle. With right sides together, place the rectangle directly over the buttonhole on the garment. Pin in place, pinning away from the marked lines.

4 Starting on a long side, sew along the marked lines, pivoting at the corners and overlapping your stitches at the end.

5 Cut through the center of the rectangle, cutting through both layers of fabric and the interfacing. Stop just short of the ends and snip Y-shapes into the corners, taking care not to cut through the stitching.

6 Carefully pull the bias-cut piece through the slit and press it flat.

7 To create the first lip, fold the top edge of the bias-cut rectangle over, so that the fold lies down the center of the opening. Press and pin in place.

8 Repeat Step 7 to create the other side of the lip. Then press the buttonhole from the right side.

9 Fold back the garment to reveal the small triangle at each end of the buttonhole and sew across all the layers. You can sew with a zipper foot to keep close to the edge of the opening.

10 Sew the seam allowance of the first lip to the bias rectangle, sewing directly over the previous line of stitching. Repeat for the other lip.

11 Trim off any excess fabric on the bias rectangle and press it flat. Baste the lips of the buttonhole closed to prevent it from warping as the rest of the garment is sewn together.

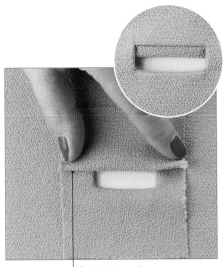

7   Fold back top edge.

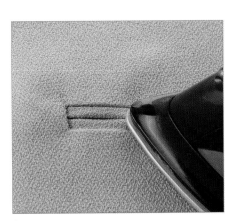

8   Right side

9

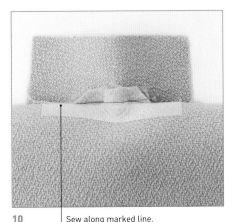

10   Sew along marked line.

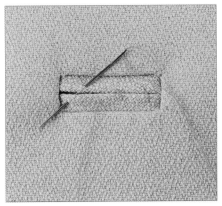

11

THE FACING

To make the buttonholes, see pages 122–123.

1 Cut a rectangle of iron-on interfacing about 2½ in. (6 cm) wider and 1½ in. (4 cm) longer than the buttonhole and mark the buttonhole in the center of the rectangle.

2 Place the non-adhesive side of the interfacing to the right side of the facing, directly over the buttonhole marks, and sew just inside the marked line with a shorter than usual stitch. Start on a long side, pivot at the corners, and overlap your stitching at the end.

3 Cut through the center of the buttonhole, stopping just before the ends, and snip Y-shapes into the corners, taking care not to cut through the stitching.

4 Pull the interfacing through the gap and arrange neatly before pressing the interfacing to the facing. The facing now has nice neat little windows already matched up to the buttonholes.

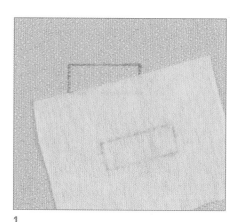

1

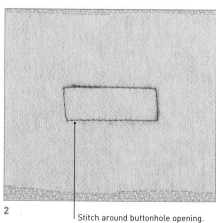

2 — Stitch around buttonhole opening.

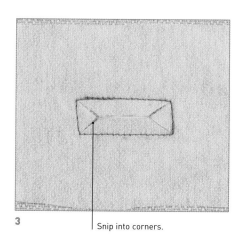

3 — Snip into corners.

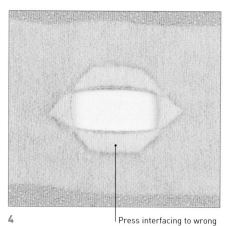

4 — Press interfacing to wrong side of facing.

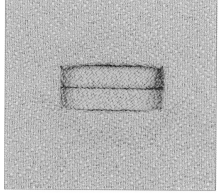

Finished facing

→ The contrast buttons provide a striking detail to this skirt.

Hooks and eyes

Hooks and eyes are usually made from twisted wire and can be minuscule or enormous, depending on their purpose. They can be plain nickel or colored black or white, and it is important to make sure that they are as invisible as possible.

Hooks and eyes are most commonly found at the tops of zippers; alternatively, they can be used to fasten a delicate fabric that doesn't have a lot of stress placed on it. Both the hook and the eye have two loops at the base through which you sew them to the fabric.

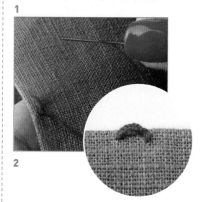

2

3

4

1

2a

2b

Finished hook and eye

SEWING THE HOOK

1 Begin by sewing a locking stitch into the fabric to mark the position of the hook.

2 Hold the hook in position with your thumb and forefinger, and wrap the threads under the hook. Sew through the fabric back under the hook. Sew a few more stitches; this will hold the hook in place while you stitch the base.

3 Slide the needle from the top of the hook through the fabric to come out in one of the loops. Sew with a buttonhole stitch all around the loop. This not only looks more attractive, but makes it nice and strong, too.

4 Slide the needle through the fabric so that it comes through the other loop. Continue to sew around the loop with a buttonhole stitch. Fasten off with a couple of locking stitches.

SEWING THE EYE

1 Sew a locking stitch as before to mark the position of the eye.

2 Sew a bar across the base of the large loop to hold it in place **(a)**, while you sew the smaller loops in place with a buttonhole stitch **(b)**, as before.

SEWING A WORKED LOOP

Sometimes a more delicate finish is required; in this instance, it is best to use a hand-stitched loop with a metal hook.

1 With a double thread sew a couple of locking stitches, then thread the needle through the layers of fabric the width of the required loop. Sew a couple of stitches in this way to create the thread bar of the loop.

2 Starting at the end, sew a buttonhole stitch around the thread bar. Make sure each stitch is nice and close to its neighbor. Again, this not only looks more attractive, but also makes the worked loop stronger. Finish with a couple of locking stitches.

Snap fasteners

Snap fasteners, or press studs, are little used now, but can be extremely useful in the right place. Sometimes used in place of hooks and eyes, they can be used in places that can be hard to reach and they are often found on vintage clothing to secure a side opening on a skirt or dress. They can also be used underneath large decorative buttons, where a large buttonhole would be impractical.

Snap fasteners come in a variety of sizes and are comprised of two elements: a ball side and a socket side. The ball "snaps" inside the socket, holding the two sides together. They are hand sewn onto the fabric using a double thickness of thread.

1 Mark the position of the snap fastener on the garment. There may be placement marks that can be transferred from the pattern onto the fabric.

2 Start by sewing a couple of locking stitches on the placement point.

3 Now bring the needle through one of the four large holes on the ball side of the snap fastener. Hold the snap in place with your finger and thumb.

4 Pass the needle down through the fabric and back up through the hole in the snap. You can sew a buttonhole stitch here, but an over stitch will suffice.

5 Sew four or five stitches, then pass the needle down through the fabric and up into the next hole. Continue to sew several stitches in each hole to firmly attach the snap.

6 When the last hole has been sewn down, sew a couple of locking stitches through the fabric.

7 From underneath, pass a pin through the center of the ball part of the snap, so that it protrudes. Hold the socket side of the snap so that the pin passes through the center. Overlap the other side of the garment: the pin will stitck through, marking the spot where you need to attach the socket side of the snap.

8 Repeat Steps 2–6 to attach the socket part of the snap, then remove the pin.

1–3

4

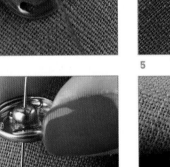

5

6

7

8

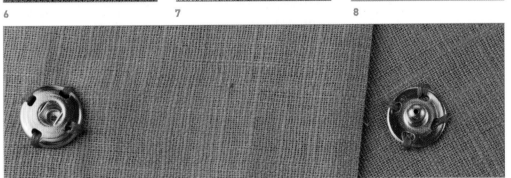

Finished snap fastener

Zippers

Zippers have been around in one form or another for longer than you might imagine. There were several iterations along the way before the product that we recognize today came into being. The first patent was in 1851, but it took 40 years to get the product to market. And even then it wasn't until 1913 that the modern zipper, designed by a gentleman named Gideon Sundbeck, was developed.

Zippers were mainly used on boots and tobacco pouches, and it took another 20 years for the fashion industry to cotton on to what a splendid idea they were. The first zippers were made with interlocking metal teeth. Now, however, there are many variations that are suited to particular fabrics or functions. The most common is still the nylon dress zipper, which is the traditional choice for most dressmakers.

Centered zipper

This is perhaps the most traditional method of inserting a zipper and is best used down the center back of a dress or skirt, using a traditional dress zipper.

1 With the back pieces right sides together, apply a strip of very lightweight interfacing down the seam allowances where the zipper is to be inserted to stabilize the opening and prevent the seam from warping or stretching as the zipper is sewn in. If the garment is to be unlined, it is also better to neaten the seam allowances of both center back pieces with your choice of finish before you insert the zipper. Trying to neaten a seam allowance after a zipper has been sewn in is a job worth avoiding.

2 Lay the zipper down along the seam allowance, with the zipper head just under the seam allowance at the top edge of the garment. Mark a point on the seam allowance just under the zipper stop, then set the zipper aside.

3 Machine baste down the center back seam from the top edge of the garment down to the mark for the zipper stop. At this point, drop the needle down into the fabric and change the stitch length back to normal. Backstitch under the mark and carry on sewing to the end of the seam.

4 Press the seam open and flat. Transfer the zipper stop mark to the seam allowance of both pieces. Draw in the stitching lines on to the right side (see Try this, opposite).

5 Lay the zipper right side down over the seam allowance, centering the zipper teeth over the seam line, and pin in place. Hand baste the zipper in place to stop it from shifting. This may seem longwinded, but it is far better to take time now than to have to unpick later.

6 Attach a zipper foot to your machine. For most machines the zipper foot has two sides; make sure that the needle drops to the RIGHT of the foot. You may need to adjust your needle position, depending on the model of your machine.

7 With the right side uppermost and starting at the top of the left-hand side of the zipper, sew down along the marked stitching line, pivot at the corner, sew across the base of the zipper, pivot again at the other corner, and sew back up the right-hand side of the zipper to the top.

8 Carefully open up the seam and remove all the basting stitches. Give the seam a gentle press.

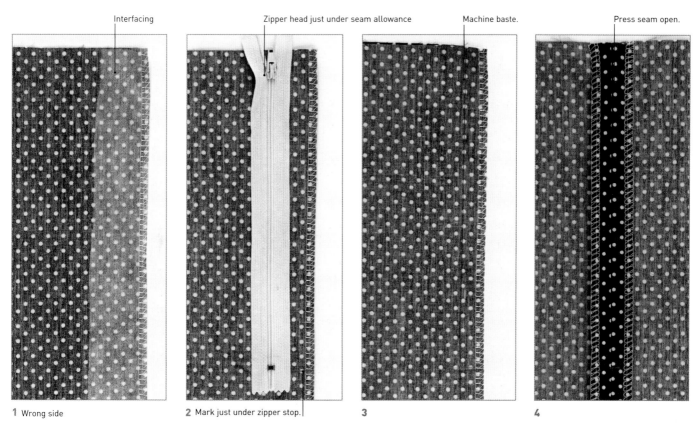

Interfacing

Zipper head just under seam allowance

Machine baste.

Press seam open.

1 Wrong side

2 Mark just under zipper stop.

3

4

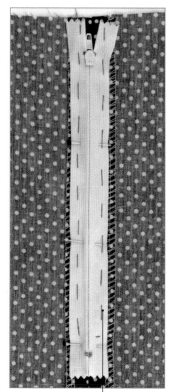

5   Hand baste.

7 Right side   Sew over stitching line.

8

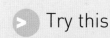
Try this

You can use the machine foot as a guide to sewing in the zipper, but for a really crisp finish, draw in the stitching lines first. Draw one on either side of the seam allowance, ¼ in. (6 mm) from the seam, and the third across the base of the zipper opening, where the zipper stop mark is.

Fly zipper

This seems to be the zipper that causes most apprehension, as it is assumed to be the most complicated. It can be tricky, but with careful consideration it is very straightforward to insert.

Fly zippers are often sewn in facing different directions for men and women's clothing. Similarly, buttons and buttonholes are on opposite sides of a garment in men and women's clothing. This is due to the rather old-fashioned concept of a lady being dressed by her maid. Most servants were assumed to be right-handed, so the fastenings were on the left of the garment, meaning the servant's right.

Nowadays, it is really up to personal preference; most of my jeans have the zipper opening on the right-hand side. So, as with a lot of sewing techniques and processes, go with what you feel most comfortable with. There are few hard-and-fast rules.

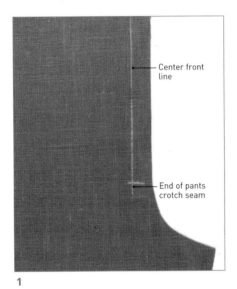

1

Center front line

End of pants crotch seam

2 Fly facing   Fly extension

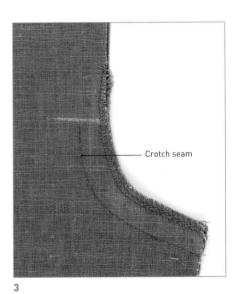

3

Crotch seam

In this sample I have sewn the fly opening on the right, as that is how I prefer to wear my pants. Patterns will differ: Some may include a "grown-on" fly extension, while others use separate fly pieces. I have used separate fly pieces, as I feel this better explains the function of the individual elements of the fly.

1 Mark in the center front line on both front pants pieces. Mark the end of the pants crotch seam on the fabric. You can use chalk or tailor's tacks if you prefer.

2 Apply interfacing to the wrong side of both the fly facing and the fly extension. Neaten the curved edge of the fly facing. Fold the fly extension in half, with wrong sides together, and neaten the curved seam.

3 Place the pants front pieces right sides together and sew the crotch seam up to the marked dot, reverse stitching to secure your sewing.

4 Lay the fly facing right side down on the left pants front, aligning the straight edges, and pin in place. Taking a ⅝-in. (1.5 cm) seam allowance, sew from the start of the crotch seam up to the waist.

5 Layer the seam (see page 91) and understitch (see page 232) the fly facing to the seam allowances.

6 Place the closed zipper right side down on the fly facing, lining up the zipper tape with the seam and making sure that the zipper stop is ¾ in. (2 cm) from the bottom of the fly facing. Pin in place.

7 Machine baste along the right-hand edge of the zipper tape, with the end of the zipper tape folded up. This will prevent the end of the zipper from getting caught in the topstitching later. Then switch back to a normal stitch length and sew a double row of stitching along the left side of the zipper tape close to the zipper teeth and the edge of the zipper tape. This keeps everything really secure.

8 Fold the fly facing back to the wrong side and press along the seam line. Following the curved line of the fly facing, machine baste ¼ in. (6 mm) in from the edge. This will act as a guide for the topstitching.

9 From the right side, topstitch along the line of machine-basting stitches. Remove all the machine-basting stitches and any loose threads.

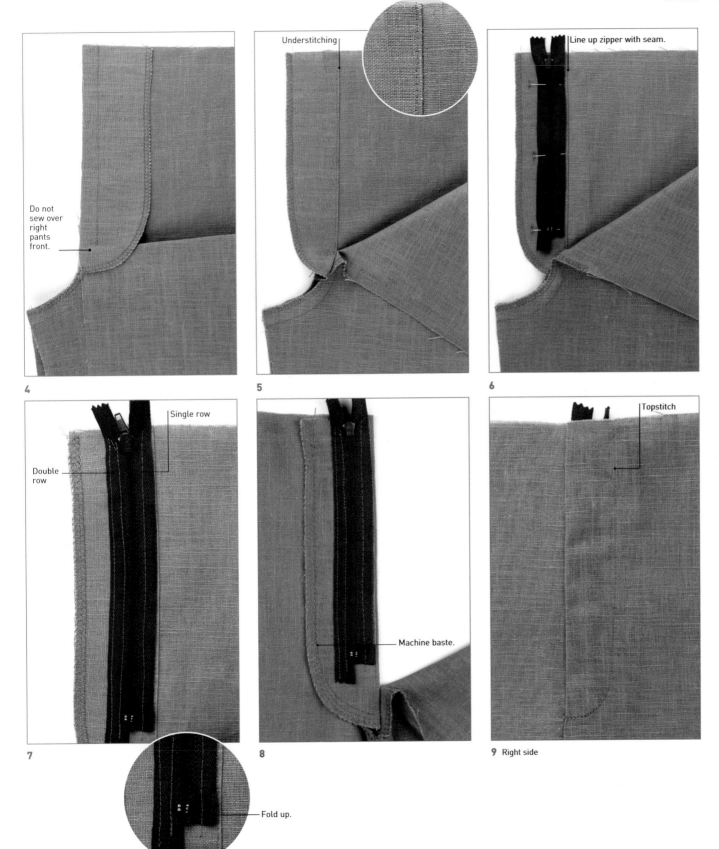

4 Do not sew over right pants front.

5 Understitching

6 Line up zipper with seam.

7 Double row | Single row | Fold up.

8 Machine baste.

9 Right side | Topstitch

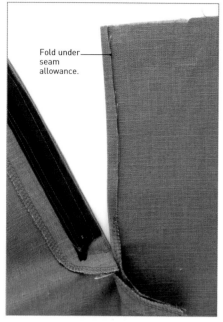

10 Wrong side

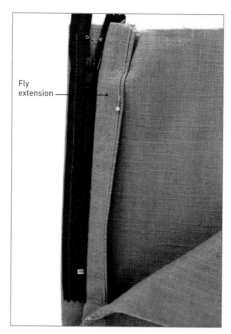

11a

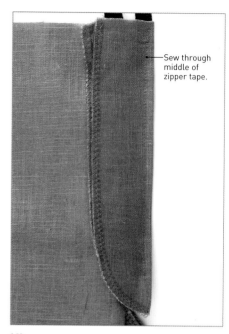

Fold under seam allowance.

Fly extension

Sew through middle of zipper tape.

11b

12

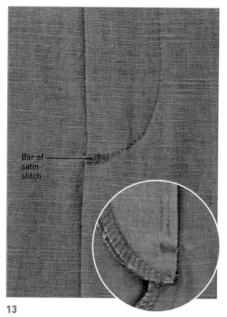

Bar of satin stitch

13

Try this

It is a good idea to neaten the front crotch seam allowance first, as that allows for a cleaner finish inside your garment.

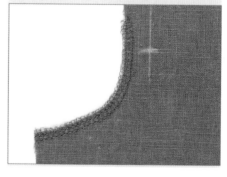

10 On the right pants front, press under a scant ¼ in. (5 mm) to the wrong side.

11 Lay the left side of the zipper tape along the folded edge of the fly extension, making sure that the zipper head is just under the top waist seam allowance. Pin in place **(a)**. Sew from the bottom of the zipper up to the top, through the middle of the zipper tape **(b)**.

12 Tuck the zipper and fly extension underneath the pressed-under seam allowance on the right-hand side of the pants front, making sure that the fold is butted up to the zipper teeth. Pin in place. Topstitch close to the folded edge from the top of the zipper down to just fractionally past the large dot.

13 Sew a bar of satin stitch across the bottom of the fly through all layers.

Lapped zipper

The lapped zipper, or semi-concealed zipper as it is sometimes known, is another more traditional way of inserting a zipper. As the alternative name implies, it is partially concealed and works very effectively on a skirt or as a side fastening on a pair of pants. Make sure that the lap of the zipper sweeps over toward the back of the garment for a smooth finish.

1 Apply a strip of very lightweight interfacing down the seam allowances where the zipper is to be inserted to stabilize the opening and prevent the seam from warping or stretching as the zipper is sewn in.

2 If the garment is to be unlined, it is better to neaten the seam allowances with your choice of finish before you insert the zipper.

3 Lay the zipper along the seam allowance, with the zipper head just under the seam allowance at the top edge of the garment. Mark a point on the seam allowance just under the zipper stop.

4 With right sides together, machine baste from the top edge down to the mark for the zipper. At this point, drop the needle down into the fabric and change the stitch length back to normal. Backstitch under the mark and carry on sewing to the end of the seam.

5 Press the seam open and flat. Transfer the zipper stop mark to the seam allowance.

Tip: You can use the machine foot as a guide to sewing in the zipper, but if you would like a really crisp finish draw in the stitching lines first. On the right-hand side of the seam allowance, draw a line ⅜ in. (1 cm) from the seam line to the zipper stop mark and another line across the base of the zipper opening where the stop mark is.

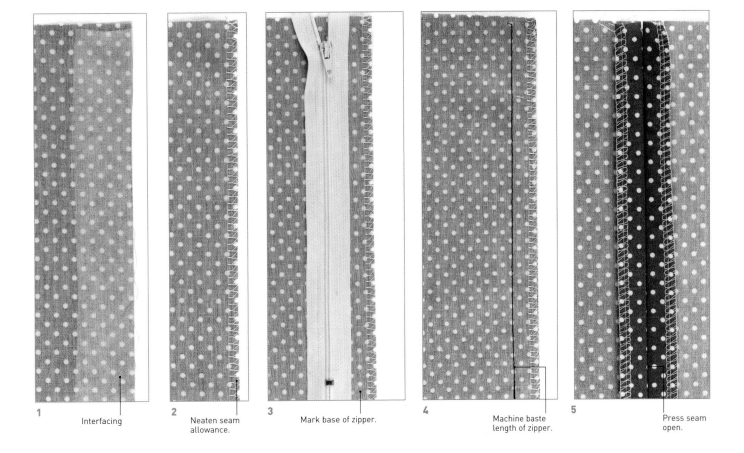

1 Interfacing

2 Neaten seam allowance.

3 Mark base of zipper.

4 Machine baste length of zipper.

5 Press seam open.

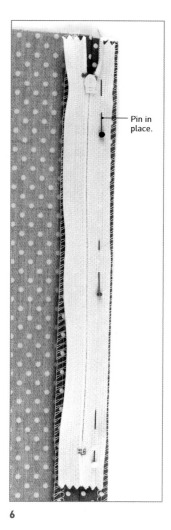

Pin in place.

6

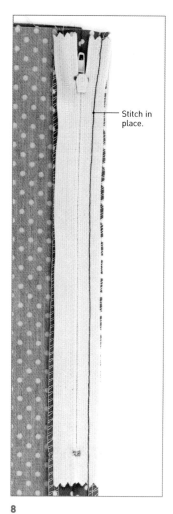

Stitch in place.

8

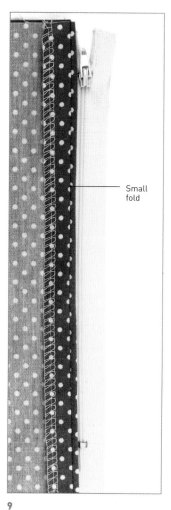

Small fold

9

Topstitch zipper in place.

11

6 Fold the garment away from the right seam allowance, but leave the seam open. Lay the zipper right side down on the seam allowance, centering the zipper teeth over the seam line, and pin in place through the right seam allowance only.

7 Attach a zipper foot to your machine. For most machines the zipper foot has two sides; make sure that the needle drops to the LEFT of the foot. You may need to adjust your needle position, depending on the model of your machine.

8 Starting at the bottom of the zipper, machine baste through the middle of the zipper tape up to the top of the zipper.

9 Turn the zipper over so you can see the right side, and fold the garment away from it. This will create a small fold in the seam allowance, close to but not touching the zipper teeth. Gently press this fold in place.

10 Adjust the needle position so that it now drops to the RIGHT of the foot.

11 From the right side of the zipper, topstitch from the top of the zipper to the bottom along the fold. Only sew through the fold and the zipper tape, not through the garment.

12 Turn the garment to the right side. Hand baste through all the layers to secure the zipper tape to the left-hand side of the seam.

13 Starting from the top of the zipper, sew from the right side down the stitching line, pivot at the corner, and sew across the base of the zipper opening to the seam, backstitching to lock in your sewing.

14 Carefully open the seam and remove all the basting stitches.

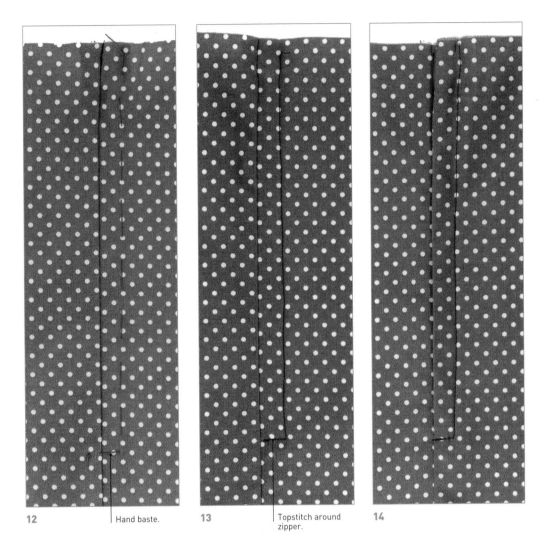

12 | Hand baste.

13 | Topstitch around zipper.

14

> ## Try this

You can achieve a better result with this technique if the zipper goes into a waistband; we will cover how to finish the top of the zipper in the Facings section, see pages 140–142.

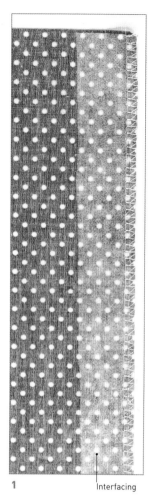
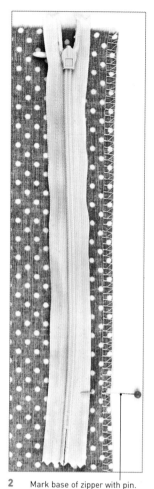
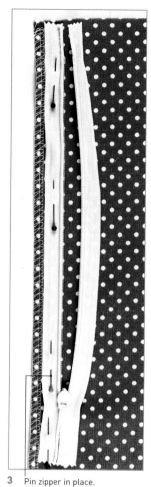

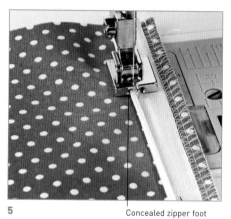

1   Interfacing   2   Mark base of zipper with pin.   3 Pin zipper in place.   5   Concealed zipper foot

Concealed zipper

Concealed, or invisible, zippers are found in a lot of commercially produced garments and are just that—concealed; all you should see is the zipper pull. The big difference with putting in this type of zipper is that, instead of being inserted into a gap in the seam, the zipper is inserted first and then the seam is stitched afterward.

It is possible to sew a concealed zipper with an ordinary zipper foot, but to get the best results you will need a special concealed zipper foot for your machine. This helps to roll out the coil of the zipper teeth so that the needle can sew just into the groove. No zipper tape should be visible from the right side of the garment after the zipper has been sewn in.

1 Apply a strip of very lightweight interfacing down the seam allowances where the zipper is to be inserted to stabilize the opening and prevent the seam from warping or stretching as the zipper is sewn in. If the garment is to be unlined, it is better to neaten the seam allowances with your choice of finish before you insert the zipper.

2 Lay the zipper along the seam line, with the zipper head just below the top seam allowance. Measure down and mark with a pin where the bottom of the zipper opening will be. You won't be able to stitch right to the end of the zipper, so the zipper will need to be at least ¾ in. (2 cm) longer than the opening.

Tip: Prepare the zipper by opening it and gently rolling the zipper teeth back. Press with a warm iron. This just helps flatten the zipper coil slightly and enables the needle to get in closer.

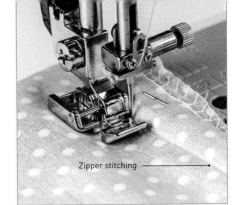

Concealed sewing either side

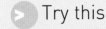

Zipper stitching

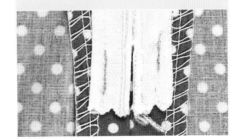

8

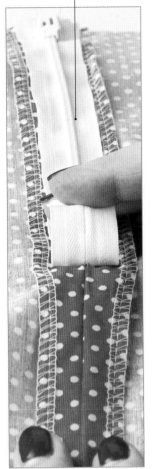

> **Try this**

As there can be a lot of stress placed on the bottom of a zipper, sew the last ¾ in. (2 cm) of zipper tape to the seam allowances only. This will secure the base of the zipper and take the pressure off the stitching holding the zipper in place.

6

7 Pin zipper tail out of way.

The finished concealed zipper: inside

The finished concealed zipper: outside

3 Open the zipper and place it right side down on the left-hand side of the garment, with the edge of the zipper tape parallel with the raw edges of the seam allowance and the zipper teeth on the stitching line. Pin in place.

4 Make sure that the right-hand coil of the zipper sits under the right-hand groove on the concealed zipper foot. Backstitch to start and then sew down the zipper, gently rolling back the zipper coil as you go. Sew down until you are level with the mark for the zipper opening.

5 Close the zipper and line it up along the other side of the garment, with the left-hand side of the zipper tape parallel with the seam allowance. Stitch down the left side of the zipper, this time with the zipper coil in the left-hand groove of the concealed zipper foot.

6 Both ends of stitching should finish at the same level to secure the zipper.

7 Pin the rest of the seam, making sure that the ends of the zipper are pulled up and out between the seam allowances so that the zipper is out of the way when the seam is stitched.

8 Change to a normal zipper foot, with the needle to the right of the foot. Sew up from the hem and sew a couple of stitches past the end of the stitching in order to secure the zipper. Press the seam open, then flip everything over, and give it a good steam from the right side.

Concealed zipper with a facing

The concealed zipper on its own is great, but more usually it will need to be finished off along the top edge, either within a neckline or a waist seam.

There are several ways of finishing off an edge with a zipper, and a facing is a common one. This method of sewing in a facing with a concealed zipper gives a really professional finish, as everything is machine sewn.

2

Finish edges of facing.

1 Concealed zipper

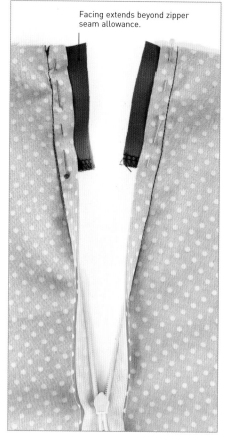

3

Facing extends beyond zipper seam allowance.

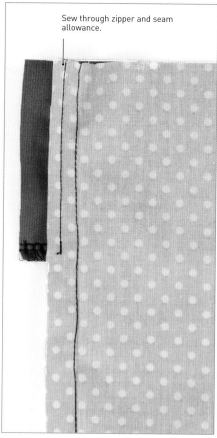

4

Sew through zipper and seam allowance.

1 Start by sewing in a concealed zipper in the usual way.

2 Stabilize the facing with a layer of interfacing; either iron-on or sew-in is fine. Finish off the visible edge of the facing with a bound edge or a zigzag stitch.

3 Place the facing and garment right sides together, matching up the raw edges along the top and any side or shoulder seams. Instead of stitching around the top edge first and then down the sides of the zipper, as is most common, pull the facing out past the zipper opening so that it overhangs by ⅜ in. (1 cm).

4 Using a normal zipper foot, stitch down the center of the zipper tape and across the facing through all the seam allowances. The stitching should be about ¼ in. (6 mm) away from the zipper.

5 Pull the facing away from the zipper and press it flat. Here's the clever part:

6 Fold the facing back toward the garment, using the zipper as the crease of the fold. You should see two rows of sewing. Now you can stitch across the top edge, making sure to go right to the edge of the fabric to keep the corners sharp.

7 Snip off the corners and clip into the top edge seam if you need to, to release the tension in any curves.

8 Pop out the corners and understitch the facing through all the layers of seam allowance, a scant ⅛ in. (2 mm) from the seam. You won't be able to get right into the corners, so just go as far as is comfortable.

9 Give everything a really good press and don't be frightened of the steam button.

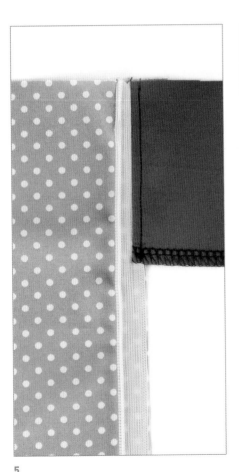

5

Stitch across top edge.

6

7

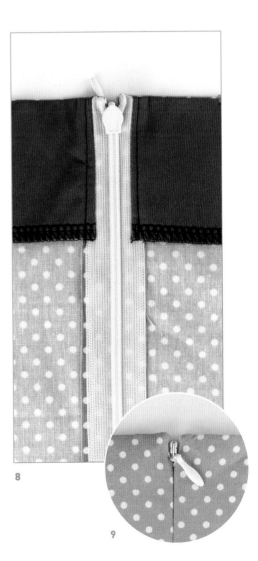

8

9

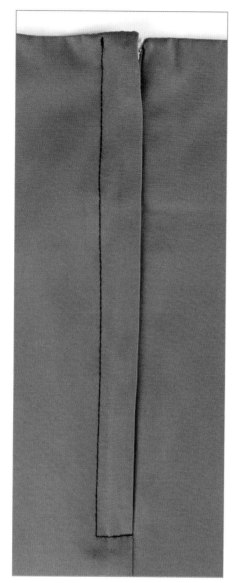

Lapped zipper with a facing

This is a different method for inserting a lapped zipper than the technique shown on pages 133–135, as it incorporates the facing during the process of inserting the zipper. It also uses a wider than usual seam allowance of ¾ in. (2 cm) down the center back opening. This caters for the overlap required for the zipper. You will also need to trim down the seam allowances and facing pieces to make everything fit together more easily.

1 Stabilize the facings with a layer of interfacing; either iron-on or sew-in is fine. Draw in the center back lines on the wrong side of the facings, too.

2 Mark in the center back line on the left and right sides of the garment. Also mark the base of the zipper with a dot on the ¾ in. (2 cm) seam line. Sew up the center back seam from the hem as far as the dot.

3 On the right-hand side of the garment, trim the center back seam allowance so it measures ½ in. (1.2 cm) from the center back line.

4 Pin the zipper face down to the center back seam allowances, so that the edges of the zipper tape lie flush with the raw edges of the seam allowances.

5 Sew down the zipper tape and past the zipper stopper on each side of the zipper, using the zipper foot on your machine.

6 Trim the center back edges of the facing pieces. On the left-hand facing, trim the seam allowance back to the center back line

so that there is no seam allowance at all. On the right-hand facing, trim the seam allowance so it measures ½ in. (1.2 cm) from the center back line.

7 With right sides together, pin the facings to the zipper and center back seam allowances. Sew down the facings along the zipper stitching line.

8 Fold the facings back away from the garment and understitch (see page 232) through the facing and seam allowance.

9 On the left side of the garment fold the facing back to the right side, using the center back line as the fold line. Pin in place around the top edge.

10 On the right-hand side of the garment fold the facing back to the right side—but this time use the zipper as the crease of the fold. Pin around the rest of the top edge.

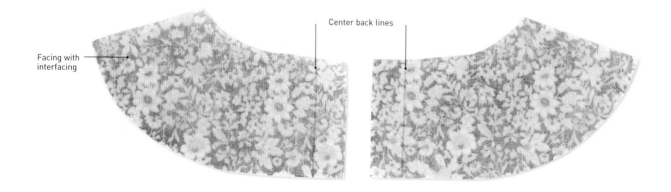

Facing with interfacing

Center back lines

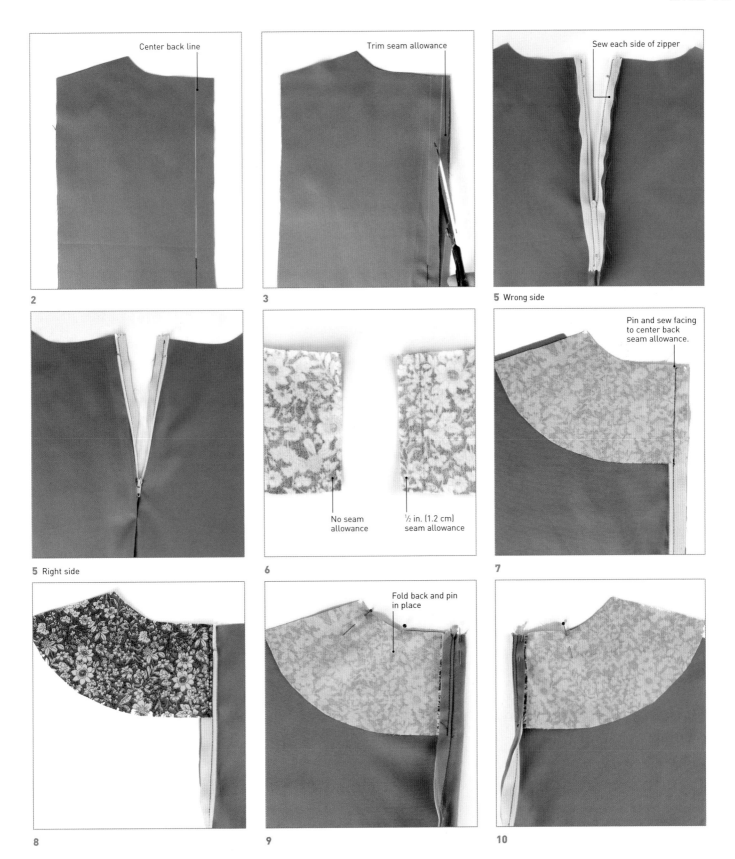

2 Center back line

3 Trim seam allowance

5 Sew each side of zipper
Wrong side

5 Right side

6 No seam allowance — ½ in. (1.2 cm) seam allowance

7 Pin and sew facing to center back seam allowance.

8

9 Fold back and pin in place

10

> **Try this**

To get beautifully neat, flat corners, give them a bash with a sewing hammer. This will flatten out the fabric without the need to press.

11 Sew all the way around the top edge of the garment from one side of the zipper to the other, reversing at the start and finish of your sewing to secure the stitching.

12 Trim off the corners, making sure you don't cut too close to the stitching. Snip into the seam allowance by a scant ¼ in. (5 mm) to allow the small pleat to sit flat.

13 Turn the facing right side out. You will notice that from the wrong side the zipper looks off center. That is a good thing!

14 On the right side of the garment, topstitch the underlap close to the zipper tape. You can see how it naturally sits under the lapped side.

15 Topstitch down the left side of the garment to the base of the zipper and across the bottom to the center back seam, being careful not to hit the zipper stop.

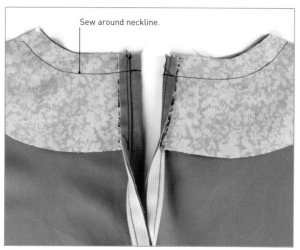

Sew around neckline.

11

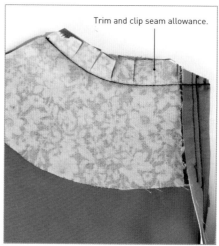

Trim and clip seam allowance.

12

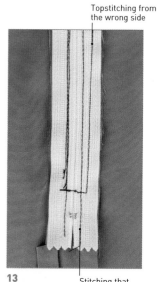

Topstitching from the wrong side

Stitching that attaches the zipper

13

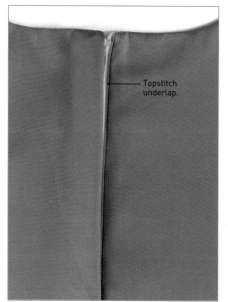

Topstitch underlap.

14

Topstitch left side.

15

Exposed zipper with a facing

An exposed zipper can be an interesting design detail to add to a dress or top. This method includes a facing, which will hide the raw edges of the seam allowance and the zipper tape.

1 Measure the width of your zipper and how much you would like to be exposed. This is measurement A; the zipper teeth will sit in the center of this line. Measure down the length of the zipper from top stopper to bottom stopper. This is measurement B. Mark these measurements on your garment, with one line B at each end of line A, so that you have a rectangle marked out.

2 Cut a small piece of iron-on interfacing and fold it over the bottom of the zipper. Iron it in place. This helps to keep the zipper tails together to make it easier to sew later.

3 Fold over the tops of the zipper tape diagonally and stitch them in place. This holds the zipper tape out of the way when the top edge is sewn.

4 Sew down one side of the rectangle marked out in Step 1, across the bottom, and back up the other side.

5 Cut down the middle of the two stitching lines, but stop ⅜ in. (1 cm) before the end. Then snip diagonally into the corners right up to, but not through, the stitching lines. This will create two small seam allowances to attach to the zipper.

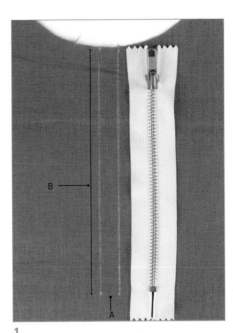

1

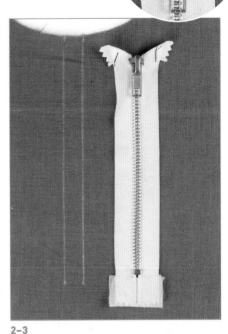

2–3

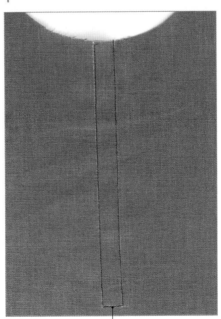

4

Sew around zipper opening.

5

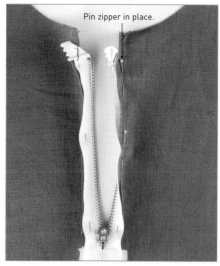

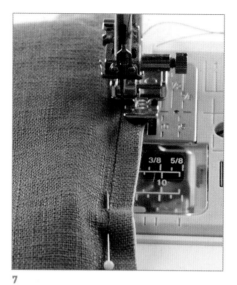

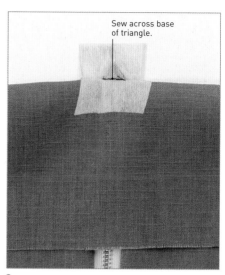

6

7

8

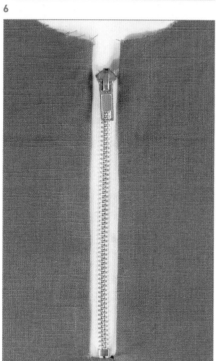

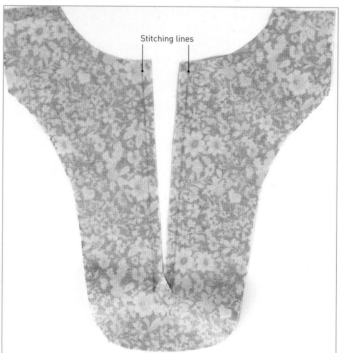

9

10

6 With right sides together, place the right-hand side of the garment seam allowance down on the right-hand side of the zipper. Pin in place and sew down the zipper tape on top of the first row of sewing (stitched in Step 4), keeping the folded-over top edge of the zipper just out of the way.

7 Flip the garment over so that the other seam allowance will lie along the zipper tape. Pin in place and sew on top of the first row of sewing again.

8 Fold the garment back so that the small triangle at the base of the zipper slot flips out and sew across the base of the triangle, again on top of the first row of sewing.

9 Press carefully from the right side.

10 Using the same measurements from Step 1, mark the stitching lines onto the wrong side of the facing. Carefully snip into the corners as you did in Step 5.

11 With the right sides together, match up one side of the facing with the corresponding side of the garment. This will mean that the zipper is in between the garment and the facing. Sew directly on top of the first row of stitching.

12 Do the same with the other side of the facing and garment, then follow Step 8 to sew across the bottom of the zipper. Press everything flat once it has been stitched.

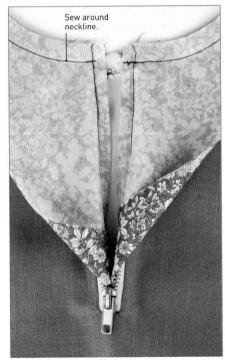

11

Zipper between facing and garment

12

Sew around neckline.

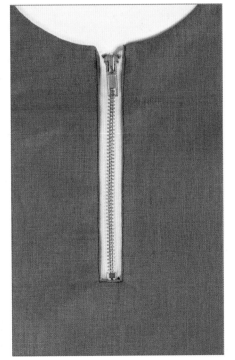

13

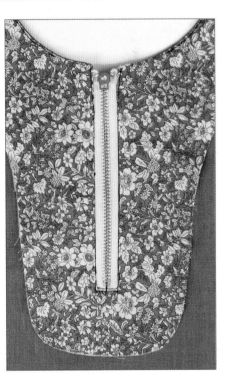

14 Right side finished

Wrong side finished

13 Turn the facing and the garment so the right sides are together and sew around the neckline, making sure to reverse over the ends of the zipper.

14 Turn so that the wrong sides are together. To finish off the zipper edge, stitch around the opening of the zipper a scant $1/16$ in. (2 mm) from the edge.

Sleeves

Sleeves have appeared in all manner of permutations over the centuries and have been revived and adapted according to current trends and practicalities.

Early medieval sleeves were often cut in one with the body of the garment, similar to the kimono or magyar sleeves of today. Sleeves became tighter and more in line with the body shape and were a separate tube of fabric that was laced onto the body of the main garment. As tailoring and sewing skills developed, sleeves became an integral part of the garment and developed into tubes of fabric that were inserted into the holes allowed for the arms.

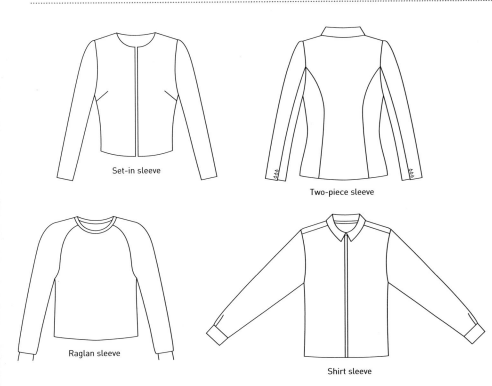

Set-in sleeve

Two-piece sleeve

Raglan sleeve

Shirt sleeve

Set-in sleeve The sleeve shape can be changed to create flare or gather, but the basic method for inserting it remains the same.

Two-piece sleeve This is also a "set-in sleeve" but with added shaping along the back seam to echo the natural fall of the arm. This gives extra comfort and ease of movement in more structured garments like jackets.

Raglan sleeve This sleeve has a diagonal seam line from the neckline to the underarm. The sleeve can be in two pieces with a seam along the shoulder and down the sleeve, or in one piece with a curved dart to shape over the shoulder. It works very well for more casual styles like sweatshirts or T-shirts.

Shirt sleeve A shirt sleeve is sewn onto the body of the garment first. This enables the seam to be finished flat for extra comfort. The side seam and underarm seam are then sewn in one go.

← The back seam gives extra shaping in a two-piece sleeve.

Set-in sleeve

A set-in sleeve, as the name suggests, is a sleeve that is set into an armhole. The sleeve itself can be varied in shape and length, but the basic method for sewing one is the same.

Most set-in sleeves are a slightly different shape at the front than the back; this is to allow for ease of movement so that the sleeve will not feel restrictive in wear. The front and back are differentiated by notches—typically a single notch for the front and a double notch for the back.

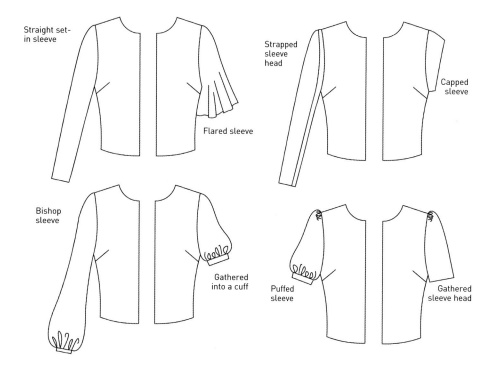

Straight set-in sleeve

Flared sleeve

Strapped sleeve head

Capped sleeve

Bishop sleeve

Gathered into a cuff

Puffed sleeve

Gathered sleeve head

Straight set-in sleeve
This looks great in all types of garment.

Flared sleeve This is very pretty in soft, floaty fabrics and works well in summer or evening dresses.

Bishop sleeve This sleeve gives an interesting shape to blouses or tunic tops.

Gathered into a cuff This sleeve works well in lighter fabrics as the gathers can be too bulky in heavier fabrics.

Strapped-head sleeve This sleeve is most effective in a tailored jacket with emphasis on the structure of the design.

Capped sleeve This sleeve looks cute in a pretty dress or top.

Puffed sleeve This is pretty in children's garments as it can add a softness to the silhouette of the garment.

Gathered sleeve head This can be effective at adding a bit of detail without looking fussy.

> **Try this**

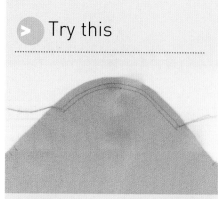

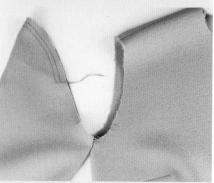

If the fabric you are working with is not sitting properly, then use an extra row of easing stitches below the seam line. These stitches can be removed later on.

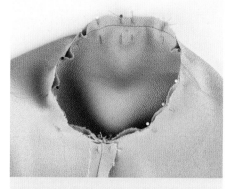

Pin around the sleeve head vertically, with the heads of the pins over the edges of the fabric. This will make it easier to take the pins out as you sew—and you won't catch yourself on the pins when handling the garment.

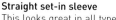

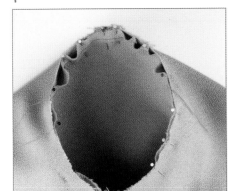

1 Easing stitches

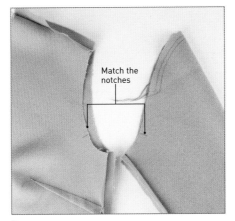

2 Match the notches

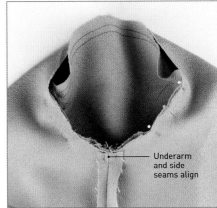

3 Underarm and side seams align

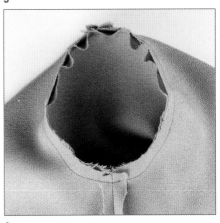

4

5 Sleeve is top layer.

6

HOW TO SEW A SET-IN SLEEVE

1 The sleeve head between the notches is slightly larger than the space into which it has to fit in the armhole. This is to allow for ease of movement.

To help the sleeve to fit into the armhole, sew a row of easing stitches across the sleeve head inside the seam allowance. Then gently pull the bobbin thread to ease up the fabric to fit into the armhole.

2 Sew the underarm seam together to make the sleeve. Sew the bodice together to create the armhole. The seam allowances can be neatened if the garment is not lined.

3 With the sleeve right side out and the bodice inside out, slide the sleeve into the armhole. Match up the underarm seam on the sleeve with the side seam on the bodice. Match up the single front notches and double back notches and pin around the lower section of the armhole.

Tip: If you are unsure which sleeve goes into which armhole, lay the garment right side out in front of you and place each sleeve next to the corresponding armhole. Look for the notches! Pinch the side seam and sleeve underarm seam together and pin. Now when you turn the bodice inside out you know which sleeve fits into which armhole.

4 Match up the dot on the sleeve head with the shoulder seam on the bodice and pin. Gently pull up the bobbin thread of the easing stitches to make the sleeve head fit into the armhole. Even out the fabric and pin in place.

Tip: Keep the sleeve head at the shoulder point flatter, as the grain of the fabric on the sleeve will not allow the fabric to be eased in as much here. Rely on easing the fabric over the curves of the sleeve head, as this is where the grain of the fabric is more flexible.

5 Place the garment on the sewing machine, with the bodice underneath and the sleeve on top. Sew inside the circle of the armhole so that you can see where you have eased the sleeve head.

6 Sew all the way around the armhole, overlapping the stitching when you get back to the beginning. Fasten off your sewing.

7 Press the seam toward the sleeve. You can neaten the seam if the garment is not lined.

Two-piece sleeve

The two-piece sleeve is still a set-in sleeve, so the basic method of insertion is the same. However, there are a few issues to consider.

If you stand side on and look into a mirror, you'll notice that your arms do not hang completely straight. A relaxed arm will hang with a slight curve to it. The two-piece sleeve caters for that curve.

There will usually be an underarm seam, as in other set-in sleeves, but there will also be a second seam that runs down the back of the arm to shape the sleeve through the natural bend in the elbow. In traditional tailoring, there can often be a third seam to help shape the sleeve—but that's a story for another day.

TO MAKE UP THE TWO-PIECE SLEEVE

1 With right sides together pin the upper sleeve and lower sleeve together along the outside edge seam. Stretch the lower sleeve between the notches to fit the upper sleeve. Distribute the ease evenly. Sew from the lower sleeve side to make sure that there are no tucks or wrinkles as you go.

Tip: To distribute the ease evenly, find the center points of each layer, match them up, and pin together. Now find the centers of the remaining sections and match those up, too. So you are halving and quartering the area to be eased and therefore distributing the ease evenly.

2 Pin and sew the underarm seam. Press both seams open by sliding the sleeve onto a sleeve board or sleeve roll.

3 Sew two rows of easing stitches over the sleeve head between the marks. Make sure that one is above and the other below the seam line. The one below the seam line will be removed later.

4 Insert the sleeve into the garment and match up the balance marks.

5 Pin the rest of the sleeve in place (a) and gently pull up the easing stitches (b). Fasten off the threads by winding them around a pin in a figure eight.

6 Starting at the underarm point, place the garment and sleeve under the machine, with the sleeve on top. Sew inside the circle around the armhole, taking care over the sleeve head and the easing stitches.

7 Remove the visible row of easing stitches and press the seam toward the sleeve.

Help!

The underarm seam on the sleeve does not match up with the side seam on the garment.

Don't worry—this often happens. Make sure to match up the mark or dot that shows the underarm point on the sleeve with the side seam on the garment.

Try this

Two-piece sleeves are often used in jacket and coats. If the fabric you are using is wool or a wool mixture, you can steam much of the ease out of the fabric before sewing in the sleeve. After fastening off the easing stitches, carefully remove the sleeve from the garment and then place the sleeve head over a tailor's ham and gently steam the fabric to shrink out the ease through the sleeve head. This will help the sleeve to sew in perfectly and keep that lovely curved shape over the sleeve head.

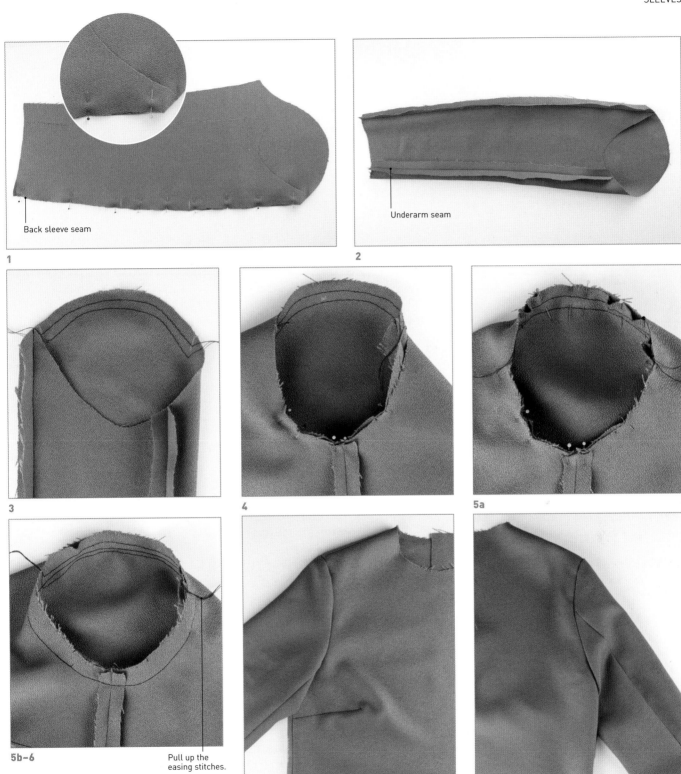

1

Back sleeve seam

2

Underarm seam

3

4

5a

5b–6

Pull up the easing stitches.

Front

Back

Raglan sleeve

The raglan sleeve is named after Lord Raglan, who lost his arm after an injury gained at the Battle of Waterloo. While he was healing from this injury, his tailors devised a way for him to dress himself more easily by creating a sleeve that extended into the neckline of his coat. This allowed for more room to move his able arm and thus to dress himself with greater ease.

Because of the greater flexibility of movement allowed with this design of sleeve, it is a style that can be found on a great deal of utility clothing, particularly within country pursuits. It also works extremely well with more casual clothing such as T-shirts or sweatshirts.

As with all sleeves, the sleeve is marked with a single notch for the front and double notches for the back. These correspond to the notches on the body of the garment.

1 Sew up the side seam on the bodice and then make up the sleeve **(a)**. If you are working with a two-piece sleeve, sew the shoulder seam and underarm seam first **(b)**. If you are using a one-piece sleeve, stitch the dart first and press it carefully over a tailor's ham to maintain the curve, then stitch the underarm seam **(c)**.

2 With right sides together, match up the underarm seam on the sleeve and the side seam on the bodice. Pin the layers together from the side of the sleeve, as this is the side you will sew from.

3 Bend the sleeve around the armhole, matching up the front and back notches and making sure that all the raw edges are level. Pin with the pin heads hanging off the edge of the fabric.

4 Place the garment under the machine, with the sleeve on the top. This will enable you to see how the sleeve fits to the garment.

5 Start sewing at the neckline and sew around the armhole back up the neckline again. Make sure to secure your stitching at the start and finish of your sewing.

6 You can neaten the seam if the garment is not lined, then complete the neckline as per your pattern instructions.

 Try this

To avoid catching the bodice of the garment underneath, lift up your sewing every couple of inches to check that it is all sitting flat. You can also feel with your fingers to see if anything has got caught in the stitching.

Check nothing is caught underneath your sewing.

> **Try this**

The curve of the sleeve may curve against the shape of the armhole—a convex curve sitting against a concave curve. Or you may like to think of it as a "happy" curve and a "sad" curve. Either way, gently ease the sleeve onto the armhole by rolling the fabric layers over your thumbs to help both layers curve together.

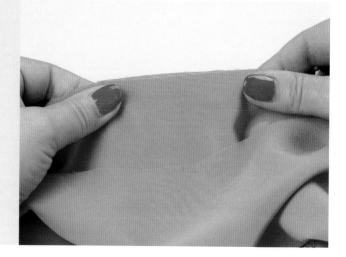

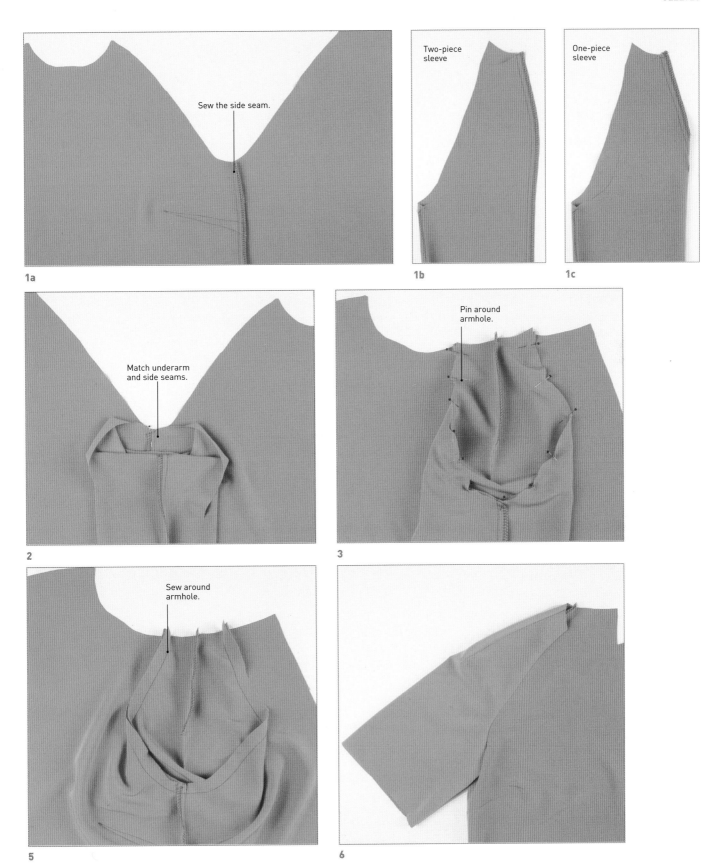

1a Sew the side seam.

1b Two-piece sleeve

1c One-piece sleeve

2 Match underarm and side seams.

3 Pin around armhole.

5 Sew around armhole.

6

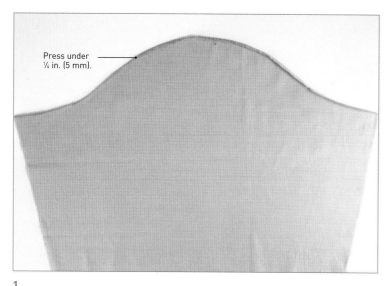

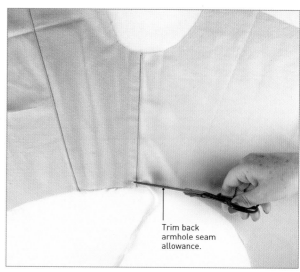

Trim back
armhole seam
allowance.

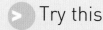

1

2

Shirt sleeve

Shirt sleeves are usually sewn into the body of the shirt before the sleeve itself is sewn up. This enables the seam attaching the sleeve to the garment to be sewn as a flat-felled seam, which keeps all the raw edges inside the seam. As this particular seam is double stitched, it also makes the seam much stronger; armholes are a particular area of stress.

As with all sleeves, the sleeve is marked with a single notch for the front and double notches for the back. These correspond to the notches on the body of the garment.

1 With the right side of the sleeve uppermost, press under a scant ¼ in. (5 mm) to the wrong side around the sleeve head.

2 On the garment, trim away a scant ¼ in. (5 mm) from the armhole.

3 Match up the dot on the sleeve head with the shoulder seam on the garment. With right sides together, pin in place, with the folded, pressed-under edge of the sleeve in line with the raw edge of the garment.

4 Match up the edges of the sleeve with the edges of the garment. The corners of the sleeve will hang over the edge of the garment to enable the seam lines to match up. Pin the ends in place, then match up the balance marks and continue to pin the rest of the sleeve in place.

5 Sew the seam with a ⅜-in. (1 cm) seam allowance, securing your stitching at the start and finish of the seam.

6 Trim the garment seam allowance down by a scant ⅛ in. (2 mm), so that the raw edge is just under the folded, pressed-under edge of the sleeve head.

Tip: If there is some slight puckering or dimpling in the sleeve head after you have sewn it, press the seam flat as it was stitched. Use the toe of the iron to guide you, then slide on about half of the sole plate in order to give the sleeve head a good steam.

7 Press the seam toward the garment, away from the sleeve. Pin the pressed-under edge of the sleeve head over the trimmed-down seam allowance to enclose the raw edge.

8 Edge stitch to hold the seam allowance down.

9 With right sides together, match up the armhole seams and pin in place. Match up the hem and the wrist and pin those as well. Pin along the sewing line.

► Try this

When sewing a flat-felled seam on the shirt, start at the hem and sew up the side seam. As you sew across the armhole seam and down the sleeve, gradually turn the sleeve into itself so that you keep everything flat underneath as you sew.

10 Sew from the hem up the side, across the armhole seam, and down to the wrist. Complete the steps for a flat-felled seam (see page 93).

Match the dot on the sleeve to the shoulder seam.

3

Make sure that the pin heads hang over the edge of the sleeve head.

4

Sew in the sleeve.

5

Trim seam allowance.

6

Pin seam allowance to garment.

7

Edge stitch along seam allowance.

8

Sew along side seam and underarm seam.

10

A contrast fabric used for the placket shows off the design detail on the sleeve.

Cuffs

Cuffs are rather like a period at the end of a sentence—they give your garment a final punctuation point. They can be a specific design feature that completely changes the look of a shirt or they can avoid attention and simply finish the garment in a subtle way.

Shirt cuff

A normal shirt cuff (or, as it is sometimes known, a barrel cuff) wraps around the wrist and overlaps with a button fastening, although the fastening you choose is entirely up to you; a snap fastener, for example, would work just as well.

The shirt cuff has two pieces to it—an outer cuff and an inside cuff. The outer cuff should be interfaced before the cuff is made up or attached to the sleeve. The inside cuff is not interfaced.

1 With right sides together, pin the outer cuff to the sleeve, making sure that the placket opening (see pages 114–115) on the sleeve sits along the cuff seam line to ensure that there is a smooth line from the sleeve into the cuff.

2 Sew along the seam, securing your stitching at the start and finish of the seam.

3 Press the seam toward the cuff.

4 Along the straight edge of the inside cuff, turn over just slightly less than the seam allowance to the wrong side, and press.

5 With right sides together, pin the inside cuff to the outer cuff around the curved outside edge, making sure that the pressed-under edge of the inside cuff sits just beyond the previous row of stitching to ensure that, when the cuff is turned right side out, it will just cover the stitching line.

6 Sew around the outer edge of the cuff, making sure that the stitching starts and finishes in line with the sleeve placket.

7 Clip the corners and turn the cuff right side out.

8 Roll the seam so that it sits on the edge of the cuff and press it in place.

9 Pin the inside cuff down along the open edge, pinning at right angles to the sewing line. Make sure the pin heads are away from the sewing area so that you can topstitch from the right side.

10 From the right side topstitch around the cuff, carefully sewing over the pins underneath and overlapping the stitching when you get back to the beginning. Fasten off your sewing.

11 Press the cuff, using plenty of steam. Mark in and sew the buttonholes (see pages 120–124).

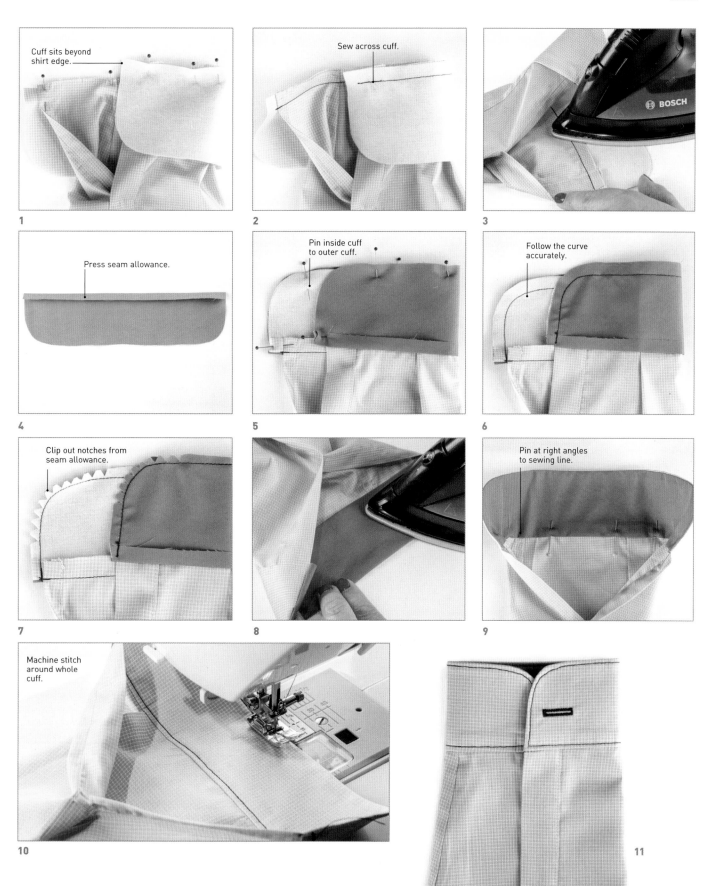

1 Cuff sits beyond shirt edge.

2 Sew across cuff.

3

4 Press seam allowance.

5 Pin inside cuff to outer cuff.

6 Follow the curve accurately.

7 Clip out notches from seam allowance.

8

9 Pin at right angles to sewing line.

10 Machine stitch around whole cuff.

11

French cuff

French cuffs, sometimes known as double cuffs, are an extended version of the shirt cuff. They should be double the depth of a shirt cuff, plus a scant ¼ in. (5 mm). This extra scant ¼ in. (5 mm) is very important, as it allows for the fabric fold depth, or "bend ease"—the small amount of extra fabric required to go around the bend in doubled-over or folded fabric.

Like the shirt cuff, a French cuff has two pieces to it—an outer cuff and an inside cuff. The outer cuff should be interfaced before the cuff is made up or attached to the sleeve. The inside cuff is not interfaced.

1 With right sides together, pin the inside cuff to the sleeve. A shirt cuff overlaps to be able to fasten, but a French cuff sits flat on itself, so the buttonholes sit on top of each other. This means that, in order to

prevent a twist in the placket (see pages 114–115), the thinner side of the placket should be folded under before it is lined up with the stitching line of the cuff.

Tip: As the placket has been folded under, there will be less fabric available to go around the wrist. It is a good idea to check the wrist measurement is still viable beforehand.

2 Press under the seam allowance along the bottom edge of the outer cuff.

3 With right sides together, pin the outer cuff over the inside cuff.

4 Now you can finish the French cuff in the same way as the Shirt Cuff from Step 5 onward.

1

Pin inside cuff to shirt.

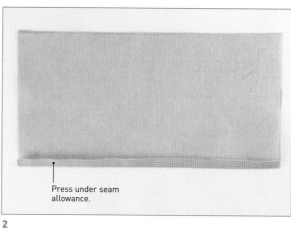

2

Press under seam allowance.

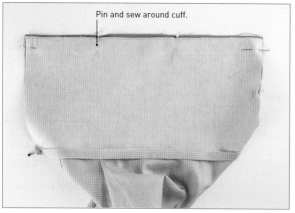

3

Pin and sew around cuff.

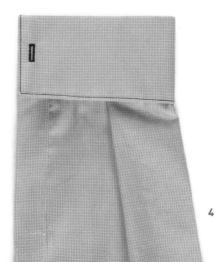

4

Collars

Collars in the form we now know them have only really been around since the early part of the 20th century. Before that, they were a separate item of clothing and have been every conceivable shape and size you can imagine: from huge, pleated ruffs that were completely impractical for the wearer to small, neat Nehru collars, fashion has seen it all.

It is only since World War I that collars, as an integral part of a garment, have been commonplace. Soldiers were provided with a "soft" collared shirt as part of their uniform. On return from the war, men found this to be a much more comfortable alternative, although it took a while for the establishment to catch on.

Shirt collars seem technical at first, but once you understand the components they are pretty straightforward. The main collar is attached to the collar stand and the collar stand is attached to the garment. The collar stand needs to sit level with the button stand, which lays along the center front of the shirt. There are many different shapes and styles of collar, but from a sewing and construction point of view there are four main categories.

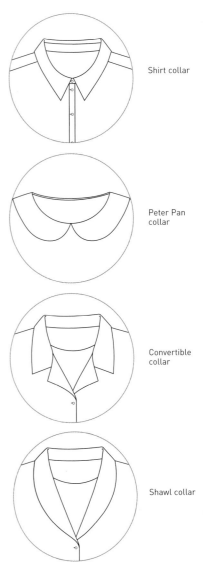

Shirt collar

Peter Pan collar

Convertible collar

Shawl collar

Contrast facings on this convertible collar give added detail to the collar shape.

Shirt collar The traditional two-piece shirt collar, with a separate button stand, is technical, but deeply satisfying when you get it right.

Peter Pan collar This sits flat against the body with no rise at all at the back neck. A very pretty shape.

Convertible collar This rises at the back neck but, when left open, falls at the front to create the reverse. It can also be buttoned up at the neck to create a softer version of the shirt collar.

Shawl collar This has a soft shape that sits close to the neck, but the outer edge of the collar can be any shape you choose rather than the traditional gentle curve.

Shirt collar

There are as many ways of attaching a shirt collar as there are styles of collar, but I feel this method is easy to follow and gives an excellent result. There are a couple of tricks that you can try, as well.

MAKING UP THE COLLAR

1 Both collar pieces need to be interfaced to give the collar some rigidity. Cut the interfacing to slightly smaller all around than the collar pieces, then apply it to the wrong side of the fabric pieces, following the manufacturer's instructions. Transfer all the markings from the pattern to the fabric pieces (see pages 62–63).

2 Lay the pieces on top of each other and trim ⅛ in. (3 mm) from each short end of the under collar. Match up the center points on the outer edges of both collar pieces and ease out the under collar to fit the upper collar, pinning as you go.

3 Sew from the center out to the end, gently stretching and easing the under collar to fit. Then start in the center again and sew the other side.

Tip: If the remaining part of the neckline is a fraction too tight to fit the collar, make a couple of small snips in the seam allowance of the garment to release the tension in the curve and allow the neckline to fit smoothly onto the collar.

4 Trim the seam down ⅛ in. (3 mm) and press it open.

5 This is a trick that I learned from a professional shirt maker and I love it! Take a length of thread and double it over. Lay it in the ditch of the seam, with the loop hanging over one end.

6 Fold over the collar, with right sides together so that the thread is still tight in the crease of the seam, and sew down one short end of the collar. Start with very

small stitches; once you are ¾ in. (2 cm) down the seam, change to a normal stitch length and sew to the end.

7 Trim the seam allowance down to ⅛ in. (3 mm) and trim the corner—BUT DO NOT CUT THE THREAD LOOP. Move the thread well out of the way before you trim anything. Repeat the process for the other short end of the collar.

8 Open up the collar and grab BOTH loose ends of the thread. Pull to turn the collar right side out and keep pulling to turn the corner through. Just keep pulling!

9 Once the corner is nice and pointy (no need for a pokey point turner here!), pull just one of the threads to pull the thread out completely.

10 Press the collar and topstitch around the outer edge.

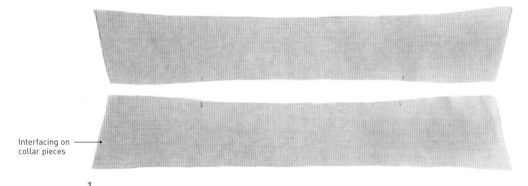

Interfacing on collar pieces

1

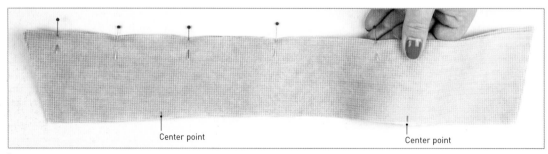

Center point   Center point

2

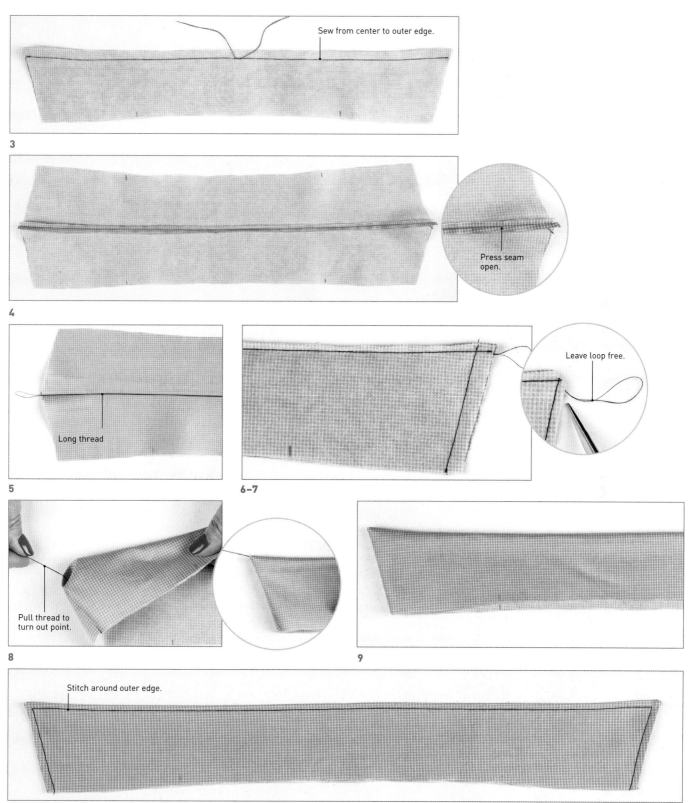

3

Sew from center to outer edge.

4

Press seam open.

5

Long thread

6–7

Leave loop free.

8

Pull thread to turn out point.

9

10

Stitch around outer edge.

Outer collar stand with interfacing

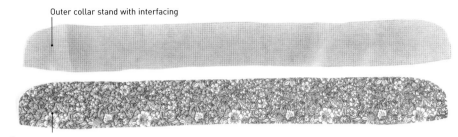

1   Inner collar stand

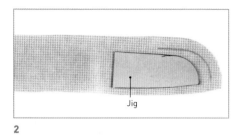

2   Jig

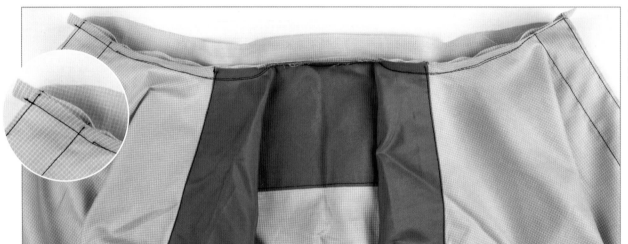

3

The outer collar is attached to the neckline with the front edge of the shirt in line with the seam allowance on the collar stand.

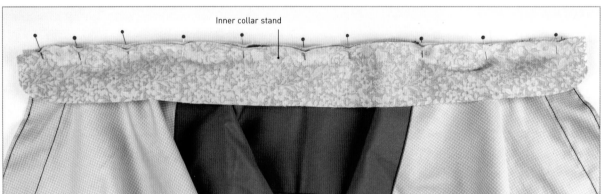

Inner collar stand

4

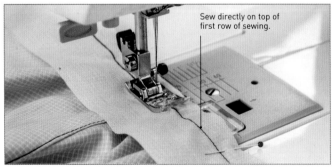

Sew directly on top of first row of sewing.

5

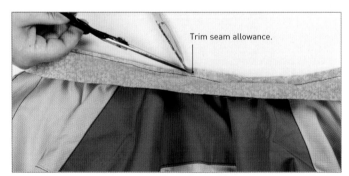

Trim seam allowance.

6

Mark where front edge of collar sits.

7

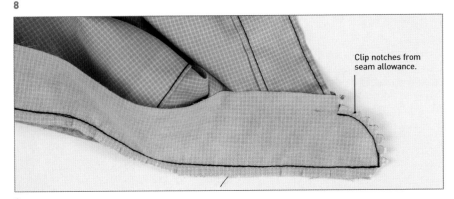

Sew around curved edge.

8

Clip notches from seam allowance.

9

10

ATTACHING THE COLLAR STAND

Staystitch around the neckline of the garment just inside the seam allowance before you start.

1 Only the outer collar stand needs to be interfaced. As before, cut the interfacing slightly smaller all around than the collar stand, then apply it to the wrong side of the outer collar stand, following the manufacturer's instructions.

2 Make a cardstock template (or jig) of the curved end of the collar stand and use this to draw the curved shape on the interfacing. This will help you to get a nice smooth curve when sewing.

3 Place the right side of the outer collar stand (the one with the interfacing) to the right side of the garment and pin the center backs together. Match up the notches and make sure that the front edge of the shirt is in line with the stitching line on the curved end of the stand. Sew around the neckline.

4 Place the right side of the inner collar stand (the one with no interfacing) to the wrong side of the garment and pin the center backs together. Gently stretch the inner collar stand out toward the curved edges so that the ends hang about ⅛ in. (3 mm) past the outer stand. Pin as you go.

5 From the right side, sewing on top of the row of sewing done in Step 3, sew from one button stand edge across to the other; don't sew into the stand seam allowances.

6 Trim the neckline seam allowance down to ⅛ in. (3 mm).

7 Pin the already-made-up collar along the outer stand, matching up the center backs, and mark where the collar comes to on the outer stand with a pin. Remove the collar.

8 Sew around the curved edge of the stand, but only up to the pins marking the position of the collar.

9 Trim the seam allowance down to ⅛ in. (3 mm) around the curve but not past the stitching. Snip out small V-shapes to allow the seam allowance to sit flat inside the curve of the collar stand.

10 Flip the collar stand out and pull it up away from the garment. Press the curved edge in place, but leave the unstitched seam allowances protruding.

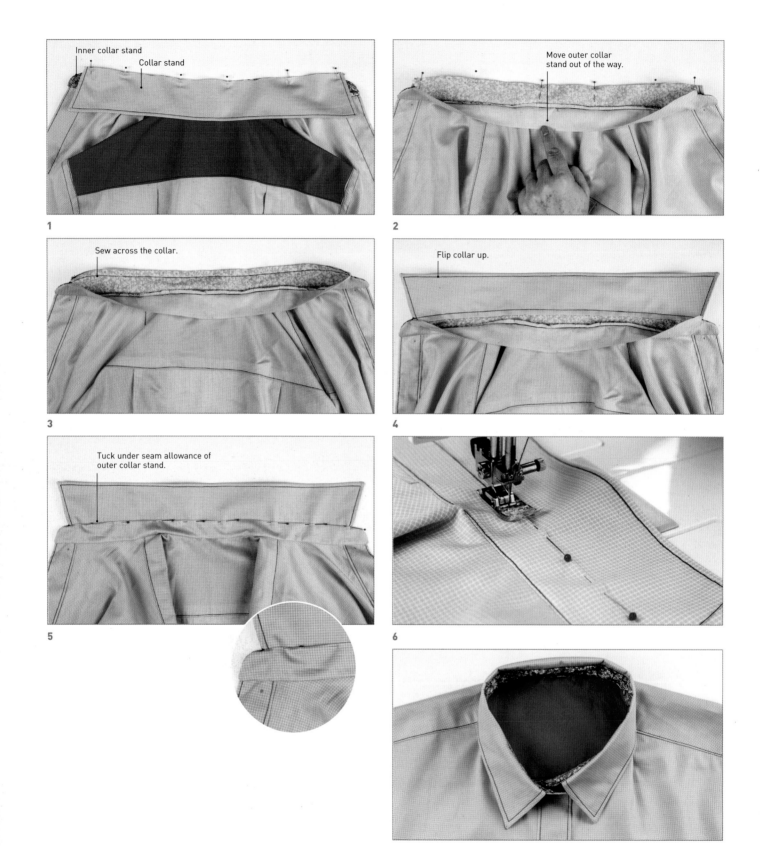

Inner collar stand

Collar stand

1

Move outer collar stand out of the way.

2

Sew across the collar.

3

Flip collar up.

4

Tuck under seam allowance of outer collar stand.

5

6

The finished shirt collar

ATTACHING THE COLLAR

1 With the wrong side of the garment facing you, lay the collar on the INNER stand, with the upper collar uppermost.

2 Match up the center backs of the inner collar stand and the under collar and pin together. Line up the ends of the collar with the ends of the protruding seam allowance and then pin in the rest of the collar to the stand. Keep the upper collar out of the way; it is important that you don't sew both layers together.

3 With the stand uppermost, so that you can line up the needle with the previous row of sewing, sew across the stand to attach the collar, making sure you don't go over onto the stitching on the stand.

4 Flip the collar seam allowance down inside the stand and trim it back to ⅛ in. (3 mm).

5 On the outer collar stand, press under the seam allowance along the top edge. Trim the seam allowance back by half, then pin in place to the underside of the collar.

Tip: Use a tiny amount of fabric glue stick to fix the inner stand to the collar. You can be old school and baste if you prefer, but this is quick and really easy!

6 Topstitch all around the collar stand. Start in the center, just under the collar, as that is the area least likely to be seen. Sew all the way around to where you started. You will close the opening left by the outer collar stand.

This is not a conventional way of attaching the collar, but it does give a really good result.

The two-piece shirt collar is technical, but looks very impressive when you get it right.

Peter Pan collar

The Peter Pan collar is probably the simplest to sew together. It is a curved, shaped collar that sits flat around the neckline and can give a very neat and pretty finish to a dress or blouse. Its name, as you may have guessed, comes from a production of Peter Pan first shown on Broadway in 1905, where Maude Adams played Peter and her costume featured this style of collar. It consists of just two pieces—an upper and a lower collar.

1 The upper collar needs to be interfaced to give the collar some rigidity. Cut the interfacing to slightly smaller all around than the collar piece, then apply it to the wrong side of the fabric pieces, following the manufacturer's instructions. Transfer all the markings from the pattern to the fabric pieces (see pages 62–63).

2 Place the two collar pieces right sides together and sew around the outer edge.

3 Trim the seam allowance down to a scant ¼ in. (5 mm) and snip small V-shapes all the way around. This will allow the collar to sit flat and smooth.

Tip: It is really important to get the snipping right on the Peter Pan collar. If you don't, you could end up with an angled collar instead of a smoothly curved one, so make sure your snips are close enough to each other. Check by turning out the collar and pressing it flat with your fingers first and then add in any extra snips if you need to.

4 If the collar isn't too small (a child's or baby's collar, for example), you can understitch (see page 232) through the lower collar and seam allowance. This will ensure that the upper collar rolls slightly and makes it easier to press.

5 Press the collar and steam it flat, making sure that the curved edges are nice and smooth.

6 Match up the dots or small triangles on the collar with the shoulder seams of the garment. Match up any other notches and ensure that the front edge of the collar sits on the center front line. Pin the collar in place.

Tip: Remember that the front edge of the collar will be at an angle, so it is the stitching line on the collar that needs to sit on the center front line or dot.

7 Sew around the neckline, reversing at the start and end of your sewing, to secure the collar in place.

Finish the collar off with a facing (see pages 170–171).

The lace trim outlines and defines the shape of this pretty Peter Pan collar.

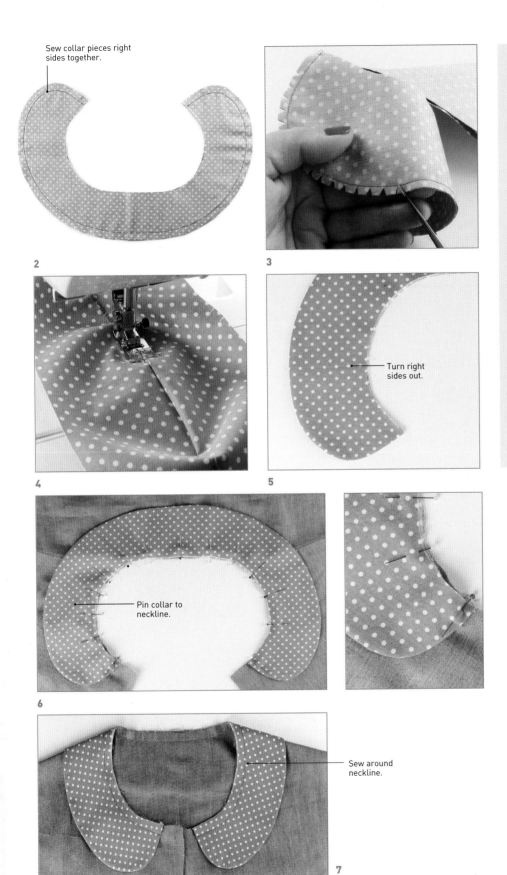

Sew collar pieces right sides together.

2

3

4

Turn right sides out.

5

Pin collar to neckline.

6

Sew around neckline.

7

Try this

To encourage the collar to sit in the correct shape, you can make a pressing jig. Trace the collar pattern piece onto cardstock, then draw in the seam allowance. Trim off the seam allowance, cutting just inside the drawn line so that you are trimming off just a fraction more than the seam allowance.

Insert the cardstock jig into the collar so the cardstock sits above the seam allowances and press. This will stop the bulge of the seam allowances pressing in to the upper collar and marking it, and will encourage the fabric to sit in the required curved shape.

Convertible collar

This is another type of shirt collar that is often used on blouses and dresses. It also looks good on men's casual shirts, as it can give quite a retro look.

A convertible collar is made up with a front facing to neaten the lapel, which is folded back. This means that it can be worn either closed or open, giving it the name "convertible collar." It can be finished with or without a back neck facing.

Depending on your pattern, there will often be an upper collar and an under collar. The under collar will be slightly smaller than the upper collar. This allows the under collar to pull the seam line under slightly, giving a neat rolled edge. Sometimes the under collar is cut in two pieces and on the bias to enable the collar to roll and sit better.

> **Try this**

If your pattern only has one pattern piece for the collar you can decide which is to be the under collar and trim off ⅛ in. (3 mm) from each of the short edges and ⅛ in. (3 mm) from the outer edge.

1 Both the collar pieces and the facings need to be interfaced to give the collar some rigidity. Cut the interfacing slightly smaller all around than the collar and facing pieces, then apply it to the wrong side of the fabric pieces, following the manufacturer's instructions. Transfer all the markings from the pattern to the fabric pieces (see pages 62–63).

2 With right sides together, match up the centers of the long outer edge of the upper and under collar. Sew from the center out to one end, gently stretching and easing the under collar to fit **(a)**. Then start in the center again and sew the other end. The under collar should be stretched just enough to make sure the short edges are level **(b)**.

3 Trim the seam down to a scant ¼ in. (5 mm) and press the seam toward the under collar.

4 Understitch (see page 232) through the under collar and seam allowances.

5 Fold the collar right sides together and sew across the short edges. Clip the corners and turn right side out. Press and steam the collar flat.

Tip: You can use the method described for the shirt collar here to get neat points to the collar (see pages 160–161).

6 On each side of the raw neckline edge of the upper collar only, clip through the seam allowance up to the small dot. The

dots indicate the shoulder seams and the snips into the dots allow the back neck part of the collar to be finished separately from the rest of the collar. It is very important to be accurate here, as a larger snip will mean you have a hole in the collar later on.

7 Machine or hand baste across both layers of the collar from the ends to the snips, but not across the center section between the snips.

8 Staystitch around the garment neckline just inside the seam line.

9 Place the collar to the garment, matching up the center backs and making sure that the under collar is next to the garment. Match up the notches and then

make sure that the snips on the upper collar line up with the shoulder seams on the garment. Lift the center section of the upper collar out of the way and pin the collar to the garment.

Tip: To help the collar fit the neckline you may need to make small snips into the garment back neck seam allowance. This releases the tension in the curve and allows the neckline to better fit the collar.

10 Sew across the neckline, making sure that you don't catch the upper collar seam allowance, but that you get close enough to the shoulder dot for there not to be a hole in the upper collar later.

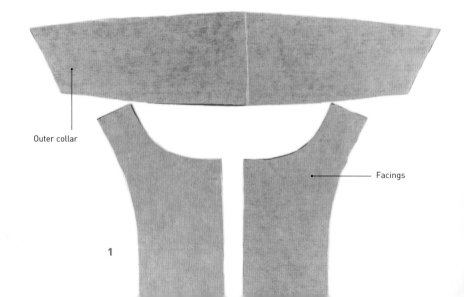

Outer collar

Facings

1

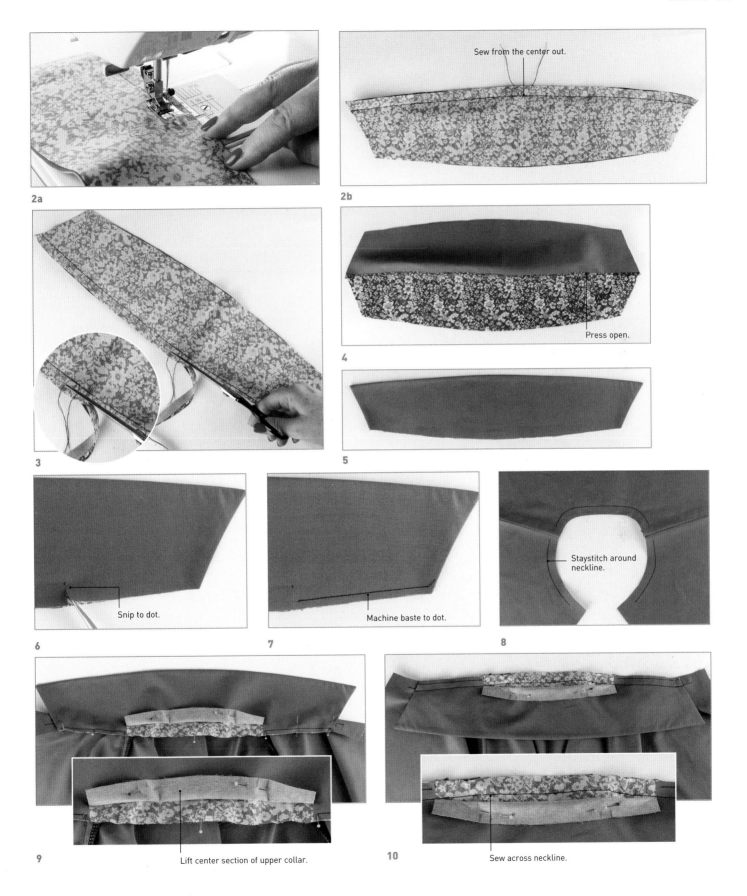

2a

2b
Sew from the center out.

3

4
Press open.

5

6
Snip to dot.

7
Machine baste to dot.

8
Staystitch around neckline.

9
Lift center section of upper collar.

10
Sew across neckline.

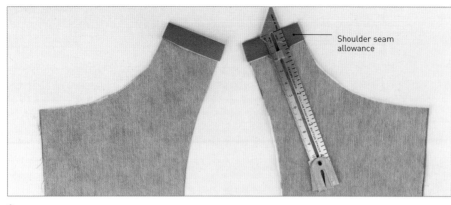

Shoulder seam allowance

1

FINISHING WITH A FRONT NECK FACING

1 Press under the shoulder seam allowances on the front facings.

2 If your pattern has separate front facings, pin and sew them to the garment up to the shoulder seams. You can layer the seam allowances on the garment and collar to reduce the bulk.

3 Turn the collar through to the right side and press the facings in place.

4 Fold under the seam allowance of the top upper collar so it just rolls over the line of stitching joining the under collar to the garment neckline and either pin or hand baste it in place.

5 From the under collar side, stitch in the ditch to close the gap from shoulder seam to shoulder seam across the back neck.

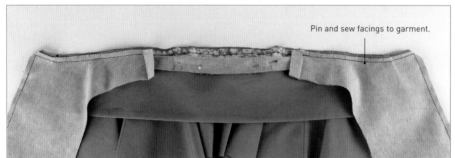

Pin and sew facings to garment.

2

Baste in place.

3–4

5

> ## Try this

Sometimes a facing is "grown on" to the center front—in other words, it is part of the garment front and not cut as a separate piece. If this is the case, fold back the front facing so that the right sides are together.

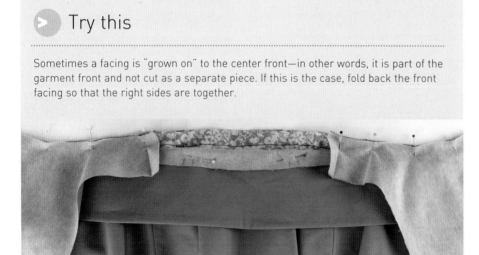

The finished facing

FINISHING WITH A FRONT AND BACK NECK FACING

1 Stabilize the back neck facing with a suitable interfacing and staystitch around the neckline of the garment just inside the seam line.

2 Pin and sew the back neck facing to the front facings at the shoulder seams. Press the seams open.

3 Place or fold back the front facing so the right sides are together with the garment. Pin the front facing and the back neck facing around the neckline.

4 Sew around the neckline. Clip into the seam allowance and layer the seam allowances on the collar and garment to reduce the bulk.

5 Turn the collar through to the right side and press the facing in place.

6 Pin the shoulder seams of both facing and garment together. Hand or machine sew the facing to the seam allowance of the garment to hold it in place.

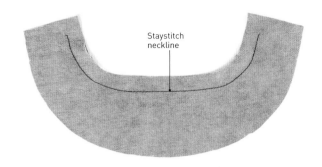
Staystitch neckline

1

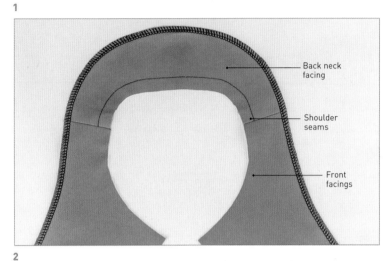

Back neck facing

Shoulder seams

Front facings

2

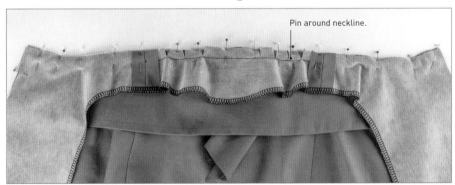
Pin around neckline.

3

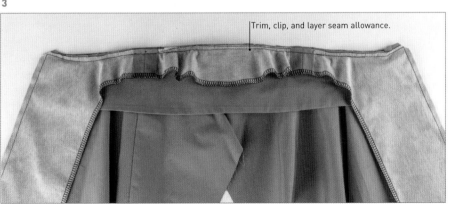
Trim, clip, and layer seam allowance.

4

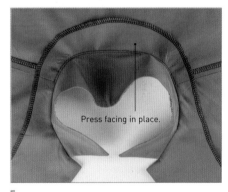
Press facing in place.

5

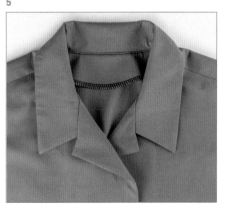

Collar with front and back facing

Shawl collar

This type of collar is one that has the lapel grown on to the front of the garment and then extends around to the back of the neck. So the whole collar is an extension of the front of the garment, which then rolls over to form the back of the collar and the upper collar is actually part of the front facing.

The traditional shape of a shawl collar is a gentle curve, but fashion has seen all sorts of differently shaped lapels.

1 The facing needs to be interfaced to give it some rigidity. Cut the interfacing slightly smaller all around than the facing piece, then apply it to the wrong side of the fabric pieces, following the manufacturer's instructions. Transfer all the markings from the pattern to the fabric pieces (see pages 62–63).

Tip: If you are making a jacket or coat, you will need to stabilize both the garment and the facing. But if you are making a blouse or dress you may only wish to stabilize the facing.

2 Staystitch around the corner of the neckline of both the garment and the facing on the seam allowance line, making sure to pivot on the small dot.

3 If there are darts in the front of the collar and the facing, sew these next (see page 73). (Darts will help to give the collar a smooth shape, but not all patterns will have them.)

4 Sew the center back seams on both the garment **(a)** and the facing **(b).** Press the seams open.

5 Clip into the corners of both the garment and facing neckline up to the small dot, being careful not to cut through the staystitching.

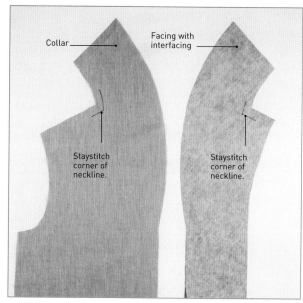

Collar   Facing with interfacing

Staystitch corner of neckline.

Staystitch corner of neckline.

1–2

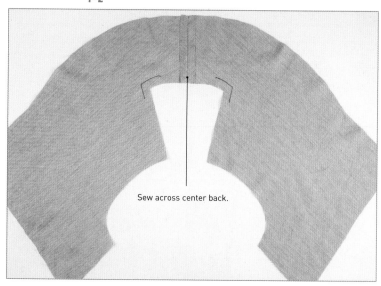

Sew across center back.

4a

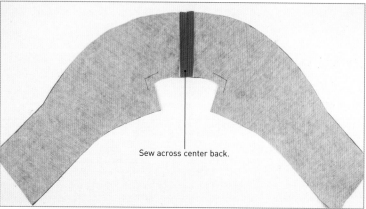

Sew across center back.

4b

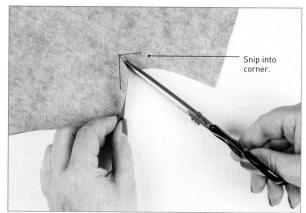

Snip into corner.

5

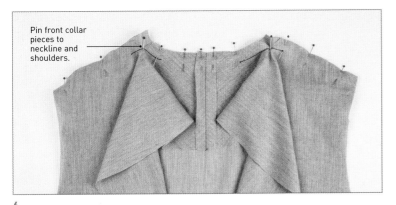

6

7

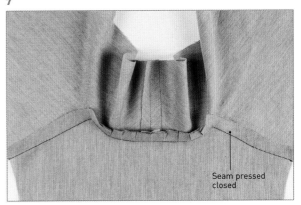

Seam pressed open

8a

Seam pressed closed

8b

9

6 With right sides together, pin the back neckline of the collar to the back neck of the garment. Match up the center back seam on the collar with the center back of the garment. Pin the shoulder/neck points together, too. Pivot the collar/garment front so that the shoulders of both the garment back and the front seams will line up.

Tip: Put a pin in vertically right at the small dot to ensure that the collar doesn't shrink back from the point of the corner as you sew.

7 Starting at the center back, sew to the pivot point, drop the needle down into the fabric, pivot everything around (making sure no fabric is caught under the foot), and continue sewing across the shoulder. Repeat for the other side.

8 If you are finishing the collar with a back neck facing, press the shoulder and neck seam open **(a)**. If you are finishing it without a back neck facing, press the seams closed and toward the collar **(b)**. This will help to neaten it all later.

9 With right sides together, pin the collar facing to the garment along the outer edge of the collar and down the center front.

In image 6: Pin front collar pieces to neckline and shoulders.

10 Starting at the center back, sew around the collar and down the center front. Then repeat for the other side.

11 To layer the seam allowance, trim one side down by half and then the other by half again. Clip into the seam allowance to remove the excess fabric; this will help the collar sit flat in a smooth curve.

12 Understitch through the garment side of the collar and the seam allowance, starting at the center back but stopping about 1½ in. (4 cm) from the breakpoint. (The breakpoint is where the collar folds back. If the understitching continues it will be visible on the garment front.)

13 Turn the collar right side out and press the outer edge.

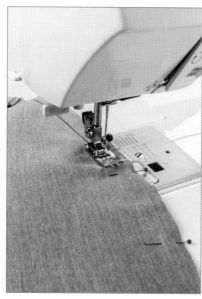

10

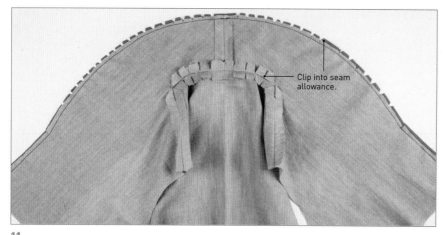

Clip into seam allowance.

11

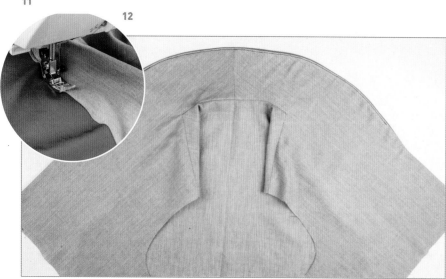

12

13

FINISHING WITH A FRONT NECK FACING

1 Fold under the seam allowance on the shoulders and neckline of the facing. Match up the corner points and the darts. Pin through the shoulder seam to hold in place.

2 Slip your hand through the gap at the armhole between the garment and the facing and pinch the shoulder seam allowance. Pull it through the armhole. This will turn the shoulder seam inside out so that you can line up the shoulder seams of the garment and facing.

3 Sew along the shoulder seam from the corner to the shoulder point just inside the original row of sewing. Turn the shoulder right side out again and press the shoulder seam. Repeat for the other shoulder.

4 Make a few small snips in the back neck seam allowance to enable it to sit flat when folded under. Lay the folded edge to the row of sewing along the back neck and hand or machine sew in place.

FINISHING WITH A BACK NECK FACING

1 The back neck facing needs to be interfaced to give it some rigidity. Cut the interfacing slightly smaller all around than the facing piece, then apply it to the wrong side of the fabric, following the manufacturer's instructions. Transfer the dots for the pivot points from the pattern to the facing (see pages 62–63).

2 With the right sides together, match up the center backs and pin. Pivot at the smalls dots as before and line up the shoulder seams.

3 Sew starting from the center back and dropping the needle to pivot at the corners before sewing across the shoulders. Snip into the seam allowance and press the seams open.

4 Match up the darts and pivot points on both the garment and the facing. Slipstitch along the dart and across the back neck seam allowance to hold the collar and facing in place.

5 If you are not including a lining, make sure that the edges of the facing are neatened and hand caught to the shoulder seams.

Tuck under shoulder seams.

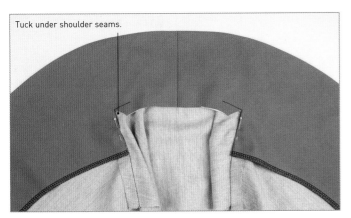

1

2

Sew across shoulder seams.

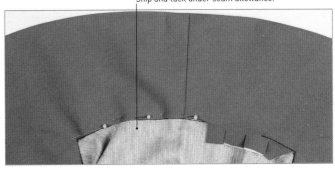

3

Snip and tuck under seam allowance.

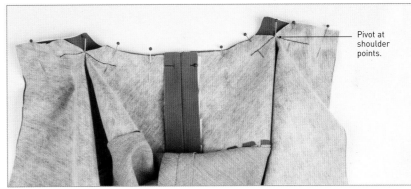

4

Pivot points

1

Pivot at shoulder points.

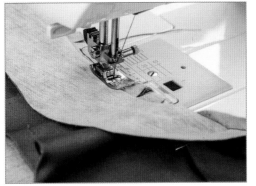

2

Center back   Shoulder

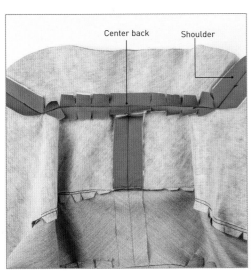

3

4

Catch facing to shoulder seam.

5

Yokes

A yoke is a piece of fabric that lies over the shoulders and sits between the front and back of a garment joining the two. It can extend from the shoulder blades to just over the shoulder line or can continue over the shoulder to the chest. Designs vary as fashion dictates.

A yoke can be a single layer of fabric, but is more commonly made up of a yoke and a facing. This means that all the raw edges are enclosed and provides a clean finish inside the garment.

Most casual shirts have a yoke cut in one piece, but a formal dress shirt can have a split yoke, which allows for a more tailored fit over the shoulders, as the yoke can be cut on the bias. A split yoke cut on the bias can also be used to great effect on a casual shirt in a checked fabric, for example.

Double yoke

This is a yoke that has two layers—an outer yoke and a yoke facing. It is sometimes called a shirt yoke, as this is where it is most often found.

Depending on your pattern, you will need to create any gathers, pleats, or tucks in the garment back before you add the yoke.

1 With right sides together, matching the notches, pin and sew the outer yoke to the garment back. Press the seam toward the garment back.

2 With right sides together, matching up the front edges, pin and sew the outer yoke to the garment front pieces.

3 With the right side of the yoke facing against the wrong side of the garment, match up the front edges of the yoke facing to the garment front. Pin through all layers. Sew across the front edges through all layers directly on top of the first row of stitching.

4 Fold the outer yoke and yoke facing away from the garment front and press **(a)**. Edge stitch through both layers of the outer yoke and yoke facing, a scant ⅛ in. (2 mm) from the seam **(b)**.

5 With the right side of the garment back uppermost, roll up the garment back from the hem onto the outer yoke. Fold the yoke facing down over the rolled-up garment so that the yoke seam allowances line up.

6 Pin and sew through the back yoke seam allowances along the first row of sewing across the yoke and garment seam.

7 Put your hand into the gap between the outer yoke and yoke facing and grab the rolled-up garment. Pull it through the gap; the rest of the garment will follow **(a)**. Keep pulling so that the front pieces follow, too, and turn the garment through to the right side **(b)**.

8 Pull the yokes away from the garment back and press **(a)**. Edge stitch the yoke a scant ⅛ in. (2 mm) away from the seam **(b)**.

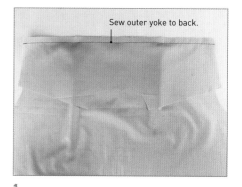

Sew outer yoke to back.

1

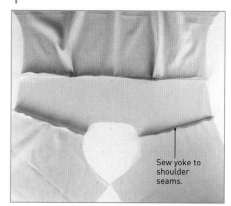

Sew yoke to shoulder seams.

2

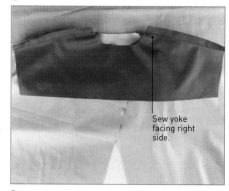

Sew yoke facing right side.

3

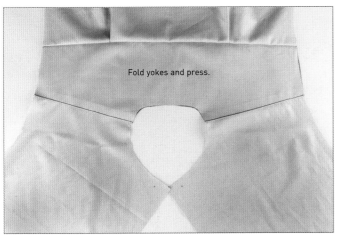

Fold yokes and press.

4a

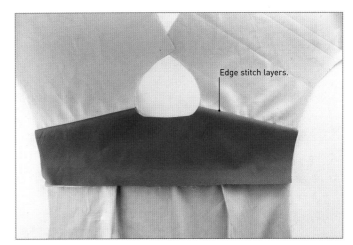

Edge stitch layers.

4b

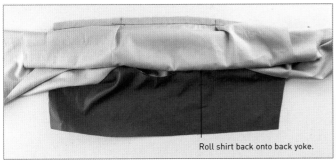

Roll shirt back onto back yoke.

5

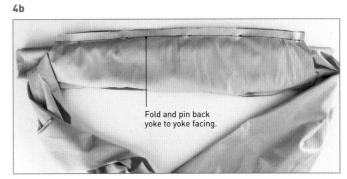

Fold and pin back yoke to yoke facing.

6

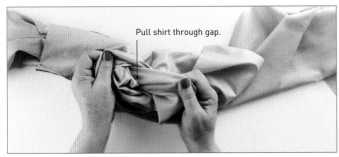

Pull shirt through gap.

7a

Pull shirt through to right side.

7b

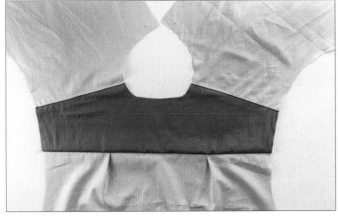

8a Wrong side

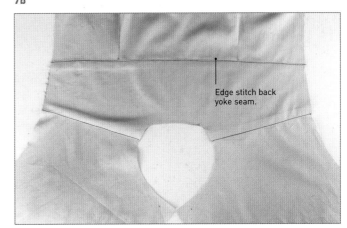

Edge stitch back yoke seam.

8b

Waistbands

A waistband is not only a way of finishing a waistline, but it also allows the skirt or pants attached to it to sit correctly on the body. Fashion dictates the depth of waistbands and also where they sit around the body. The natural waistline may seem uncomfortably high, given the current penchant for lower waistlines. So this is a secure way of making sure the garment fits correctly around the body, wherever the "waist" is supposed to be.

A neatly finished waistband helps the pants to hang correctly.

Straight waistband

There are many ways to finish off the waist on a garment, but one of the simplest is a straight piece of fabric doubled over to create a waistband.

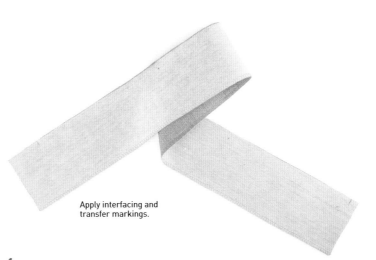

Apply interfacing and transfer markings.

Depending on the fabric being used, a firm or medium-weight interfacing will be required to support the waistband and ensure that it doesn't warp out of shape. If you are using a heavier fabric such as denim, interfacing will only be required to support the area where a buttonhole is to be sewn. This is also the reason why the waistband is cut on the straight grain.

A straight waistband usually extends past the waist length to create an underlap to hold the chosen method of fastening (buttonhole or hook and bar). This extension is usually 1–1½ in. (3–4 cm), but check your pattern.

1 Attach interfacing to the wrong side of the waistband. Transfer any markings from the pattern to the wrong side of the waistband, too (see pages 62–63).

2 With right sides together, matching up the notches, pin the waistband to the garment. One end of the waistband should overhang the garment by ⅝ in. (1.5 cm) and the other by 1–1½ in. (3–4 cm) to allow for the underlap.

3 Sew around the waistline, making sure to go right to the end of the garment and reverse stitch at the start and finish.

4 Layer the seam allowance (see page 91) and press the seam up toward the waistband.

1

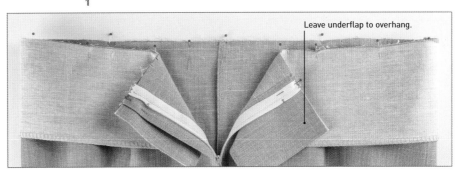

Leave underflap to overhang.

2

Reverse stitch at start and finish.

3

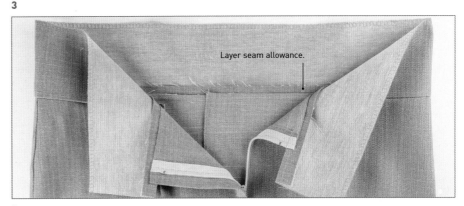

Layer seam allowance.

4

TO FINISH THE WAISTBAND

Method 1

This will give a clean machine finish to the inside of the waistband.

1 Neaten the remaining long edge of the waistband using an overlocker, zigzag, or mock overlock stitch.

2 At the end with the ⅝ in. (1.5 cm) overhang, fold up the seam allowance, then fold the waistband over so that the right side is inside and the folded-up seam allowance is just below the waist seam. Pin in place.

3 Sew across the short edge in line with the garment opening.

4 Trim the seam allowance back to half and turn out the corner.

5 On the end with the longer overhang, fold the waistband over so that the right side is on the inside and the waist seam allowances are flat. Pin in place.

6 Sew across the short edge of the waistband until you are level with the waist seam. Then drop the needle and pivot around the corner. Continue to sew until you meet the stitching for the waist seam—but do not overlap the rows of sewing, as this will prevent you from turning the waistband to the right side.

7 Snip off the corners and trim the seam allowance down by half, then turn the waistband to the right side.

8 Press the waistband in place so that the neatened edge lies flat over the waist seam. Pin in place.

9 At either end, tuck up a small amount of seam allowance to enable the waistband to sit flat.

10 From the right side, stitch in the ditch through the waist seam to hold the waistband in place.

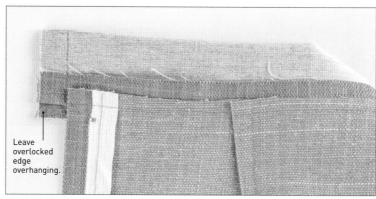

Leave overlocked edge overhanging.

2–3

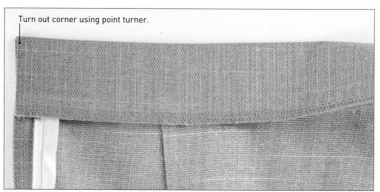

Turn out corner using point turner.

4

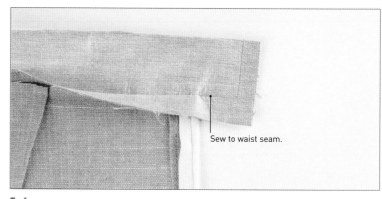

Sew to waist seam.

5–6

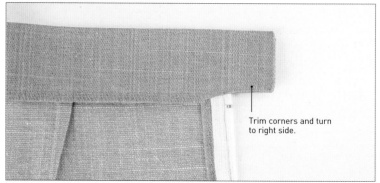

Trim corners and turn to right side.

7

Pin horizontally to flatten waistband.

8–9

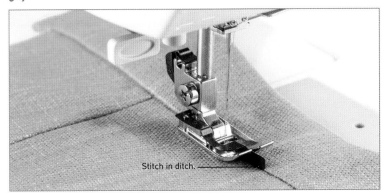

Stitch in ditch.

10

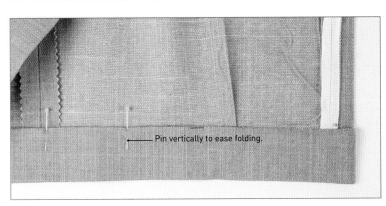

Pin vertically to ease folding.

1

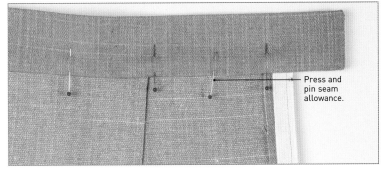

Press and pin seam allowance.

2

 ## Try this

To get a completely machine-finished waistband, use a blind-hem foot to sew the waistband to the waist seam allowance.

With the garment right side up, fold the garment back from the waistband so that the waist seam is on the edge of the fold and you can see about ¼ in. (6 mm) of waistband peeking out. Run the blind-hem foot along the waistband so that the needle has to hop across to catch the waist seam allowance. You won't be able to get right to the ends, but as the stitches are so secure that really doesn't matter. If you really want to, you can hand sew a few stitches at either end.

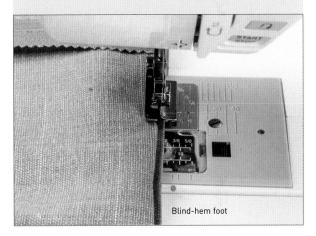

Blind-hem foot

Method 2

If you prefer to have a completely clean finish inside the waist of the garment, you can tuck under the seam allowance of the waistband rather than leaving it flat.

1 Press under the seam allowance on the long edge of the waistband and follow steps 1–7 of Method 1.

2 When the ends of the waistband have been stitched, press the waistband along the top edge and pin the folded-under seam allowance so that it sits just over the waist seam.

3 Slipstitch the waistband in place to finish.

Curved waistband

Curved waistbands look like an integral part of the garment and not a separate piece added on like a straight waistband. They sit just on or below the natural waistline, which means that they follow the natural curves of the body over the high hip and do not extend above the waist of the garment.

Fashion and personal choice dictate how deep the curved waistband will be. As the curved waistband is integral to the main part of the garment, use a lightweight interfacing to stabilize the piece and help to support the curved shape.

There are two parts to a curved waistband—the outer waistband (front and back) and the inner waistband facing (front and back).

1 Attach interfacing to the wrong side of the outer waistband pieces and, if you are using a lightweight fabric such as cotton poplin, to the waistband facing pieces, too. Transfer the markings from the pattern to the wrong side of the fabric pieces.

2 Join the front and back waistband pieces together along their short edges to create a long strip and press the seams open. Do the same with the facing pieces.

Tip: Remember! If you have the opening at the side of your garment you will need to make the facing a mirror image of the waistband so that, when the wrong sides are together, the openings on both the waistband and the facing are on the correct side.

3 With right sides together, matching the seams and notches, pin the waistband to the garment.

4 Sew around the waist seam, making sure to reverse stitch at the start and finish of your sewing.

5 Layer the seam allowance (see page 91) to reduce the bulk. Snip into the seam allowance to remove any excess fabric and allow the seam to sit flat.

6 Press the seam toward the waistband.

7 With right sides together, matching the notches, pin the facing to the waistband and sew around the top edge.

8 Layer the seam allowance and snip into it to release the tension in the curve.

9 Lay a narrow tape or ribbon along the seam allowance so that it sits just next to the seam line. Follow the curve of the waistline and allow the snips in the seam allowance to splay open. Sew the tape

close to the seam line, stitching through the seam allowances only, but not through the skirt. This will help to support the waist of the garment.

10 Understitch through the facing and all the seam allowances, a scant ⅛ in. (2 mm) away from the seam.

11 Finish the rest of the waistband according to the type of fastening to be used and Methods 1 or 2 from the straight waistband instructions.

1 Apply interfacing to outer waistband.

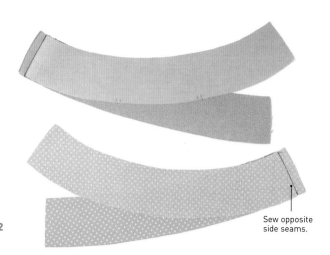

2

Sew opposite side seams.

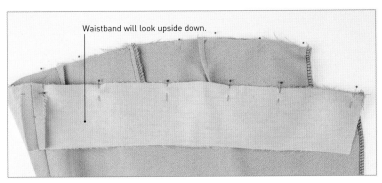

Waistband will look upside down.

3–4

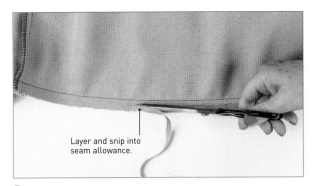

Layer and snip into seam allowance.

5

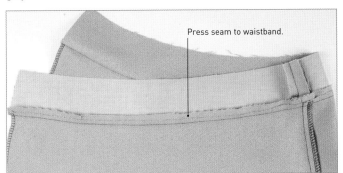

Press seam to waistband.

6

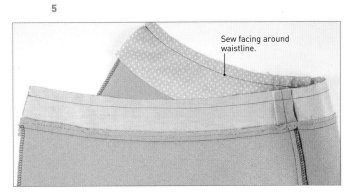

Sew facing around waistline.

7

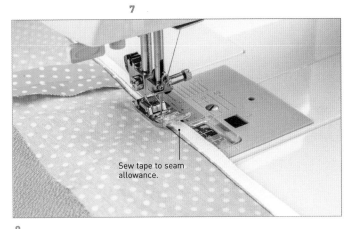

Layer and clip into seam allowance.

8

Sew tape to seam allowance.

9

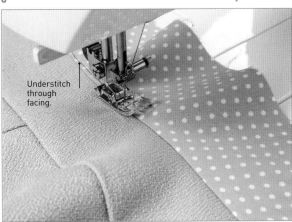

Understitch through facing.

10

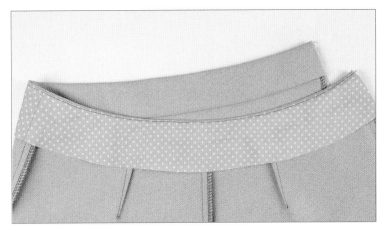

11 Finished waistband

Belt loops

Belt loops, or carriers, are sewn evenly around a waistband to hold a belt in place. They can also be a wonderful decorative feature on a garment and give extra definition to the waist.

There are usually five belt loops on a garment—two on the front, two close to the side seams, and one at the center back—but there can be more if you wish, Two either side of the center back can look good, too. Most belt loops are about ⅜ in. (1 cm) wide, but they can be wider if you prefer.

1 To make five loops ⅜ in. (1 cm) finished width, you will need to cut a strip of fabric on the straight grain about 20 in. (50 cm) long by 1½ in. (4 cm) wide. Overlock or zigzag stitch one long edge.

2 Fold the strip into thirds, with the overlocked edge on the top. Press in place.

3 Edge stitch or topstitch down both long sides of the strip.

4 Cut the strip into five equal lengths. These can be trimmed later if need be.

5 Pin the waistband to the garment and then slide in the belt loops between the garment and the waistband. Make sure they are in the correct positions before you sew around the waist seam.

6 Finish the waistband and then fold up the belt loops and tuck them under the raw edge, level with the top of the waistband. Adjust the length of the belt loops now if you need to.

7 Sew across the top edge of the belt loop using a strong needle; a size 90 or a jeans needle are best. Stitch though all the layers of the waistband.

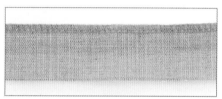

1 Finish one edge.

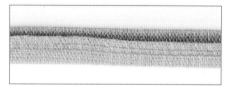

2 Fold into thirds.

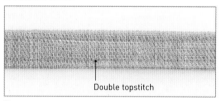
Double topstitch

3

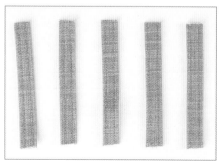

4 Cut into five equal lengths.

Tuck loop between waistband and garment.

5

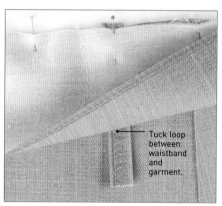

6

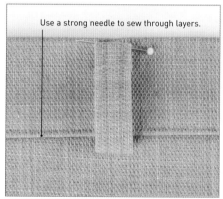
Use a strong needle to sew through layers.

7

> Try this

You can use a narrow, close zigzag stitch for strength and decoration.

Zigzag stitch

Elastic casing

Elastic is often seen as quite a modern invention, although natural rubber in the form of latex has been used for thousands of years.

However, it wasn't until 1820 that Englishman Thomas Hancock patented the first elastic fastenings for gloves, suspenders, shoes, and stockings.

Elastics now vary widely and come in many different qualities suitable for specific purposes. The most common type of elastic is corded into different widths. This is an all-purpose elastic used for most dressmaking projects, although there are other softer elastics that are more suited to lingerie or childrenswear.

During garment manufacturing processes, elastics are usually sewn directly onto the fabric as this saves time. The edge of the elastic lies along the edge of the waist or cuff and is sewn directly to the garment, neatening and elasticating the garment at the same time.

However, there can be occasions when a casing to house the elastic is more appropriate. In children's clothes it is easy to alter the elastic in a waistband if it is sewn into a casing, while an elasticated cuff has a cleaner finish if the elastic is in a casing.

Casings can have single or multiple channels for the elastic, depending on the function and look required.

← Elasticated waistbands are both comfortable and very easy to sew.

Method 1

This is a good method to use if the amount of elastication needs to be adjusted—for children's clothes, for example.

Measure the width of the elastic being used.

1 Make up the garment and press under ¼ in. (6 mm) to the wrong side along the top edge. Fold the top edge over again by just a fraction more than the width of the elastic to create the casing. (Don't make the casing too wide, otherwise the elastic could twist.)

2 Pin the casing in place and edge stitch around the waistline, stopping about 2 in. (5 cm) from the beginning to leave a gap.

3 Edge stitch around the top of the waist to help prevent the elastic from twisting; this gives a neat finish to the waist, too.

4 Measure the length of elastic by holding it around your waist or wrist, making sure it is firm but not uncomfortably taut. Allow a ⅜-in. (1 cm) overlap, then cut the elastic to the required length.

5 Pin a safety pin to one end of the elastic and thread the safety pin though the casing. Keep going until you get back to the gap again.

6 Pull both ends of elastic out through the gap and make sure that the elastic is not twisted. Overlap the ends by ⅜ in. (1 cm) and machine sew around the overlap in a rectangle or square shape to join the ends together. Make sure to reverse stitch at the start and finish a couple of times so that the stitching is secure.

7 Tuck the elastic back inside the casing and sew across the gap.

Try this

Pin a second safety pin to the loose end of the elastic and then pin this to the garment. This will stop the elastic from being accidentally pulled into the casing so that you lose the end.

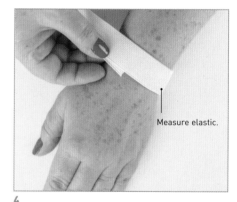

Method 1

Press over twice.

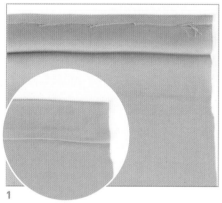

1

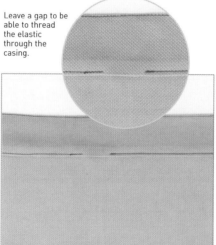

Leave a gap to be able to thread the elastic through the casing.

2–3

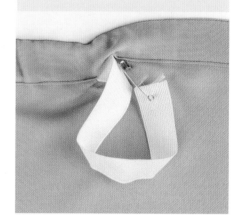

Measure elastic.

4

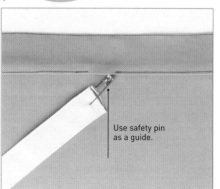

Use safety pin as a guide.

5

Secure ends together.

6

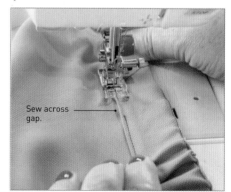

Sew across gap.

7

Method 2

This method requires the elastic to be measured and sewn into a circle before being sewn into the casing. It is a quicker method and the one that I prefer to use when I can.

1 Make up the garment and press under ¼ in. (6 mm) to the wrong side along the top edge. Fold the top edge over again by just a fraction more than the width of the elastic to create the casing and pin in place. (Don't make the casing too wide, otherwise the elastic could twist.)

2 Edge stitch around the top of the waist to help prevent the elastic from twisting; this gives a neat finish to the waist, too.

3 Tuck the elastic circle inside the casing and pin the casing down, enclosing the elastic.

4 Work your way around the waist, hiding the elastic inside the casing and pinning in place as you go. There will be gaps and bubbles of fabric as the garment gathers up, but these will disappear when the casing is sewn down.

5 Edge stitch the casing down, being careful not to catch the elastic. Sew 2 in. (5 cm) or so at a time, removing the pins as you go.

6 When you get back to the beginning overlap the stitching to secure your sewing.

> ## Try this
>
> For thinner elastic, sew more channels (making a wider casing and sub-dividing it into several channels), with a length of elastic running through each one.

Method 2

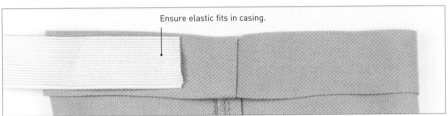

Ensure elastic fits in casing.

1

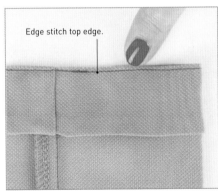

Edge stitch top edge.

2

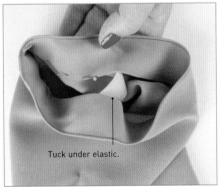

Tuck under elastic.

3

Pin casing over.

4

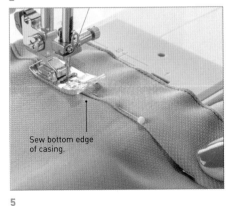

Sew bottom edge of casing.

5

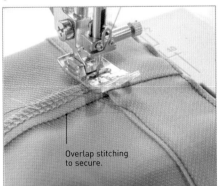

Overlap stitching to secure.

6

The finished casing

Decorative features

There are a whole range of decorative features and processes that can add definition or detail to your clothing. They can be used to highlight a seam, add decoration to a neckline, or even trim a hemline.

Bias strips

A woven fabric has three grain lines: the straight grain, the cross grain, and the bias (see page 39). The bias grain has the special ability to stretch slightly and we can exploit this wherever we use bias tape made from cutting bias strips.

There are several methods of cutting and joining bias strips. You may choose one over another, depending on the length of bias tape you require.

Method 1: Individual strips

This method is fine if you only need a small amount of bias tape.

1 Find the straight grain on your fabric, either by using the selvage or by following the threads in the fabric. Draw a line along the straight grain. Draw another line at right angles to this.

2 Fold the horizontal line down so that it sits on top of the vertical line. You can use a pin to make sure you are accurate.

3 The folded edge of the fabric is now on the bias grain. Cut through the fold, measure out the width of strips from the bias edge, and draw in parallel lines to mark the strips. Then cut along the lines to create your bias strips.

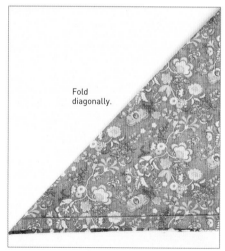

Right angle

1

Fold diagonally.

2

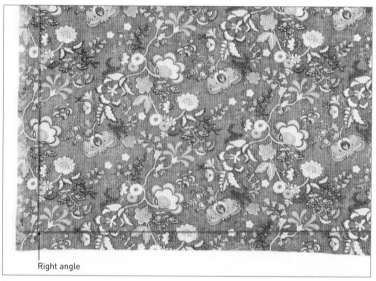

Draw in lines for bias strips.

3

To join bias strips

1 Place one strip horizontally in front of you, right side up.

2 Place the next strip right side down at right angles to the first.

3 Sew from top left to bottom right, starting and finishing at the points where the two fabrics cross.

4 Press the seam open and trim back the excess fabric to about ¼ in. (6 mm).

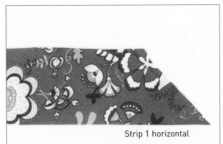

Strip 1 horizontal

1

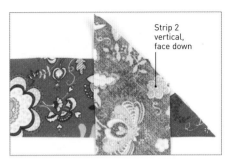

Strip 2 vertical, face down

2

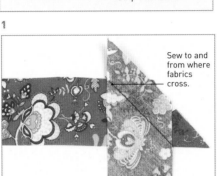

Sew to and from where fabrics cross.

3

Trim seam and press.

4

Method 2: Continuous strips

Cutting continuous bias strips is much easier and quicker, as the seams to join the strips are done first. Also if you are using a lot of bias, it just makes sense.

1 Place a square of fabric right side up and fold down one corner diagonally. Cut through the fold to create two triangles.

2 Flip one triangle over so that the right sides are together and slide it along so that the diagonal lines cross in the middle.

3 Sew a ¼-in. (6 mm) seam and press it open.

4 On the wrong side, draw in the lines to mark out all the bias strips. Make sure to keep them equal and parallel.

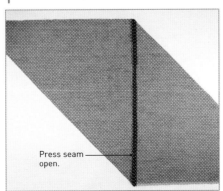

Cut through fold.

1

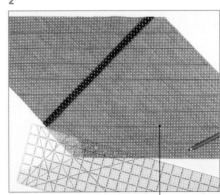

Flip so triangles cross in middle.

2

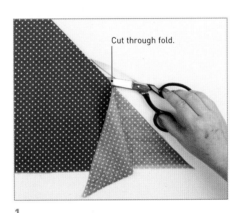

Press seam open.

3

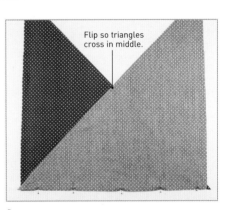

Draw in lines for bias strips.

4

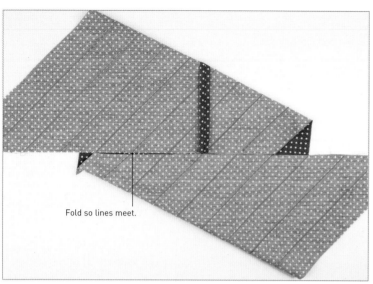

Fold so lines meet.

5 Fold over the ends of the fabric so that the lines all match up.

6 Slide the fabric so that the top edge of one side now lines up with the first line drawn on the other side. This will create a step in the fabric.

7 Pin the fabrics right sides together, making sure that all the lines match up. Sew with a ¼-in. (6 mm) seam and press the seam open.

8 Starting from one step, cut along the lines and through the seams **(a)**. Effectively you are cutting a spiral around the tube of fabric **(b)**.

Now you have a continuous length of bias strip, you can make it into binding, use it to finish a hem, turn it into a ruffle, or make it into piping or rouleau cord.

5

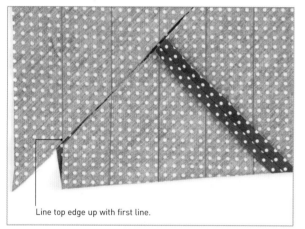

Line top edge up with first line.

6

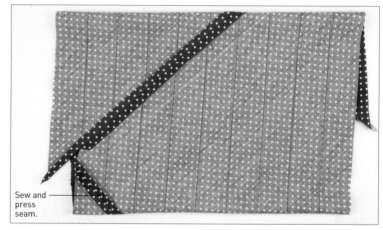

Sew and press seam.

7

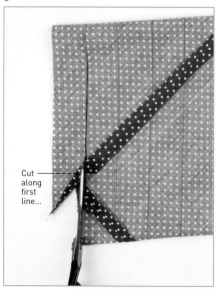

Cut along first line...

8a

... and keep going.

8b

Align raw edges.

Piping

One of the many uses for a bias strip is to make it into piping. This technique is wonderful for highlighting seams or creating a solid finish to an edge. Often used on cushions or soft furnishings, it also has its place in dressmaking both as flat piping and filled with a cord.

FLAT PIPING

Flat piping should be narrow and give definition. It can be used in a seam, around a pocket, or even along an edge. With a bit of careful measuring, it can be easy to achieve an accurate finish.

Piping along an edge

To work out how wide the bias strip needs to be, decide how much piping you would like visible—usually a scant ¼ in. (5 mm). Add this to the seam allowance required for the seam and then double it, as the piping is folded over and used double.

e.g. a scant ¼ in. (5 mm) visible piping + ⅝-in. (1.5 cm) seam allowance = ⅞ in. (2 cm)

Double this = 2 in. (4 cm)

Measure the length of piping needed and cut the bias strip with an inch or so spare.

1 Fold the bias strip in half lengthwise and press it.

2 Aligning the raw edges, lay the bias strip down on the right side of the fabric.

3 Sew along the seam line, stitching through both the bias strip and the garment. Don't pin the bias all the way around first; instead, position the bias strip as you sew and hold it in place with your fingers. As the bias has more ease in it, if you pin the length of it first you will end up with a bulge of piping at the end where the fabric has stretched slightly as it is sewn.

4 Lay the other side of the garment right side down on top of the piping. Pin in place.

5 Turn the garment over, so that you can see the first row of sewing. Stitch directly on top of this row of sewing.

6 Press the seam one way and layer the seam (see page 91) to reduce the bulk.

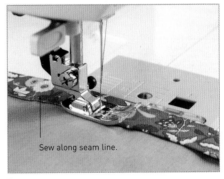

Sew along seam line.

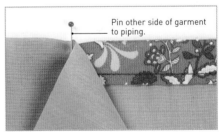

Pin other side of garment to piping.

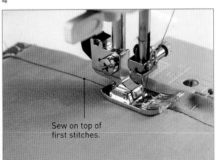

Sew on top of first stitches.

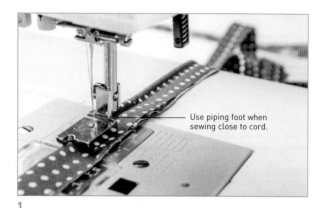

1 — Use piping foot when sewing close to cord.

2 — Align raw edges.

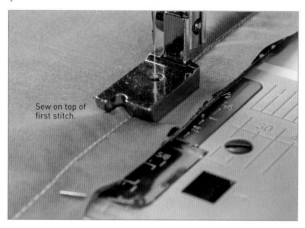

3 — Sew on top of first stitch.

CORDED PIPING

A length of cotton cord can be sewn inside a bias strip to make the piping more three-dimensional. This gives a really firm edge to a garment and looks great around the edges of collars or even along the top edge of a corset bodice.

To work out how wide the bias strip needs to be, decide on the size of piping cord you're using. Most cords are described by their diameter—for example, a ⅛ in. (4 mm) or a ¼ in. (6 mm) cord.

Multiply this by 3 to give an amount of fabric to go around the piping cord. Then add double the seam allowance.

A ⅛ in. (4 mm) cord would need about ⅝ in. (1.5 cm) of fabric to go around it. And then double the seam allowance (⅝ in./1.5 cm), as the bias strip is used double.

So the width of the bias strip needed is 1⅜ in. (4.5 cm).

To sew the piping cord into the bias strip, the stitching needs to be nice and tight into the cord itself. A single-toe zipper foot allows you to stitch really close. You can also use a specific piping foot that has a groove along the underside for the cord to sit in and a single hole as the needle aperture to enable you to stitch close to the cord.

Attaching the piping cord

By working out how wide to make the piping and cutting the bias strip the correct width to start with, you can leave the right amount of seam allowance, or "flange," to be able to sew the piping to the garment accurately.

1 Lay the piping cord along the center of the folded bias strip. Sew along the piping nice and close to the piping cord inside the bias strip.

2 Lay the bias strip along the seam allowance of one side of the garment, aligning the raw edges. As with flat piping, do not pin the piping all the way around first; just start sewing and hold it in place with your fingers as you sew directly on top of the piping stitching.

3 As for flat piping, lay the other part of the garment with the right side down onto the piping cord. Flip over the garment and sew along the previous line of sewing.

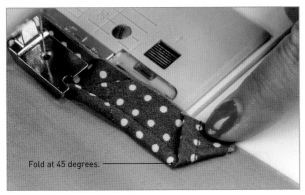

Cut excess cord.

1

Fold at 45 degrees.

2

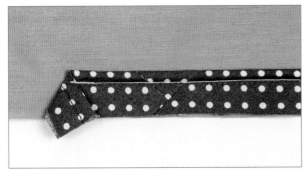

The finished, attached piping

Clean finish

A clean end is useful for butting the piping up to another seam or at the end of a seam.

1 Pull out about 1¼ in. (3 cm) of the cord and trim it off so that it slips back inside the bias casing.

2 Fold the empty section of bias strip down at 45° to create a neat finish, then sew along the strip.

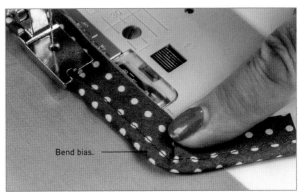

Bend bias.

1

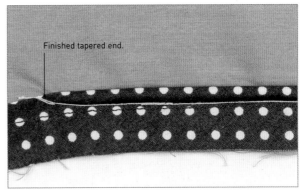

Finished tapered end.

2

Tapered end finish

Tapering the piping allows it to blend into another seam or if the piping seam folds under into a hem or cuff.

1 Stop about 4 in. (10 cm) before the end of the seam. Pull out about 1¼ in. (3 cm) of cord and trim it off so that it slips back inside the casing level with the end of the seam.

2 Pull the bias casing down so that it gently curves into the seam allowance and sew across to the end.

Rouleau cord

A rouleau is like piping cord, but without the flange to attach it to a garment. The excess fabric is actually turned inside the casing and creates the cord from itself. Because of the way a rouleau is made, it really only works with lightweight, closely woven fabrics such as silk charmeuse, cotton poplin, or lawn.

A rouleau cord works very well as a surface decoration, as you can bend and twist it into some interesting shapes. It can even be turned and twisted into a traditional frog fastening.

Rouleau also makes very neat little button loops and can be a traditional decorative feature on wedding dresses and evening wear, although you might not want quite so many on a day dress or blouse.

 ## Try this

At the end/beginning of the channel sew from the edges in toward the folded edge to create a funnel. This will help the fabric to turn in on itself.

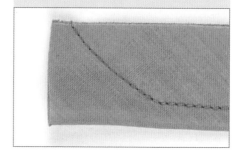

TO MAKE ROULEAU CORD

Method 1

1 Cut the bias strip between 1½–2½ in. (4–6 cm) wide.

2 Fold the bias strip in half lengthwise, right sides together, and sew a channel a scant ¼ in. (5 mm) from the folded edge.

3 Insert a rouleau turner all the way through the casing. Inset: Catch the top edge of the fabric firmly inside the hook.

4 Gently work the fabric back down inside the casing. This is a bit fiddly and requires a gentle but firm pressure to ease the fabric down inside.

5 Keep pulling until the end of the hook appears at the bottom. Remove the hook and continue to ease the rest of the fabric through to create the rouleau cord.

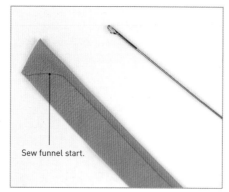

Sew funnel start.

2

Hook loop turner in bias end.

3

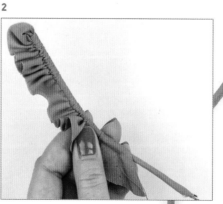

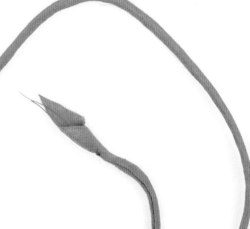

4 Pull rouleau through.

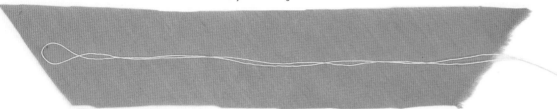

Lay thread along bias.

3

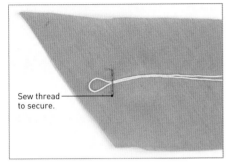

Sew thread to secure.

4

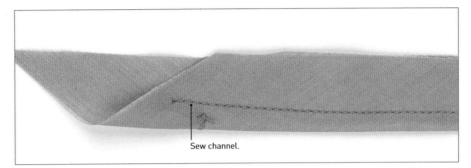

Sew channel.

5

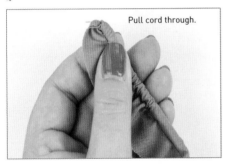

Pull cord through.

6

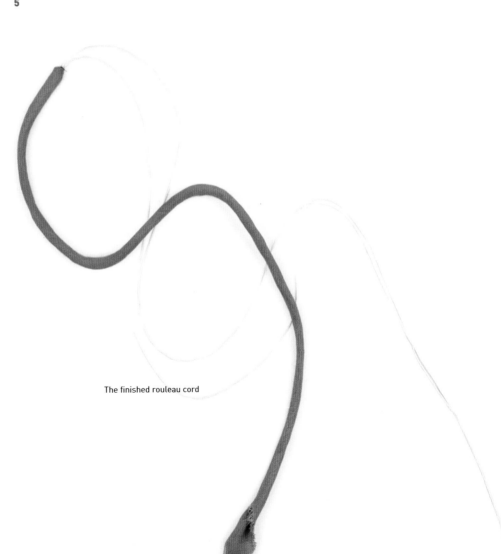

The finished rouleau cord

Method 2

1 Cut the bias strip between 1½–2½ in. (4–6 cm) wide.

2 Pull off enough strong, thick thread or yarn to lie along the length of the bias strip. You may need a couple of strands.

3 Lay this thread along the center of the right side of the bias strip.

4 Sew back and forth to secure the thread to one end of the bias strip.

5 Fold the bias strip over to encase the thread and sew a channel a scant ¼ in. (5 mm) from the folded edge, making sure not to catch the thread in the stitching.

6 Gently but firmly pull on the thread to turn the fabric in on itself to create the rouleau cord.

Lace is a delicate way of adding detail and interest to a garment, either within the garment itself or as an edging.

Adding lace

This is such a pretty way to add detail to your clothes.
It works well on light to medium-weight fabrics, so it is
perfect for lingerie or silk dresses and skirts.

If you are adding this decoration within a
garment, you will need to do a bit of
pattern alteration first to accommodate the lace if
you don't want to add extra length.

1 Mark on your garment the width of lace
to be inserted. Cut through the garment
and neaten the edges of the seam
allowances to be attached to the lace.
Press the seam allowances back toward
the main garment.

2 With the right side of the garment
uppermost lay the lace along the
folded-under edge of the upper part
of the garment.

3 Sew through the lace and folded-under
seam allowance.

4 Lay the right side of the lower part of the
garment under the lower edge of the lace
and pin in place.

5 Sew through the lace and the folded-
under seam allowance. You can then make
up the rest of the garment as instructed in
the pattern.

Right side

2

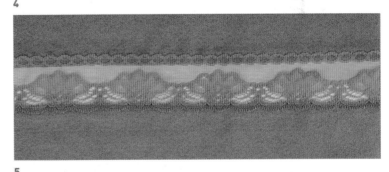

Sew through.

3

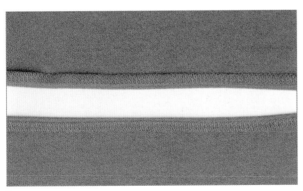

1

4

5

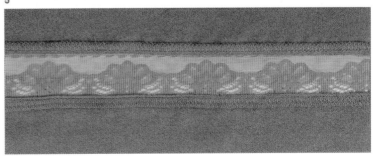

Finished insert from the wrong side

Frills and flounces

Frills, flounces, and ruffles are a wonderful way of adding softness to a garment or highlighting a particular feature or seam. The terms are often interchanged, but there is a distinct difference.

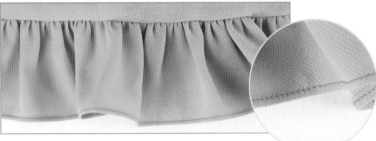

Single frill

Doubled-over frill

FRILLS

These are straight strips of fabric that are gathered or pleated up to create fullness and a rippled edge.

Frills are gathered or pleated up along one edge of a strip of fabric. Inset: It is a good idea to hem the frill first before gathering or pleating.

A doubled-over frill can add fullness and opulence, especially on evening wear and also if both sides of the frill are visible.

← A gathered frill has been used around the button placket to give definition and add a pretty detail to this dress.

RUFFLES

Ruffles are also straight strips of fabric, but the gathering or pleating often lies in the middle of the strip, creating a rippled edge on both sides of the ruffle.

The gathering or pleating can also lie off center to give an asymmetric effect.

Ruffles can look particularly effective made from a bias-cut strip of fabric, as the raw edges will give a soft, slightly frayed look.

To create your own ribbon frill or ruffle, you can use an ordinary fork to evenly space the pleats. Line up the edge of the ribbon under the sewing foot. Now insert a single tine of the fork over the fabric. Turn the fork to wrap the fabric around it and create the pleat. Line up one pleat with the edge of the pleat underneath. You can feel with your fingers where to place it. Sew to just catch the edge of the pleat and remove the fork. Now you can use this to edge or decorate your clothes.

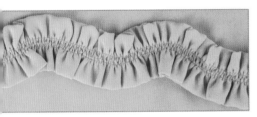

Central ruffle

Off-center ruffle

Use a pin to tuck frills under machine foot.

FLOUNCES

These are different to both frills and ruffles, in that the edge that is attached to the garment is flat and has no gathers or pleats. Used inserted into a vertical seam, flounces can create a beautiful waterfall effect in clothing.

The fullness and rippled edge are achieved by cutting the flounce as a circular piece of fabric. The inner circle is the same measurement as the length required for the flounce and the outer edge of the circle, as it is longer, creates the fullness.

As with both ruffles and frills, it is a good idea to finish the hem of the flounce before attaching it to the garment. You can use a decorative edge finish on an overlocker or pin hem (see page 239), depending on the look you want to achieve.

Measure the length you would like the flounce to be. Remember to include seam allowances. This is measurement C.

If you remember back to secondary-school algebra and the formula for working out the circumference of a circle ($C = 2\varpi r$), you can work out the radius of the circle. However, the easy way is just to divide measurement C by 6.28. This will give the radius for the inside circle of the flounce. To draw in the outer circle, add the depth of flounce to the radius and then draw that in too.

The ends of a flounce can be tapered to curve back into the seam or left blunt.

Insert the flounce into the seam using the same method as for inserting flat piping (see page 191).

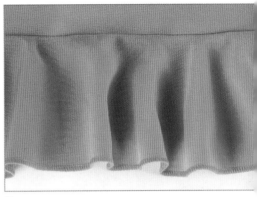

Flounce

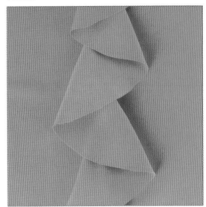

Waterfall flounce

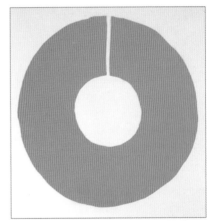

A flounce is made from a circular piece of fabric.

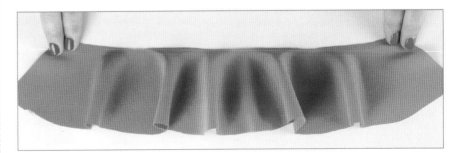

The circular fabric stretched out to create a flounce.

Topstitching

Topstitching is one of my favorite processes. It is a simple technique, but it can be the perfect way to add definition, texture, or decoration to your garment. It's also very useful, as it can hold layers of fabric together and keep seams neat and flat.

Topstitching is sometimes avoided, as it is assumed that it is rather tricky to get right, that it won't show up, or that it won't be straight. But like all techniques, a bit of thought and preparation will make it much, much easier.

There are several things to consider:

FABRIC CHOICE

A more stable fabric will cope a lot better with more rows of sewing. However, a finer fabric can still be topstitched as it can be stabilized with interfacing or even spray starch to keep the fabric flat and prevent it from puckering as it's topstitched.

 Try this

If the ends of the topstitching are going to be enclosed in another seam or hem, you don't need to reverse at the start and finish of your stitching; this can just add bulk and look untidy. Instead, pull the top thread to the bottom and trim them off flush with the fabric.

You may need to alter the top tension if you are sewing with a thick thread. Remember: The lower the number on the tension dial, the looser the tension will be. Lower = looser.

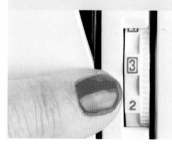

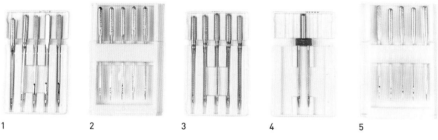

NEEDLE CHOICE

Topstitching needles (1) have larger-than-usual eyes to accommodate thicker threads.

Denim/jeans needles (2) are able to penetrate thick layers of fabric.

Embroidery needles (3) have wider-than-usual eyes to be able to cope with decorative or metallic threads.

Twin needles (4) create a double row of stitching with two top needle threads; the bobbin thread zigzags between the two.

Stretch or jersey needles (5) are used on knitted fabrics.

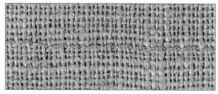

10 spi (2.5 mm) stitch length

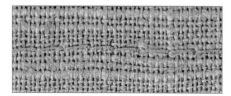

6 spi (4 mm) stitch length

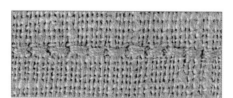

Triple stitch

STITCH

Topstitching requires a longer-than-normal stitch to really show off your stitching. Most medium-weight fabrics work well with a 10–8 spi (2.5–3 mm) stitch length, but a heavier fabric may need to go up to 7 spi (3.5 mm) or even 6 spi (4 mm).

You can use a triple stretch stitch with a normal thread if you don't want to use a specific topstitching thread. The stitch goes back and forth to create a thicker line of sewing, so the topstitching will be more defined.

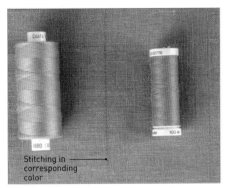

You can choose a corresponding thread (left) or contrasting thread (right).

Denim will require thicker thread.

Normal thread (left) and thicker thread (right) on linen.

THREAD CHOICE

Whether you want the topstitching to show up by using a contrasting color or if you prefer it to be more subtle, the thread you sew with should really correspond with the fabric you are working with.

If you are using a medium-weight fabric like cotton poplin, a normal thread will probably be fine. If you are sewing a denim or canvas fabric, then a thicker topstitching thread will work better. You don't need to have the topstitching thread on your bobbin; a normal thread here is fine.

MACHINE FEET

Normal sewing foot You can use a normal straight sewing foot to topstitch. However, to make it easier to sew parallel to the edge, give yourself a guide on the foot—for example, where the foot changes from metal to clear plastic. Line this up with the edge of the garment or seam and swing the needle over so that it is the correct distance away from the edge. Try not to look at the needle, but focus on aligning the marker on the foot with the edge or seam on the garment.

Blind-hem foot This foot has a blade running through the center of the foot, so it can be used to run along the edge of the garment or the seam. The needle can then be swung into the correct position.

Stitch in the ditch foot Sometimes this is known as an edge stitching foot; this is similar to the blind-hem foot but does not have the blade running through the needle aperture. This makes it more flexible for positioning the needle and the type of decorative stitching you can use.

Normal sewing foot

Blind-hem foot

Stitch in the ditch foot

> Try this

With any of these feet you can also use a quilting guide slotted into the back of the foot. This will allow you to sew in parallel lines wider than the width of the machine foot.

Stretch

4

If you go to your wardrobe or bureau and look through your clothes, I'll bet that many of them will be made of some kind of knitted fabric. Knits and jersey have become so commonplace in modern garments that we sometimes don't even notice what fabric we are wearing; a top is just a top. But these fabrics have very particular qualities that make them different to a woven fabric.

Stretch fabric characteristics

Knitted or jersey fabrics are not difficult to work with. Once you understand the properties of the particular fabric you are working with—the weight and stretch—you can make any adjustments to your sewing machine to ensure your garments are stitched correctly.

Why knit is different to woven fabric

WOVEN FABRIC

A woven fabric is made up of lots of warp threads that run the length of the fabric and the weft threads that weave in and out of the long warp ones. This gives the fabric stability. The threads or "yarns" can be all kinds of thicknesses and made from a whole range of different fibers, creating the wonderful range of textures and weights of fabric available to us.

The way a woven fabric is constructed still maintains the structure of the fabric even when it has a hole in it or several of the threads break.

KNITTED FABRIC

A knitted fabric is constructed by a single thread or yarn that is looped and twisted around itself to create the fabric. This means that if that single thread is broken or damaged, there are no other threads or yarns to support it and so the fabric unravels, creating the ladders we are familiar with in pantyhose or stockings.

The upside to a knitted fabric is that it's much more flexible. It drapes well and molds itself to the curves of the human body, making it extremely comfortable to wear.

STRETCH

Stretch is inherent in knitted fabrics and is what makes them so comfortable to wear. There are two basic types of stretch:

Mechanical stretch This is the amount of stretch that is provided by the structure of the knitted fabric itself. Knitted fabrics generally stretch most along the weft grain (from selvage to selvage), as the loops of yarn flatten and elongate when the fabric is pulled.

Yarn stretch This is when a specialty yarn is used to provide extra stretch and recovery to the fabric. Spandex (also know by the brand name Lycra) and elastane are the most common. Most dressmaking fabrics will have between 4% and 8% spandex, but some specialty fabrics can have up to 20%.

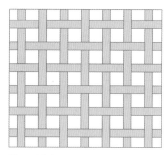

Woven fabric

Knitted fabric

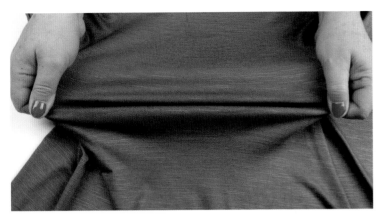

Horizontal stretch

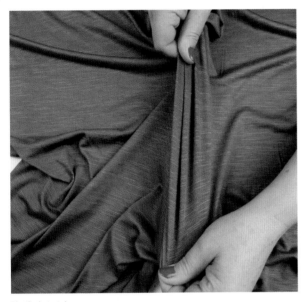

Vertical stretch

Measure out 4 in. (10 cm)

Stretch the measured fabric out to check the amount of stretch

HORIZONTAL OR TWO-WAY STRETCH

Fabrics should stretch easily from selvage to selvage. This horizontal stretch should go around the body, making it more comfortable to wear.

VERTICAL OR FOUR-WAY STRETCH

Most knitted fabrics have little or even no vertical stretch. But a four-way stretch means that additional stretch runs along the length of the fabric, making it bend in all directions with the body—perfect for active sportswear.

To check to see how much stretch your chosen fabric has, cut a piece of fabric about 4 in. (10 cm) long, place it on a ruler, and hold it in place with a finger on the 0. Now pull the other end of the fabric to see how far it will comfortably stretch. (You don't want to pull it so hard it distorts the fabric, though.) This will give you the rough percentage of stretch. For example, if 4 in. (10 cm) of fabric will stretch to 6 in. (15 cm), then the fabric has 50% stretch.

The percentage of stretch is actually more of a factor in selecting the right fabric for your project than the amount of spandex it contains, as it is the amount of stretchiness the fabric has that will determine whether or not it is suitable for your particular project.

PRESSING KNITS

It is incredibly important to use a very light touch when pressing knitted fabrics. Knitted fabrics have a life, body, and bounce to them and it is very easy to overpress and knock the life out of a fabric.

Always use a pressing cloth to diffuse some of the direct heat away from the surface of the fabric.

A light steam over the fabric will make a big difference to the way seams and hems can sit. The steam allows the fabric to relax back into shape after being sewn and what can look like a sewing failure can be saved by the iron.

Different types of knit fabric

As stretch is the most important thing to consider when choosing your knitted fabric, you will need to think about how the stretch will be used within the style of garment you want to make.

If you are choosing a close-fitting style with little ease, a fabric that has both vertical and horizontal stretch would make sense.
   If, on the other hand, the style of the garment is more relaxed and has more draping to it, then a two-way horizontal stretch would be fine.

 Try this

The best way to shop for knitted fabrics is to feel the fabrics before you decide. This way you will understand the stretch and handle of the fabric.

Jersey is susceptible to shrinking on the first wash, so it's best to prewash the fabric before cutting.

A soft four-way stretch fabric is better for more closely fitting garments like leggings. Whereas a more stable two-way stretch fabric is great for sweatshirt tops.

Tricot is often used for sportswear as it is lightweight and drys quickly.

As with woven fabrics, knitted fabrics come in a whole range of different textures, weights, drape, and fibers, and a lot of different terms and names are used to describe them. These are some of the most common.

Jersey Usually a single-yarn knitted fabric, jersey can be made from almost any fiber, including yarn, cotton, silk, and polyester, and can be made in a range of different weights. Also known as single jersey, double jersey, jacquard jersey, or interlock jersey, these names refer to the type of knitting used to make the fabric. Apart from interlock jersey, which is similar on both sides, you should also be able to tell the right and wrong side to a jersey. A single plain-knit jersey looks similar to hand-knitted stocking stitch.

Rib jersey This is the type of knitted fabric usually found on collars, cuffs, and waistbands. It is stronger and tighter than a jersey knit and looks similar to a hand-knitted rib. Lighter, softer rib knits can be used to make vests and to trim other jersey knits as bindings.

Spandex Knitted fabrics will always have a percentage of spandex included and would never be made from 100% spandex, as that would be like wearing a massive rubber band. The higher the percentage of spandex, the more likely it is that the fabric is made of other manmade fibers, such as polyester or nylon, as these lend themselves to a more high-performance type of garment.

Nylon or tricot These are lightweight fabrics mostly used in nightwear or lingerie. These fabrics range from almost sheer to completely opaque.

Lace Knitted stretch lace is also mainly used for lingerie. A four-way stretch is preferable, as it provides a closer, more comfortable fit to the body.

French Terry This is a good, heavier-weight, stable knit to work with. It has a looped wrong side, so will not pill when washed.

Brushed-back fleece This is smooth on the right side, but has a soft brushed finish on the reverse. It is a stable knit and good for sweatshirts and "bottoms."

Double knit or Ponte Roma These are often labeled interchangeably as they have a similar feel and weight, although their knit structure is different. They work very well for "bottoms" as they are stretchy but densely knitted.

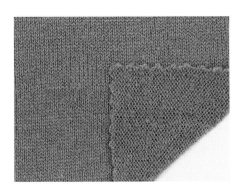

Jersey

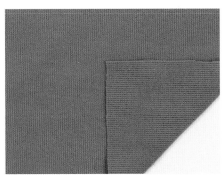

Tricot

Lace

French Terry

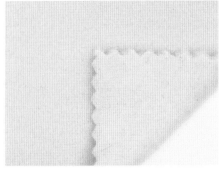

Brushed-back fleece

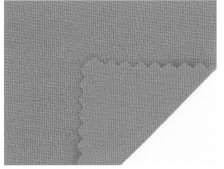

Double knit or Ponte Roma

USING THE RIGHT NEEDLE FOR KNITS

This can make a huge difference to the professional look of your finished garments and can also be the cause of sewing difficulties, including skipped stitches and large needle holes.

It is important to use either a ballpoint or a stretch needle. These needles have a slightly rounded point to enable the needle to push between the looped threads of the fabric—unlike a normal needle, which will pierce and split the threads, causing laddering and possibly holes.

Tip: The higher the number of the needle, the thicker the needle will be.
70—very lightweight silk or viscose jersey
80—light T-shirt-weight cotton jersey
90—interlock jersey, Ponte Roma

DIFFERENT FEET CAN HELP

Most of the time a normal sewing foot will work quite well, but specific sewing machine feet can really make a difference to the quality of the finish.

Overcasting foot This foot is used with the overcasting or zigzag stitches. The right-hand edge is lined up with the edge of the fabric and the fabric is held flat as the stitches are created.

Walking foot Often used for quilting, this foot has an additional set of upper dog teeth that grip the top layer of fabric and pull both or several layers of fabric through under the presser foot at the same rate.

MACHINE SETTINGS

Some machines have the ability to alter the pressure of the presser foot. The dial or control for this will be in different places on different machines, so do check your instruction manual. Lowering the presser foot pressure means that the fabric is not held as tightly when it passes under the presser foot, so the fabric is not stretched as much as the seam is sewn. Thread tension is best left alone on most occasions, but this is one situation you may have to alter it by lowering it slightly to allow the stitch a bit more flexibility.

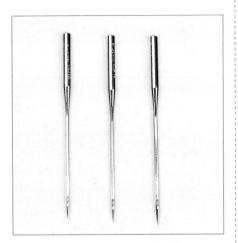

From left to right: 70, 80, and 90 sized needles

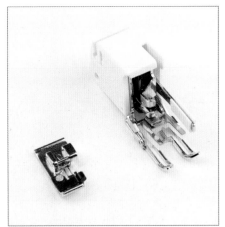

An overcasting foot (left) and a walking foot (right)

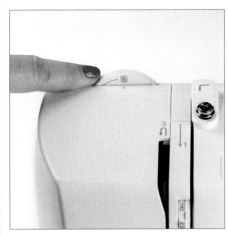

The presser foot pressure dial

Elastics and stabilizers

Elastics are the perfect partner for jersey knit fabrics and serve a variety of purposes.

Clear elastic can be used in many ways with knit fabrics. It works well both as a fully functioning elastic and as a stabilizer.

Clear elastic can also be used as a stabilizer to control the stretch in seams and prevent them from stretching out of shape. A good example is in shoulder seams. The elastic should be just a bit wider than your seam allowance so that it is caught in with the stitching of the seam.

Clear elastic (1) This is very thin polyurethane elastic tape and different from the usual corded elastics.

Plush elastic (2) This is often used in lingerie and the soft, plush finish is comfortable against the skin.

Corded elastics (3,4) This is the most common elastic with rows of latex cords sewn together. It is useful for threading through casings.

Picot edge elastic (5) This is often used in lingerie, as the decorative picot edge can be used both to trim and elasticate edges of garments like underpants.

1   2   3   4   5

HOW TO STABILIZE A SEAM

Do not skimp on the amount of elastic you buy: You will always need a bit more elastic than the length you wish to stabilize or gather. This is so that you have extra elastic to hold on to when sewing.

1 Start sewing with an overlock stitch onto the extra elastic at the beginning of the seam first, to make sure that the needles will catch the elastic. Also make sure that the elastic is on the top of, or in between, two layers of fabric and not directly in contact with the feed dogs, as this can rip the elastic.

2 Sew the seam, stitching over the elastic to hold it in place. Sew it without stretching the elastic, as if it's only one fabric. Leaving ends of elastic at the beginning and end of the seam makes it easier to handle.

Once the seam has been sewn, trim away the excess elastic.

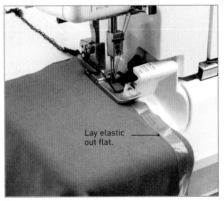

Lay elastic out flat.

1

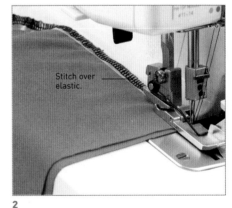

Stitch over elastic.

2

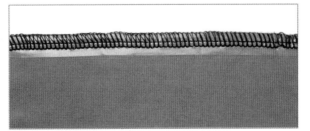

The finished stabilized seam

STABILIZING TAPE AND INTERFACING

An alternative to stabilizing with elastic is to use a stabilizing tape. This is a quick and easy way to add stability to a seam. It can also be used for areas where stretch is not required, such as hems or necklines. You can also use strips of fusible knit interfacing ironed onto the fabric.

You may also need to provide extra support for your knit fabric in areas other than seams—if you are sewing a pocket or placket, for example. An interfacing should be used here, but you will need one that has some give to it so that it will stretch with the fabric. Specific knit interfacings are available.

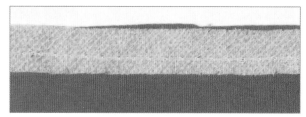

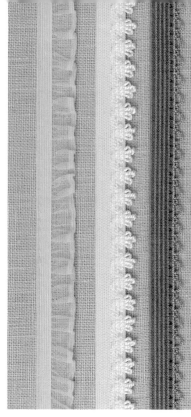

Stabilizing tapes

Use stabilizer tape for areas where no stretch is required.

Decorative elastics

GATHERING WITH ELASTIC

Method 1: Stretch as you sew

1 Mark the start and finish points on the clear elastic with a pen as well as on the fabric with pins. The elastic should be shorter than the fabric to be gathered. Make sure to have an inch or so of extra elastic at either end to give you something to hold on to as you stretch the elastic.

2 If the length you want to gather is more than about 12 in. (30 cm), mark the quarter, halfway, and three-quarter points on the elastic and the fabric to be gathered. Stretch the elastic to match each corresponding point on the fabric.

3 Place the start mark on the elastic at the start point on the fabric and sew a few stitches to hold everything in place.

4 Stretch the elastic out so that the second mark on the elastic sits on the second marker on the fabric. You can place your left index finger at the end of the flat sewing plate to help to hold the elastic in position as you sew. To keep an even distribution of gather, do not let the tension on the elastic go slack.

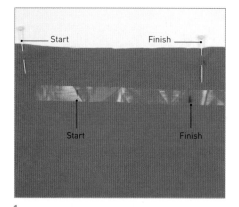

Start   Finish

Start   Finish

1

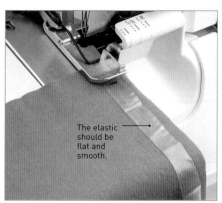

The elastic should be flat and smooth.

3

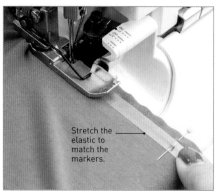

Stretch the elastic to match the markers.

4

The finished stretch-as-you-sew seam

Decorative elastic

This gives a really neat finish, especially to pieces of lingerie.

This type of elastic is attached to the right side of the fabric first. You can choose whether to neaten the raw edge of your fabric first or not. There is no right or wrong answer to this one. Knits do not need to be finished, as they will not fray, but you might wish to neaten to add a bit of stability to your fabric. Or you might choose to neaten if you are using a lightweight fabric and don't wish to add any additional bulk. The choice is yours.

1 With the right sides of the elastic and fabric together, place the non-decorative edge of the elastic along the raw edge of the garment so that the edges of the fabric and the elastic are level.

2 Stretch the elastic as you sew close to the decorative edge of the elastic with a lightning or small zigzag stitch. If you have chosen not to neaten the fabric first, trim off any excess fabric showing past the elastic.

3 Fold the elastic back to the wrong side and topstitch it in place using a triple step zigzag or large normal zigzag, while still stretching the elastic out to fit the fabric. Give it a gentle steam in order to relax it back into shape.

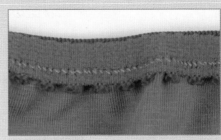

1–2

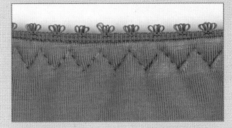

Method 2: Gather first

1 If using elastic to gather as well as to stabilize a full amount of fabric, it is better to gather the fabric first and then to add the elastic to stabilize the seam. Use the sewing machine to sew a double row of gathering threads (see pages 76–77). Then pull up the bobbin threads to create nice even gathers.

2 After the fabric has been gathered, add the clear elastic in the same way as before. Make sure that the gathered layer of fabric is uppermost to ensure that the gathers are nice and even.

This method is perfect if you want to ensure that you get an even distribution of gathers before committing yourself to the seam.

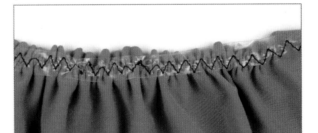

1

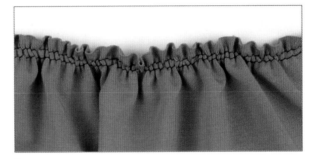

2

> Try this

Remember to remove the gathering threads after sewing in the elastic, as they may pop if the fabric is stretched.

Working with stretch fabric

Stretch fabrics are not difficult to work with, just different from woven fabrics. With a bit of consideration and minor adjustments to your sewing machine you will find working with stretch fabrics speedy and satisfying.

You don't need an overlocker

One of the most common excuses for not sewing with knits is that you need to have an overlocker or some special sewing machine. This is absolutely not true. While an overlocker will give a completely professional finish to sewing knits, it is not essential.

> Try this

Using a wider stitch throws the needle off center, so you will need to alter where you gauge the seam line. Try using a rubber band around the arm of the machine to guide your fabric to sew the correct seam allowance.

BASIC SEAMS

The first thing to be aware of is that the stitching will need to "give" with the stretch in the fabric. An ordinary straight stitch will just pop when stretched with the fabric.

Your machine will have several stitch settings that can be used with knits to sew basic constructional seams. Remember that knits don't fray, so you don't always need to neaten seams.

Lightning stitch

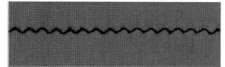

Normal zigzag stitch

Overcasting

Mock overlocking

Lightning stitch Sometimes called a "stretch stitch," this looks a bit like a slanting zigzag. This is good for heavier-weight knits.

Normal zigzag You will need to adjust the stitch length and width depending on the fabric you are working with. A small, narrow zigzag is good for seams on heavier-weight fabrics.

Overcasting This stitch will create the seams and neaten the edge of the fabric, too. You may need to reduce the tension slightly if the stitch is too tight and is causing the edge to curl under.

Mock overlocking This again creates the seam and neatens the edge in one. It looks very similar to an overlocked seam.

Edge finishes for necklines and armholes

SELF-FABRIC BAND

This is probably the easiest way to finish a neckline or armhole. You will need a band of fabric that is double the width of the finished band, plus twice the seam allowance. The most stretch in the fabric will need to go along the length of the band.

1 If you want the finished band to be ¾ in. (2 cm) and the seam allowance is ⅜ in. (1 cm), the cut width of the band should be 2¼ in. (6 cm). The band needs to be a bit shorter than the seam it is being sewn into. This allows for the sewn edge to stretch into the curve and ensure that the folded edge remains flat to the body.

2 Once the band is cut, sew the short edges together and fold over to enclose the seam.

3 Match up the seam on the band with where you want the seam to sit on the garment—usually the center back or a shoulder seam. Gently ease and pin the band to the neckline, making sure that the distribution of stretch around the band allows it to remain flat to the body. This may take some adjustment to account for the different amounts of stretch in different fabrics. And you will also find that more stretch is required on the more curved areas of the neckline.

4 Sew the band to the neckline using lightening, zigzag, or mock overlock stitch. Then give it a gentle steam to help it relax into shape.

5 The neckline should have a clean finish with the seam folded down inside the garment **(a)**. You can topstitch the seam allowance in place with a normal zigzag, triple step zigzag, or a twin needle **(b)**.

Sew across short ends.

2

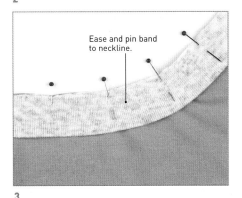

Ease and pin band to neckline.

3

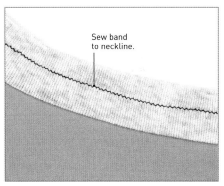

Sew band to neckline.

4

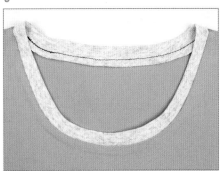

5a

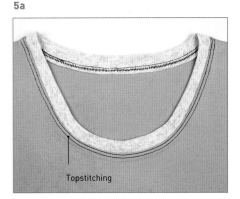

Topstitching

5b

Help!

The band puckers won't sit flat.

It is worth taking the time to adjust the band before sewing to make sure that it really is sitting flat, with no puckering along the seam line.

If the band is standing up away from the neckline, it is too large to fit into the neckline. Remove it and take it in along the short edge seam.

If you notice a puckering along the seam line, the band is too small to fit the neckline. You will need to recut the band slightly larger.

Jersey is a much easier fabric to work with than you might first assume. The stretch works with rather than against you to ease the pieces together.

CLEAN-FINISH BINDING

This method will hide the binding itself and only a row of sewing will be visible on the right side of the garment around the neckline.

1 Cut the binding so that the stretch of the fabric runs along the length. The finished width of the binding should be no more than a scant ⅜ in. (8 mm). So the cut width of the binding should be ⅝ in. (1.6 cm), plus the seam allowance, and it should be longer than the neckline.

2 Fold the binding in half, with wrong sides together.

3 To make it easier to attach the binding, it is usual to leave one seam open so that the binding can be sewn on flat and not "in the round."

4 With right sides together, aligning the raw edges, place the binding to the garment. Sew around the binding using a lightning stitch or small zigzag (other stitches leave too much thread bulk under the binding when it's finished).

5 Fold the binding over to the wrong side of the garment and edge stitch it in place. You can use a very narrow zigzag or a twin needle for more decoration. Give the neckline a gentle press to allow it to relax back into shape.

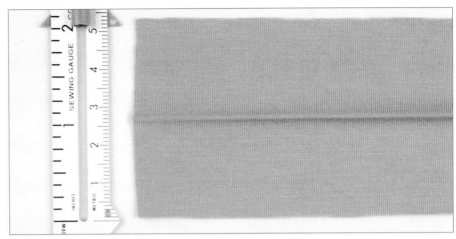
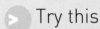

1–2

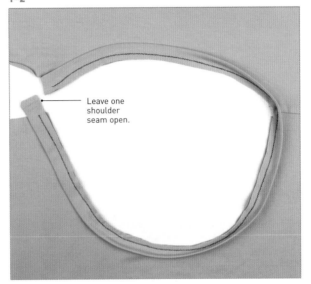

Leave one shoulder seam open.

3–4

> **Try this**

To make sure you do not stretch the fabrics as you are sewing the binding, sew a practice sample first.

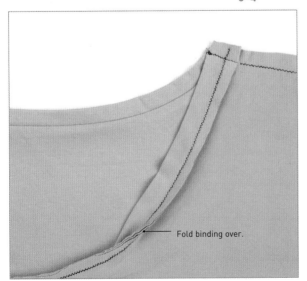

Fold binding over.

5

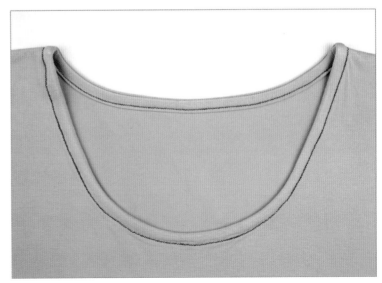

The finished clean-finish binding

VISIBLE BINDING

This method has the binding wrapped over the raw edge of the fabric and is visible on both the right and the wrong sides of the garment.

1 Cut the binding as for the clean finish (see page 215), so that the binding is double the finished width, plus twice the seam allowance, and is longer than the neckline.

2 Sew across both shoulder seams and secure with staytape.

3 Fold the binding over, wrong sides together, and make sure that it sits flat. Sew across the short ends.

4 Place the binding to the wrong side of the garment, aligning the raw edges. Gently ease the binding onto the neckline, making sure that you don't stretch the garment in the process.

5 Sew the binding to the garment with a lightning stitch or small zigzag. Give the binding a gentle steam to help it relax back into shape.

6 Fold the binding over to the right side, enclosing the seam allowances, and allow the folded edge of the binding to just cover the row of sewing attaching it to the neckline.

7 Edge stitch the binding down to the garment using a lightning stitch, normal zigzag, triple step zigzag, or twin needle. Give the neckline a gentle steam to help it relax back into shape.

1

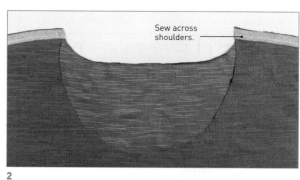

Sew across shoulders.

2

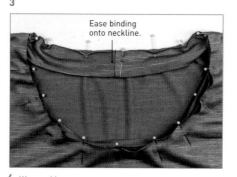

Sew across short ends.

3

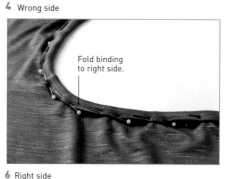

Ease binding onto neckline.

4 Wrong side

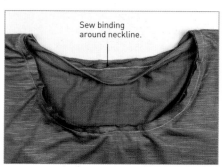

Sew binding around neckline.

5 Wrong side

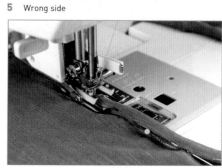

Fold binding to right side.

6 Right side

7

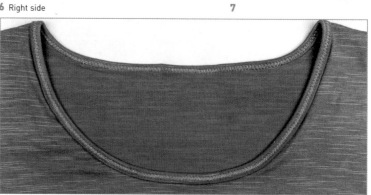

Finished visible binding

Hemming and using a twin needle

This can be an area that causes home sewers the most headaches. But with a gentle hand and a steam iron, you can achieve a good finish.

POINTS TO REMEMBER!

- Knits do not fray, so hems only need to be turned up once and then secured.
- Always use the correct needle for the type of knit fabric you are working with and make sure they are either ballpoint or stretch needles.
- Try using a walking foot to help the fabric pass through the machine.
- Stabilizing the hem by using iron-on tape or interfacing will significantly improve the sewing outcome.
- The iron is your friend. Pressing the hem gently after sewing can really make a difference to the finished look of the garment.

USING A ZIGZAG STITCH

A small zigzag stitch is less noticeable, especially if using a matching thread (I have used a contrast here to show the stitching more clearly). You can see the difference between the unstabilized hem sewn with a normal foot and the stabilized hem sewn with a walking foot.

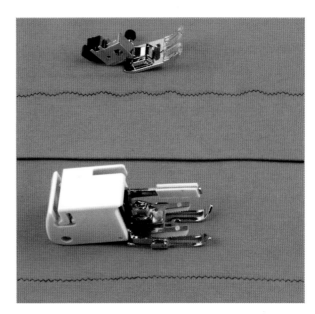

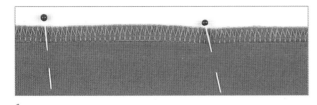

1

The blind hem should just catch the garment.

2

3

USING A BLIND HEM STITCH

This is more commonly used on woven fabrics, but a stretch version can be found on most modern sewing machines. It looks like a small zigzag that opens out into a larger stitch every so often. This means the main part of the zigzag is sewn onto the hem and the larger stitch hops over and just catches the garment.

1 Fold up the hem as usual, then fold the hem back to the right side of the garment. This should leave a little bit of the hem showing past the folded-over garment.

2 Run the stitch along the small bit of exposed hem so that the larger stitch hops over and just catches the garment. It is best to do some test samples first to work out how wide to make the stitch before sewing the garment.

3 Fold the hem back into place and press.

Try this

If you don't have a blind-hem foot, the stitch should work just as well with a walking foot.

TWIN NEEDLE

This is the closest method to a cover-stitch, which is how hems are finished using an industry method. It has two top-spool threads, each going through a needle, and the normal bobbin thread. It sews a double row of straight sewing on the right side and a zigzag stitch on the back, where the bobbin thread goes between the two top threads.

1 Unthread your machine and add the extra spool holder with the additional thread on it. Now take both threads and pass them through the machine threading system as if they were only a single thread. This helps to prevent the threads from twisting too much against each other and breaking.

2 Pass the usual thread through the left-hand needle and the extra thread through the right-hand needle.

3 You may wish to neaten the raw edge of the fabric first to make it look more like a proper cover-stitch but you don't have to.

4 Press up the hem and sew from the right side. You can mark the stitching line from the right side or just gauge where you need to sew to catch the hem in place.

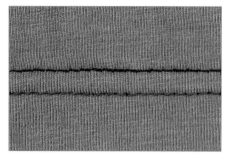
Right side

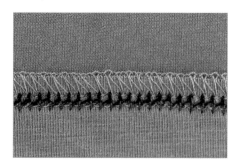
Wrong side

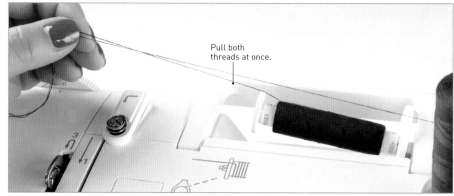
Pull both threads at once.

1

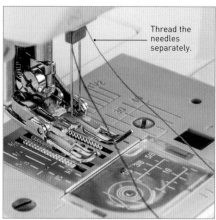
Thread the needles separately.

2

4 Right side

> **Try this**

If you don't have an additional spool holder, you can pop your extra thread into a jam jar. It will allow the spool to unwind but keep it contained.

You may want to reduce the tension slightly to prevent a ridge forming between the two lines of top-stitching. Some machines will let you alter the bobbin tension; with others just reducing the top tension slightly will have a similar effect.

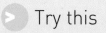

FABRIC BAND

An alternative way of giving a clean finish to hems and cuffs is to sew an additional folded-over band of fabric. This allows all the seaming to be on the inside of the garment, keeping everything neat and cleanly finished.

1 Measure the hem or cuff and cut the band just a little bit shorter. This ensures that the band will sit nice and snug, and not bag as you wear it. The band needs to be cut with the stretch running around the band.

2 Fold the band in half widthwise, right sides together, and sew across the short ends with a small zigzag or lightning stitch. Turn the band right side out, enclosing the seams, and press it flat.

3 With right sides together, pin the band to the garment, gently easing it in place.

4 Sew around the band using a lightning stitch, small zigzag, edge stitch, or mock overlock.

5 Fold the garment back down and press the seam allowance up toward the garment.

1

Garment

Band

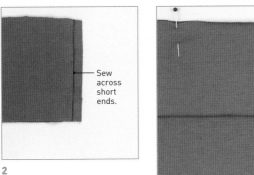

Sew across short ends.

2

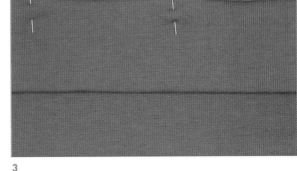

3

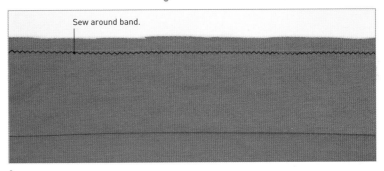

Sew around band.

4

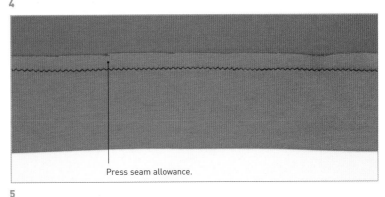

Press seam allowance.

5

Try this

You can topstitch with the twin needle for a bit of added decoration. This will make sure that the seam sits up toward the garment, too.

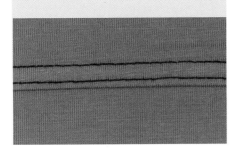

Finish

Finish is where you can make a real difference to the final look of your garments. It is the difference between your sewing looking "handmade" as opposed to "homemade." What we are trying to achieve is an individually handmade wardrobe to suit your own figure shape and personality.

When you're on the homestretch of a project, it can be tempting to rush ahead and use whatever method is the quickest to get something done, but thinking about the method and process you are going to use and selecting the best one for the fabric and garment type will pay dividends.

5

Bound edges

Bound edges are a very neat and attractive way to finish an edge. A bound edge will also help a curved neckline or armhole maintain its shape. The binding can be made from the same fabric as the garment or a contrast fabric can make a feature of the binding.

Positioning the bias strip

The bias strip will need to be sewn accurately to the garment using the correct seam allowance to preserve the fit and look of the garment.

POSITIONING THE BIAS BINDING

This method uses a single layer of bias binding, with the edges folded in to create small seam allowances—which is how ready-made binding comes.

With the wrong side of the bias strip in front of you, unfold the top edge and measure from the raw edge to the top crease. The crease will be the stitching line and must sit directly on top of the stitching line of your garment.

So, if the crease is ¼ in. (6 mm) from the raw edge and the garment seam allowance is ⅝ in. (1.5 cm), you need to move the raw edge of the tape down by ⅜ in. (9 mm) so that the crease line sits on the seam allowance line.

The same will apply if you are using a doubled-over bias strip or a bias strip you have cut yourself from your chosen fabric. Make sure that the seam allowance on the bias strip sits directly on the seam line of the garment.

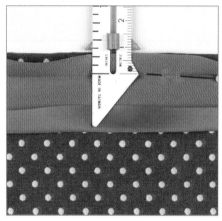

Measure from the crease to the raw edge of the binding.

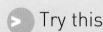 Try this

How much extra binding to allow?

You will need to cut your binding slightly longer than the finished length required, so that you can overlap the ends for a neat finish. The amount of overlap required depends on whether the ends of the binding are being closed into a continuous loop (around a neckline or armhole, for example) or left open (if they are going to be enclosed into another seam).

Closed ends

If the binding is going in a circle and the ends are going to be closed (around an armhole or a neckline, for example), allow an extra 3 in. (8 cm) at each end.

Open ends

If the ends of the binding are going to be open (if they are going to be enclosed in another seam, for example), allow an extra 1 in. (2.5 cm) of binding at each end.

Attaching the bias strip

The bias strip can be attached either as a single layer or a double layer, depending on whether you wish the binding to be visible or invisible. Either finish involves attaching the bias strips in the same way.

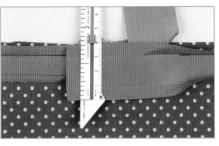

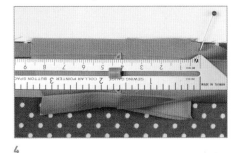

1

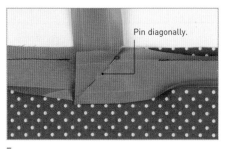

2

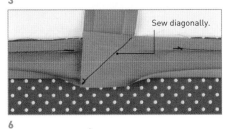

3

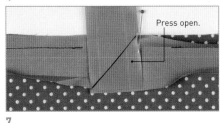

4

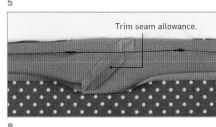

5

6

7

8

ATTACHING THE BINDING WITH CLOSED ENDS

1 Align the crease with the sewing line (see opposite) and pin the binding all the way around the opening, leaving an extra 3 in. (8 cm) of binding at each end. Stretch the binding slightly as you go around the curve. It is this slight stretching of the binding as you pin that allows the binding to sit perfectly flat when it is folded back and finished. (Think concentric circles, if that doesn't sound too confusing.) It is worth having a practice to really get a feel for this. Stitch along the crease line.

2 When the binding gets back to where it started, leave a gap of about 3 in. (8 cm).

3 Unfold the binding completely, measure the width from raw edge to raw edge, and make a note of this measurement (measurement A).

4 Keeping both ends of the bias tape unfolded, overlap them so that they sit neatly together. Mark with a pin where the bottom layer sits underneath. Then measure out the width of the binding (measurement A) from this point and mark this. You are basically making a square. Trim the top layer down to this point.

5 Lift the bottom corner of the top layer and fold it up to make a triangle. Then fold the top corner of the bottom layer down to make a similar triangle. Fold in the creases with your thumb. Fold the triangles back and pin along the creases.

The two ends of the binding will sit together at right angles.

6 Sew from bottom left to top right.

7 Open out the seam and adjust to make sure the binding is sitting neatly.

8 When you're happy with it, trim back the seam allowances to ¼ in. (6 mm) and press open. You can now either sew across the remaining single layer of bias or fold the bias strip back and sew across the double layer. The circle of binding has been made continuous and can be sewn all the way around, with the join almost invisible.

Finishing the bias binding

Binding can be finished in one of two ways to ensure a neat finish to your garment.

VISIBLE BINDING

This type of binding encases the raw edge and is visible from the right side, so no seam allowance is needed on the garment. If a seam allowance is included in the pattern, trim it off before you add the binding. The raw edge is the finished edge of the garment and if the visible binding is sewn onto the seam allowance, it will make the neck or armhole smaller. Position and attach the binding (see pages 222–223) to the wrong side of the garment. This ensures that when you edge stitch the binding you are sewing on the right side of the garment.

FINISHING VISIBLE BINDING

1 Trim the seam allowance down to ¼ in. (6 mm).

2 From the right side, using the toe of the iron, gently push the binding up away from the garment and press it in place. Use a tailor's ham to make it easier around the curves.

3 Fold the bias binding down to the wrong side, enclosing the seam allowance. Roll it down so that it sits just over the first row of stitching. Pin in place all the way around.

4 Edge stitch along the binding to enclose the raw edges and finish the binding.

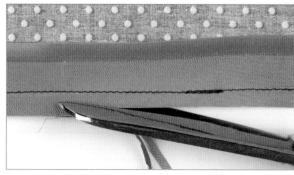

1 Wrong side

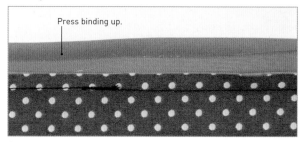

Press binding up.

2 Right side

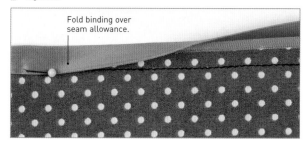

Fold binding over seam allowance.

3

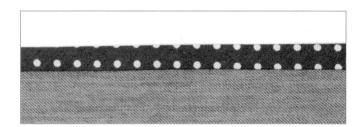

HAND-FINISHED INVISIBLE BINDING

Hand finishing a binding gives a real couture finish and is perfect for sewing fine fabrics such as crêpe de Chine or satin-backed crepe. The binding needs to be sewn to the RIGHT side of the garment first. This means that the hand sewing will be on the WRONG side and will not be visible. Once the binding has been sewn on to the garment and folded over to conceal the line of stitches, the folded edge of the bias can be slipstitched in place (see page 236).

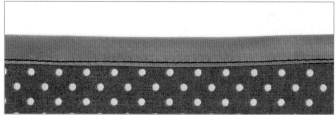

MACHINE-FINISHED VISIBLE BINDING

If you are edge stitching the binding in place, it is better to sew from the RIGHT side. This means that the binding should be attached to the WRONG side of the garment first.

Sew close to the edge of the binding. You can swing the needle over to get in nice and close, still using the guides on the foot as a marker.

INVISIBLE BINDING

Invisible binding neatens a raw edge, but is hidden inside the garment. This method is particularly effective at supporting necklines or armholes and gives a clean finish to a garment. You can use doubled-over bias strip to enable a very narrow binding to be created, but that will also sit neatly without having to tuck under any seam allowance.

This method uses a bias strip that is doubled over. The width of the strip should be twice the width of the finished binding, plus twice the seam allowance. So, if the finished width is ⅜ in. (1 cm) and the seam allowance is a scant ¼ in. (0.5 cm), then the cut width of the bias strip will be 1¼ in. (3 cm).

Position and attach the invisible binding (see pages 222–223) to the right side of the garment. This ensures that when you edge stitch the binding you are sewing on the wrong side of the garment.

PREPARING THE INVISIBLE BINDING

1 Open out the folds in the binding and press it flat.

2 With wrong sides together, fold the bias strip in half lengthwise so that both long raw edges are together and press. You will still be able to see the lines of the original fold to use as a guide for sewing.

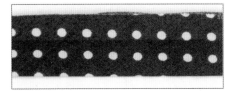

2

FINISHING INVISIBLE BINDING

1 Trim the seam allowance down to ¼ in. (6 mm).

2 From the right side, using the toe of the iron, gently push the binding up away from the garment and press it in place. Use a tailor's ham to make it easier around the curves.

3 Fold the bias binding over to the wrong side, enclosing the seam allowance. Roll it down so that you can just see a fraction of the garment and then you will know that the binding will be invisible from the right side. Pin in place all the way around.

4 Sew close to the edge of the binding.

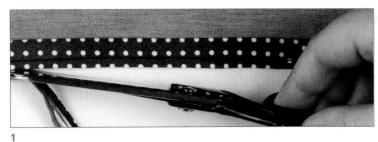

1

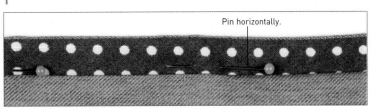

Pin horizontally.

3

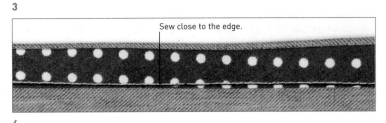

Sew close to the edge.

4

> ## Try this

You can swing the needle over to get in nice and close to the edge of the binding while still using the guides on the machine plate.

Facings

A facing is a piece of fabric that is the same shape as the open edge on a garment you wish to finish. It is sewn around the open edge and turned back inside the garment to enclose all the raw edges. It is most commonly used around the neck or waist edge to neaten, strengthen, and support the open edge of a garment.

Neck facing

These are the simplest forms of facing and will be a mirror image of the main garment. The right side of a facing faces outward on the inside of a garment, so it needs to be a "reverse" shape of the main garment—especially if the garment has an asymmetrical neckline. If there isn't a pattern, it is very easy to make your own.

1 Draw a line on your garment pattern pieces about 1½ in. (6 cm) away from the neckline of your garment, making sure it follows the same shape. Trace off the facing shapes onto a separate piece of paper. Don't forget to mark on any pattern information such as "place to fold" or the grain line.

2 Cut out the facing pieces in fabric and attach a suitable interfacing (see page 38). This will add support to the fabric and prevent it from pulling out of shape. With right sides together, sew the facing pieces together to create the whole shape of the neckline and press the seams open. Neaten the outer edge of the facing by overlocking, zigzagging, or sewing a pin hem (see page 239).

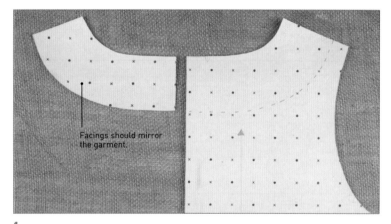

Facings should mirror the garment.

1

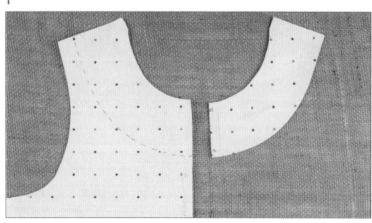

1

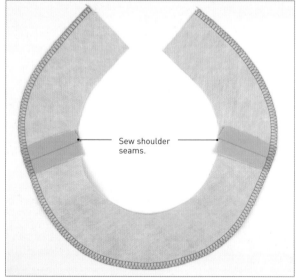

Sew shoulder seams.

2

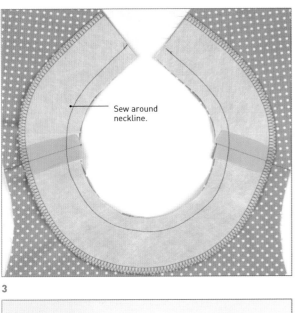

Sew around
neckline.

3

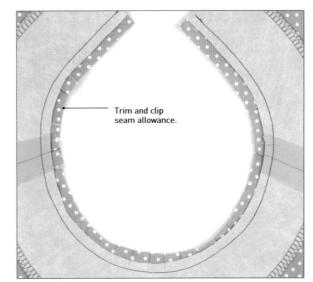

Trim and clip
seam allowance.

4

5

6

3 With right sides together, matching up the shoulder seams and any pattern notches, place the facing on the neckline. Sew around the neckline with a slightly shorter-than-normal stitch length. This will help to ensure that the stitching remains firm and that the neckline won't bag.

4 Trim and layer the seam allowance (see page 91) to reduce the bulk. Snip into the curved seam allowance (see page 91) to release the tension in the curve and to allow it sit flat.

Tip: Make sure to trim the facing down lower than the garment. This ensures there are no ugly "steps" showing on the right side of the garment.

5 Understitch (see page 232) the facing to hold it in place. Alternatively, edge stitch and topstitch around the neckline.

6 Press the finished neckline flat.

Waist facing

Finishing the waist edge with a facing not only hides all the raw edges, but also supports and stabilizes the waistline, so helping the garment to maintain its shape.

1 Again it is easy to create your own pattern for a facing if there isn't one provided. Draw a line on your garment pattern pieces about 1½ in. (6 cm) away from the waistline of the garment. Fold out any darts and trace the facing shapes off onto another piece of paper.

2 Attach a suitable interfacing (see page 38) to the facing pieces. With right sides together, sew the facing pieces together to create the shape of the waist. Press the seams open and neaten the outer edge by overlocking or using a binding (see pages 94–96).

3 With right sides together, matching up the notches, place the facing on the waistband. Pin and sew around the top edge of the waistband.

4 Trim and layer the seam allowance (see page 91) to reduce the bulk. Snip into the seam allowance (see page 91) to release the tension in the curve.

5 Lay a narrow tape or ribbon along the seam allowance so that it sits just next to the seam line. Follow the curve of the waistline and allow the snips in the seam allowance to splay open. Sew the tape close to the seam line, stitching through the seam allowances only but not the skirt. This will help to support the waist of the garment.

6 Understitch (see page 232) through the facing to hold it in place. Catch the facing down to the seam allowances by hand or machine.

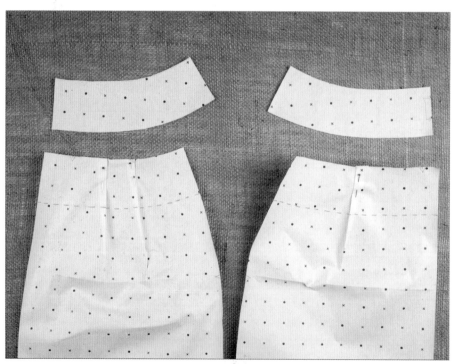

1

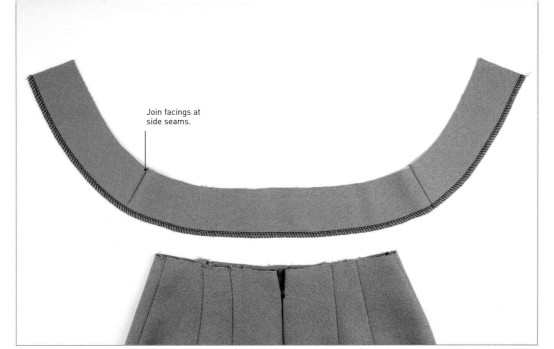

Join facings at side seams.

2

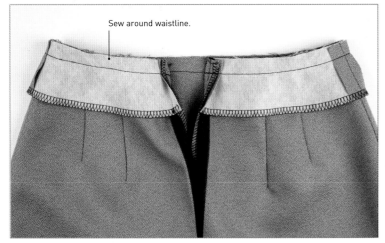

Sew around waistline.

3

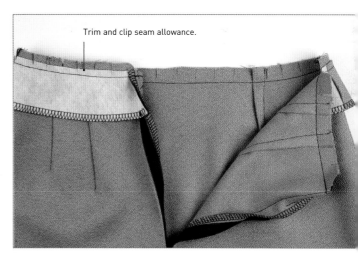

Trim and clip seam allowance.

4

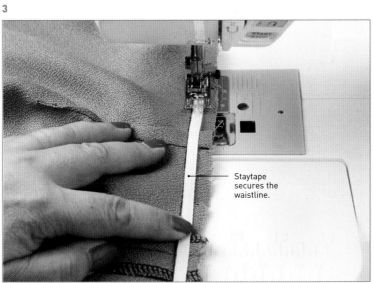

Staytape secures the waistline.

5

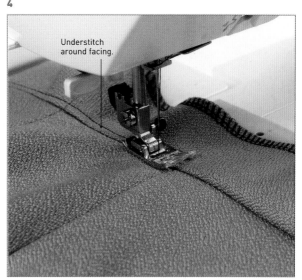

Understitch around facing.

6

All-in-one facing

This type of facing finishes off both the neckline and the armholes at the same time, thus reducing bulky excess fabric. The lower edge of the facing should curve up and over the bust to avoid creating any tension over the bust line. As with all facings, attach a suitable interfacing before sewing and neaten the lower edge with your chosen method.

1 Sew the front and back bodice pieces together at the shoulder seams, but leave the side seams and center back open **(a).** Repeat with the facing pieces **(b).** Press the seams open.

2 With right sides together, lay the facing on the bodice. Pin together and sew around the neckline and armholes.

3 Layer and clip the seam allowances to release the tension in the curves (see page 91).

4 Gently ease the back sections of the bodice through each shoulder gap.

5 Understitch (see page 232) around the neckline and armholes as far as you can. (You will not be able to get all the way around, as the shoulder will be too narrow.) Press the neckline and armholes to ensure that the facing rolls under the edge of the bodice.

6 With right sides together, pin and sew the side seams of the bodice. Make sure to fold back the facing at the underarm and sew all the way across this as well.

7 Fold the facing back down and press in place. Catch the facing to the side seam of the bodice to prevent it from riding up.

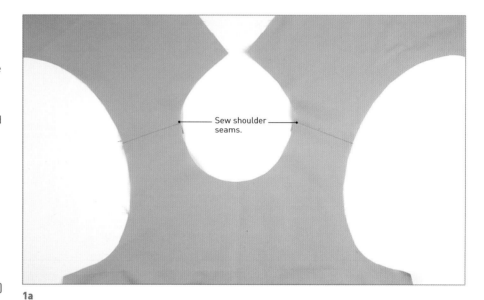

Sew shoulder seams.

1a

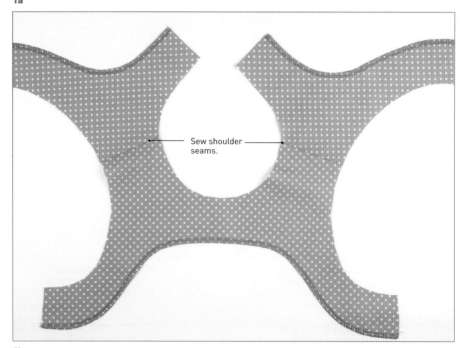

Sew shoulder seams.

1b

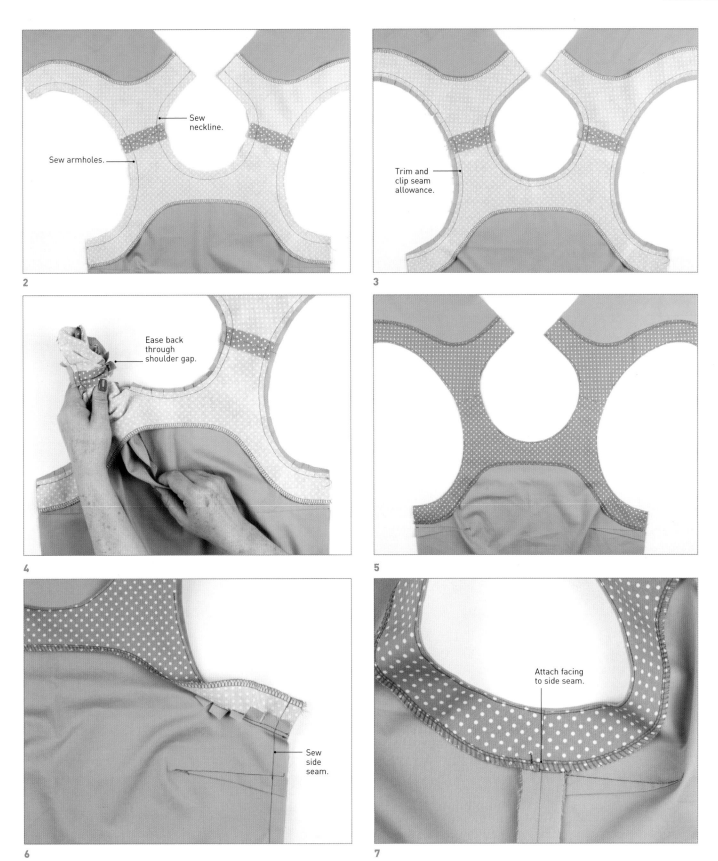

2 Sew neckline. Sew armholes.

3 Trim and clip seam allowance.

4 Ease back through shoulder gap.

5

6 Sew side seam.

7 Attach facing to side seam.

Understitching and edge stitching

These techniques are both ways of achieving a better finish to your garments. As with many sewing terms, they are fairly self-explanatory.

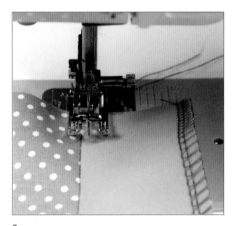

2

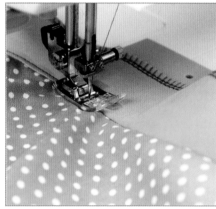

3

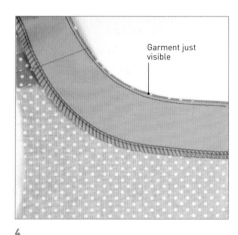

Garment just visible

4

Understitching

This literally holds a part of the garment "under" and is particularly useful when sewing a facing.

1 After the facing has been attached to a garment around the neckline or waist and the seam has been trimmed down and snipped to release the tension in the curve, push all the seam allowances toward the facing.

2 Position the facing under the sewing machine so that the needle will come down a scant ⅛ in. (2 mm) from the seam.

3 Sew around the facing, sewing through the seam allowances of both the garment and the facing.

4 Fold the facing down to the inside of the garment and press in place. A thin line of the main garment should be visible from the inside above the facing.

> ## Try this

If the facing is curved, try to keep the facing as flat as you can and let the garment ripple and curl up to accommodate the extra fabric. This will ensure that the neckline or waistline remains as flat and smooth as possible.

Edge stitching

Edge stitching is very similar to topstitching and the two terms are often used interchangeably; however, there is a difference. Edge stitching is a normal length of stitch that is used to keep several layers of fabric together. Topstitching is a longer stitch that can be used anywhere on a garment, farther away from the edge and in multiple rows.

1 Press the area to be edge stitched before stitching to make it easier to line up the machine foot.

2 Place the edge of the fabric under the presser foot so that the needle drops down just a scant ⅛ in. (2 mm) from the edge of the garment.

3 To make it easier to keep a straight sewing line, line up the edge of the fabric with the outer edge of the machine foot and swing the needle into the correct position **(a)**. Keep the edge of the fabric in line with the machine foot to maintain a consistent stitching line **(b)**.

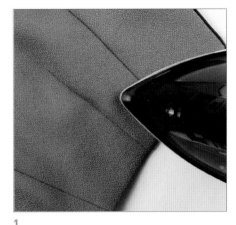

1

2

3a

3b

Edge stitching at both the lace and neckline edges gives the curve of the neckline band a smooth and clean finish.

Hems

This is another of those finishing processes that it's worth taking time over. After all, the effort you have put in to making something that fits you perfectly and that you want to wear surely deserves to have a beautifully finished hem.

Whether it's a skirt, dress, pants, or top, you may have noticed after making up a garment that occasionally the hem doesn't sit straight. This isn't necessarily the fault of the pattern; it could come down to a number of reasons.

Grain lines

Unless you are making up a pure straight rectangle of fabric, you are more likely to have the hemline sitting on different grain lines. This is more common in fuller skirts, where the center front or back is on the straight grain and the sides are on the bias or diagonal grain.

This means that those parts of the hem that are not on the straight grain line will have more flexibility and may cause the fabric to drop slightly, giving an uneven hemline.

The human form

The other main reason is that the human form has dips and curves. If you have a fuller bottom, for example, there will need to be a bit more fabric in the length of the hem at the back to accommodate this. Otherwise you might find the hem lifting up at the back.

Let the garment hang

Once you have made up your garment, leave it to hang for a day or so. This will allow the fabric to settle and "drop" if it needs to. This is more important on a garment with a fuller hem, like a circular skirt, as more of the hem is on the bias grain (see below). A garment that fits closer to the body, such as a pencil skirt, has a straighter hem that will sit more on the straight grain.

You can then level the hem, either on a dress stand or with the help of a friend while you try on the garment.

LEVELING A HEM

If you have a dress stand that is set to your own measurements, you can put your garment on this. Remember, however, that the hard shell of a mannequin won't necessarily replicate your exact shape. So do try on the garment after you've leveled the hem to make sure that it remains level and parallel to the floor.

It's also a good idea to try on the garment wearing the same type and height of shoes you'll wear with that garment, particularly pants.

Tip: If the height of the room allows, you can put your dress stand on a table to make measuring and marking the hem much easier on your back.

1 Whether you are using a dress stand or yourself, always measure up from the floor to the desired length of the hem. If possible, use a measuring stick rather than a flexible tape measure, as a stick is much easier to keep perpendicular to the floor, ensuring a level hem.

2 Mark the hem with a pin.

3 Work your way around the garment. Once you take the garment off and lay it flat, you will have a clear line of pins to follow to mark a level hem.

4 Trim off the excess fabric and finish the hem with your chosen method.

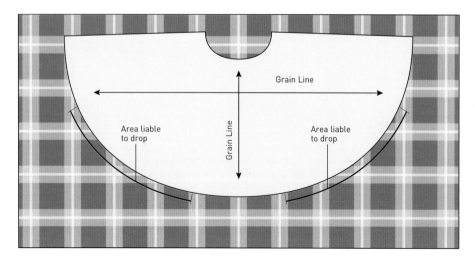

1

2

3

Hand sewing

Hand sewing gives a more couture finish to your garments, allowing the hem to become almost invisible if sewn with care and attention. Slipstitch, herringbone stitch, blind hemming, and a hand-rolled hem are all hand-sewn hems. Use a single thread to minimize the impact of the stitches on the right side of the garment.

The threads should be caught and fastened at the beginning and end of your sewing. We've used a contrasting thread to make them easier to see, but you should use a matching thread. The following photographs have been taken from the point of view of a right-handed stitcher; the instructions (in brackets) are for sewing left-handed.

STARTING AND FINISHING

1 To start, sew a couple of small stitches in the same place—but don't pull the thread all the way through.

2 Thread the needle through the loop of thread twice **(a)** and pull to tighten the stitch down to the fabric **(b)**.

3 Finish your sewing in the same way.

4 To lose the tail of thread at the end of your sewing, pass the needle through the layers of hem fabric **(a)** and snip off the thread flush with the fabric **(b)**. The tail of thread should slip down under the fabric out of sight.

5 If your stitches are going to be visible at all or you find it tricky to maintain even stitches, it is worth marking them out with a disappearing marker pen before you start to sew.

Tip: Keep your length of thread to about an arm's length. Too long a strand is more likely to get tangled up and knotted.

1

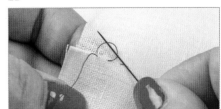

2a

2b

3

4a

4b

SLIPSTITCH

This works really well with a double-turned hem, as most of the thread is hidden inside the fold of the fabric. The small, regular stitches look good from the right side, too.

1 Work from right to left (left to right) and with the needle pointing to the left (right). Anchor the thread (see page 235). With the wrong side of the fabric facing you, slip the needle through the folded edge of the hem for about ⅜ in. (1 cm), making sure you do not go all the way through to the right side.

2 As the needle comes back through the hem fold, catch a small bit of the fabric—just a few threads really—and pull the thread through to create the stitch.

3 To create the next stitch, slip the needle back into the hem fold directly under where the previous stitch finished.

4 Slip the needle through the hem fold for another ⅜ in. (1 cm). Repeat Steps 2–4 along the length of the hem.

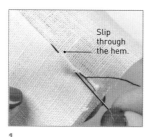
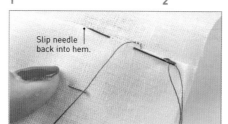
1

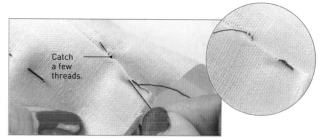
Catch a few threads.
2

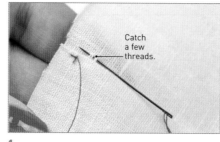
Slip needle back into hem.
3–4

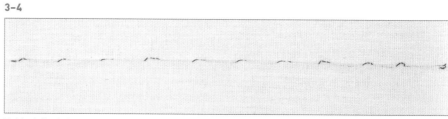

Finished slipstitch

HERRINGBONE STITCH

The way this stitch brings the thread across the stitch creates a bit of stretch and is stronger, too. Herringbone stitch works well on both a double-turned hem and a single layer of fabric, as it holds the hem completely flat to the garment.

1 Work left to right (right to left). Anchor the thread (see page 235). With the needle pointing to the left (right), catch a small piece of the garment just above the hem. Try to keep the stitch as small as you can, as it will be seen from the right side.

2 Move the needle over to the right (left) by ⅜ in. (1 cm) and catch up a small piece of the hem fold with the needle still pointing to the left (right).

3 Repeat Steps 1 and 2 along the length of the hem.

4 Your stitches should look like stretched-out crosses.

Catch a few threads.
1

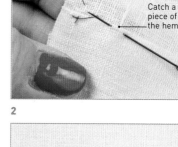
Catch a piece of the hem.
2

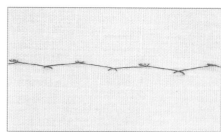
Finished herringbone stitch: wrong side
3

Finished herringbone stitch: right side

BLIND HEMMING

A blind hem should be almost invisible from the right side, especially if you use matching thread.

1 Fold up a double-turned hem and press flat. Fold the garment down onto itself. Work from right to left (left to right), with the needle pointing to the left (right). Anchor the thread (see page 235).

2 The doubled-over edge of the hem should stick out by a scant ¼ in. (5 mm). Pick up a very small amount of fabric—just a few threads—in the folded edge of the garment. This will be seen from the right side, so make sure to only sew through a single layer of fabric.

3 Move the needle over a little bit and pick up a small amount of the hem just under the folded edge.

4 Repeat Steps 2 and 3 along the length of the hem. Fold the hem back in place and press.

1

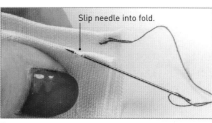

2

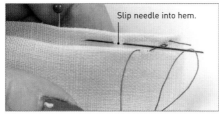

3–4

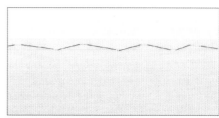

Finished blind hemming: wrong side

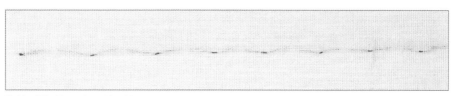

Finished blind hemming: right side

1

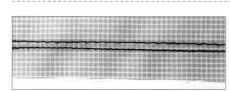

2

4 Wrong side

5

HAND-ROLLED HEM

This type of hem works well on sheer or very lightweight fabrics, but not on thicker fabrics as they just won't roll properly.

1 Trim any seams vertical to the hem down to about ¼ in. (5 mm). Machine baste around the hem at the hemline, then shorten your stitch length and sew ⅛–¼ in. (3–5 mm) below the basting line. This should help prevent the edge of the fabric from fraying too much.

2 Trim about 6 in. (15 cm) of the excess fabric back to the second row of stitching. Only do a bit of trimming at a time to help prevent stray threads from fraying.

3 Weight or pin down the end of the hem to help act as an extra hand. You can also use the presser foot on your machine to help with this.

4 Work with the wrong side facing you. Roll the trimmed edge of the hem toward you, stopping at the row of basting stitches. The other row of sewing will be tucked under, inside the roll of fabric.

Tip: Licking your fingers will really help with rolling the fabric between your fingers. Not the most hygienic tip but very useful!

5 Slipstitch down the roll of fabric, rolling the hem as you go. As you get close to the end of the trimmed-off tail, trim a bit more. Repeat Steps 4 and 5 along the length of the hem.

6 Remove the machine basting stitches.

Finished hand-rolled hem: wrong side

Finished hand-rolled hem: right side

Machine sewing

A machine-sewn hem is a quick and effective way to finish most types of garment. A neat row of machine stitching can be just as attractive as a hand-sewn hem.

SINGLE-TURNED HEM

This is probably the simplest type of hem. If only a small hem is turned up, it works very well for curved hemlines.

1 Neaten the raw edge by overlocking, zigzag stitch, or mock overlocking (see page 95). Turn up the hem by the desired amount and press in place.

2 Machine stitch through the center of the overlocking; this ensures that the edge of the hem doesn't fold back down over the hem.

3 You can do this from the right side. Pin through the hem from the wrong side where you want the line of topstitching to be.

4 Place the garment under the machine so that the needle lines up with the pin. Carefully remove the pin and note where the folded edge of the hem comes to on your machine. You can use the guidelines on the sewing plate to help you sew an accurate line.

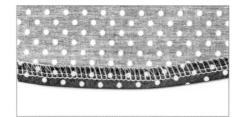
1

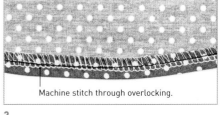
2
Machine stitch through overlocking.

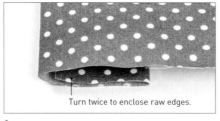
3

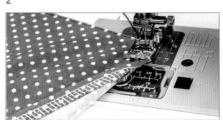

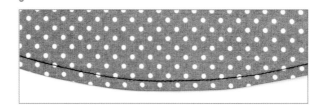
Finished single-turned hem

DOUBLE-TURNED HEM

This is very similar to the single-turned hem, but the hem is turned up twice to enclose all the raw edges.

1 Make sure that the first turn is smaller than the second, so that the fabric is not doubled up inside the garment edge.

2 Topstitch from the right side, using the guides on the machine plate to make sure your sewing stays on the edge of the hem.

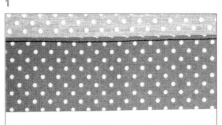
Turn twice to enclose raw edges.
1

2

Finished double-turned hem: wrong side

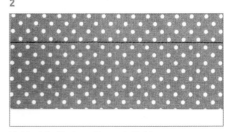
Finished double-turned hem: right side

BLIND HEM

This is a great method for sewing deeper hems on pants, skirts, and jackets. If you use matching threads, it is virtually invisible.

1 Turn up a double hem and press in place. Pin vertically so that the pinheads show above the folded edge of the hem.

2 Fold the garment back down away from the hem. This should allow the hem to stick out a scant ¼ in. (5 mm) with the pinheads showing.

3 Select the bind hem stitch on your machine. You can alter the length and width of the stitch according to your fabric.

Tip: It's best to sew a test piece first to gauge the width and length you need for the fabric you're working with. You may need to increase or decrease the width, as you should only see a small pin prick from the right side. Lengthen the stitch so that the row of small stitches is not as visible from the right side.

4 Attach the blind-hem foot to your machine and place the garment under the foot so that the blade of the foot runs along the folded-over edge of the garment.

5 The stitch will sew a couple of stitches on the visible part of the hem, then hop over and sew a catch stitch through the folded edge of the garment.

6 Continue to sew around the hem, overlapping your sewing at the end.

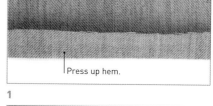
Press up hem.

1

Sew close to fold.

2

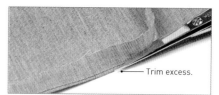
Trim excess.

3

4

Finished pin hem

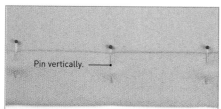
Pin vertically.

1

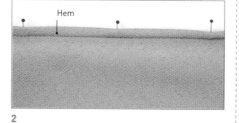
Hem

2

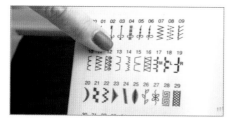

3

4

5

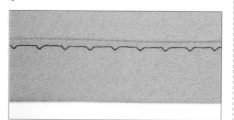
Finished blind hem: wrong side

Finished blind hem: right side

PIN HEM

This is similar to a rolled hem, but is useful if you don't have a specific rolled-hem machine foot.

1 Press up the hem a scant ¼ in. (5 mm) below the hemline.

2 Sew a row of stitching very close to the folded edge of the hemline.

3 Trim the excess fabric away as close as you can to the line of stitching, leaving a very narrow hem.

4 Fold over the narrow hem and sew directly on top of the first row of sewing.

BIAS-BOUND HEM

This method uses a strip of bias-cut fabric or ready-made bias binding to neaten the raw edge of the hem. Again, this works very well with a curved hemline.

1 Press up the hem allowance. Open up one side of the bias binding. With right sides together, line up the edge of the binding with the raw edge of the hem, leaving a 2-in. (5 cm) tail of bias binding at the beginning of your sewing. Backstitch for a few stitches, then sew around the hem in the crease of the bias binding.

2 Stop 2 in. (5 cm) from the start of your stitching, and backstitch again.

3 Bring the ends of the bias binding together and pin so that the binding fits neatly around the hem.

4 Open up all the folds of the bias binding and sew vertically across the ends.

5 Trim the ends down to a scant ¼ in. (5 mm) and press the seam open. Realign the bias binding to the edge of the hem and sew between backstitching to close the gap.

6 Fold the hem to the wrong side and tuck under the raw edge of the binding. Machine or hand sew the binding to the garment to finish the hem.

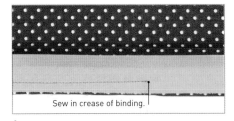

Sew in crease of binding.

1

Leave ends free.

2

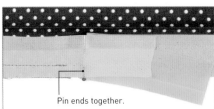

Pin ends together.

3

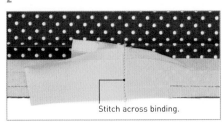

Stitch across binding.

4

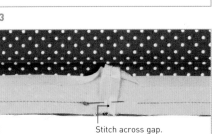

5

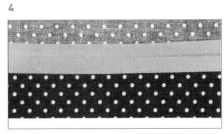

Stitch across gap.

5

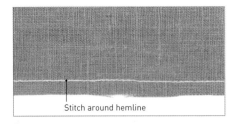

6

RAW EDGE OR UNFINISHED HEM

This can look great with a fabric that frays easily, such as a loose-weave linen. It works well on curved hems, too.

Method 1

1 Cut the garment to the finished length, as this is where the hemline will be. Set up the machine with a normal stitch and line up the edge of the fabric to sew a line of stitching about ⅜–⅝ in. (1–1.5 cm) from the raw edge. Starting at the side seam or other less visible place, sew around the hemline.

2 Allow the raw edge of the fabric to fray. A greater distance from the edge will allow more fabric to fray.

Method 1

Stitch around hemline

1

2

Method 2

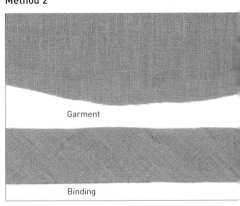

Garment

Binding

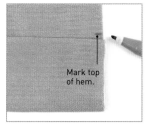

1

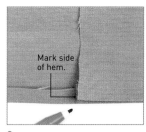

2

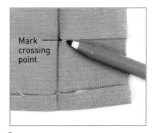

3

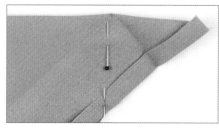

4 Wrong side

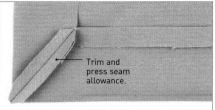

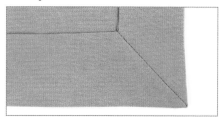

Mark top of hem.

Mark side of hem.

Mark crossing point.

5

Sew across corner.

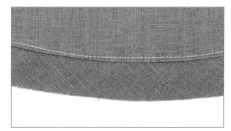

6

Trim and press seam allowance.

Finished mitered corner

MITERED CORNERS

Mitered corners give a really neat finish to the corners of a vent or split in a skirt or jacket.

1 Press up ⅜ in. (1 cm), then press up the hem allowance. Mark on the vertical seam allowance of the garment where the folded edge of the hem sits.

2 Unfold the hem, but leave in place the ⅜ in. (1 cm) fold. Fold over the vertical

seam allowance, press in place, and mark where this comes to on the horizontal edge of the hem.

3 Unfold the vertical seam allowance and mark where the pressing lines intersect. This will be the point of the corner.

4 With right sides together fold the garment so the two hem edge marks come together and the dot on the intersecting pressing lines is on the new fold. Remember to keep the ⅜ in. (1 cm) fold in place.

5 Sew from the dot on the fold to the edge marks. Backstitch at the start and finish of your sewing.

6 Trim the excess fabric down to ¼ in. (6 mm) and press the seam allowance open and flat.

7 Turn the corner to the right side, making sure the corner is nice and sharp. Press flat.

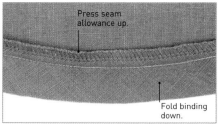

1 Right side

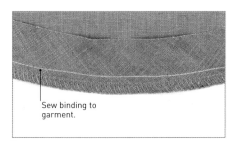

2 Right side

Press seam allowance up.

Fold binding down.

3 Wrong side

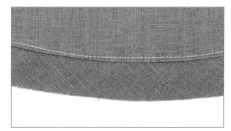

4 Right side

Sew binding to garment.

Method 2

Using the raw edge of a bias-cut strip of fabric will give a more even frayed edge, as both warp and weft threads will fray.

1 With right sides together, pin the binding to the garment.

2 Taking a ⅜-in. (1 cm) seam allowance, sew the binding to the edge of the garment. Finish the seam with your preferred method.

3 Fold the binding down away from the garment and press the seam allowance up toward the garment.

4 If the seam allowance needs to keep in its place, you can topstitch through the garment and seam allowance just above the seamline.

Linings

Linings not only look good, they also perform several useful functions. First, they enclose all the raw edges to keep everything neat and tidy. A satin-weave lining fabric will also allow the garment to slip over the body, making it much more comfortable to wear. And, finally, a lining will take a lot of the wear and tear in a garment, making it look better and last longer.

Lining fabrics

The lining fabric you choose for your garment should be a similar weight fabric to your garment to provide it with support and it should be fairly slippy to make it comfortable to wear.

Examples of lining fabrics

Habotai silk, silk charmeuse, and cotton lawn are suitable for lightweight, delicate tops, and dresses.

Viscose rayon, silk taffeta, and jacquard silk are suitable for medium-weight dresses, jackets, and pants.

Acetate bemburg and polyester twill are suitable for heavier-weight jackets and coats.

Tip: One of the main jobs of a lining is to take the daily wearing strain off the outer garment fabric. To do this, the lining should be free to move inside the garment—so although the lining is the same shape, often cut using some of the same pattern pieces, it needs to be a fraction looser. One way of ensuring this is to sew the lining on the normal seam allowance, but to swing the needle to the right by one stop. This means that each seam will be just a fraction smaller than those on the outer garment, allowing the lining to be that little bit looser.

The lining in this skirt not only provides a way of neatening the inside of the skirt, but also adds a contrast detail at the hem.

Skirt lining

The lining in a skirt is attached to the main garment at the waist, allowing the rest of the lining to move freely inside the skirt. It will also help the skirt maintain its shape and allow it to be slipped on and off easily.

1 Make up the outer skirt (the shell), sewing in all the darts and seams and inserting the zipper.

Tip: Although the skirt is to be lined, it can be worth neatening the seams as the lining is left free.

2 Cut out the lining using the main skirt pattern pieces, but trim the hem down by 1 in. (2.5 cm). Mark the base of the zipper on the lining seam allowances. This will usually be on the center back or side seam.

3 Sew up the seams of the lining, neatening the side seam allowances together but the center back (or whichever seam the zipper is inserted into) separately. Use overlocking, zigzag stitch, or mock overlocking to prevent the lining from fraying (satin-weave synthetic linings are very prone to this). Press the closed seam allowances to one side and the zipper opening seam allowance open.

Tip: To reduce bulk at the waist, only neaten the seams to halfway up. This keeps the zipper opening free from bulky sewing threads.

4 Open the skirt zipper. With both the outer skirt and the lining inside out, place them next to each other, aligning the zipper openings. Pin one side of the zipper seam allowance on the outer skirt to its corresponding lining seam allowance. Do the same with the other side of the zipper seam allowance.

1 Skirt shell

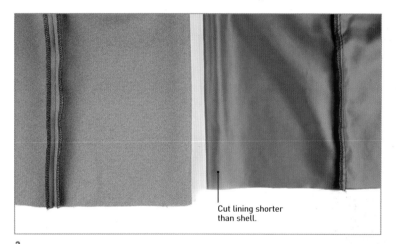

Cut lining shorter than shell.

2

3 Skirt lining

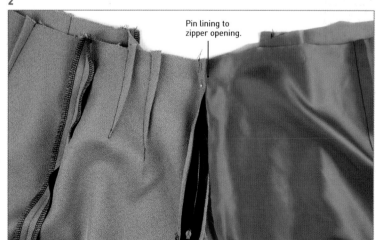

Pin lining to zipper opening.

4

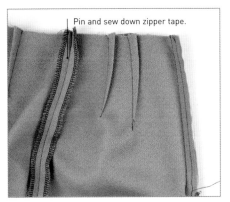

Pin and sew down zipper tape.

5

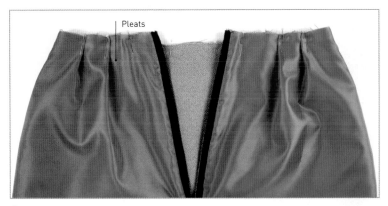

Pleats

6

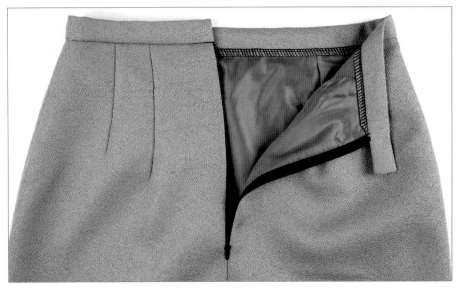

7

8

French tack

9

5 Match up the raw edge of the lining with the edge of the zipper seam allowance. Pin and sew through the middle of the zipper tape from the top of the zipper to the end of the zipper tape. Repeat for the other side. Press the lining away from the zipper.

6 Flip the lining over so that it sits right side out on top of the shell. Match up the side seams and center fronts. Smooth the lining down along the waist, creating small pleats at the darts to suppress the extra fabric. The pleats should fold in the opposite way to the stitched-in darts to reduce bulk. Baste the shell and lining together at the waist.

7 The skirt shell and lining layers can now be treated as one. Attach the waistband using your preferred method (see pages 178–181).

8 Turn up the skirt hem by the desired amount and sew in place using your chosen method (see pages 234–241). Turn up the skirt lining and sew a double-turned hem so that the lining is at least ⅜ in. (1 cm) shorter than the finished skirt.

9 To keep the lining in place at the hem, sew French tacks at the seams. These will allow the lining to move but remain anchored at the hemline.

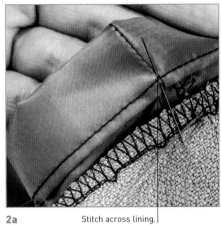

1 | Anchor stitch

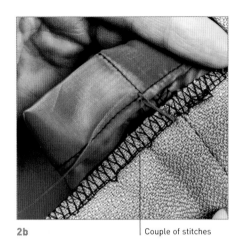

2a   Stitch across lining. |

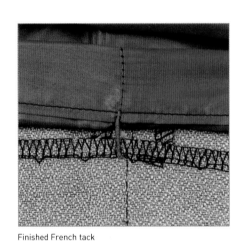

2b | Couple of stitches

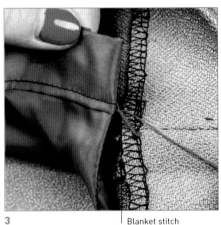

3 | Blanket stitch

4 | Secure stitching

Finished French tack

FRENCH TACKS

These are also known as chain threads and are a reinforced chain of stitches to create a thicker thread that can hold two pieces of a garment together loosely.

1 Sew a locking stitch to one side of the tack.

2 Sew a stitch through the garment on the other end of the tack **(a)**. Sew a couple of stitches in each side, leaving a gap of about ¾ in. (1.5 cm) between the two garments **(b)**.

3 Sew a blanket stitch around the line of threads to create a chain of stitches.

4 Lock off your sewing at the finished end of the tack.

Bodice or dress lining

Adding a lining to the bodice of a dress will most definitely improve the look and finish of the garment. Not only will it neaten any raw edges, but it will maintain the shape of the garment too. The style of the dress will determine the way it is made up to incorporate the lining. However, the simplest method is to join the lining to the neckline and armholes before sewing up the side seams.

1 Make up the bodice and lining separately. Sew the front and back bodice pieces together at the shoulder seams, but leave the side seams and center back open. Repeat with the facing pieces. Press the seams open.

2 With right sides together, pin the lining and bodice together and sew around the neckline and armholes. Layer the seam allowances and snip into them to release the tension in the curves (see page 91).

3 Turn the bodice right side out by pulling through the shoulder seams. Understitch (see page 232) as far as you can around the neckline and armholes through the lining and seam allowances to prevent the lining from showing on the right side, and press so that the seams lie flat.

4 Lift up the lining away from the garment. With the right sides together place the front and back bodice side seams together and match up the underarm points. Sew down along the side seam of the lining, across the armhole seam, and down the side seam of the garment.

5 Press the seams open and turn the bodice right side out. Press the underarm to keep the lining inside the bodice.

6 Lengthen your machine stitch and baste the waists of the bodice and lining together. This will make it easier to attach to a skirt.

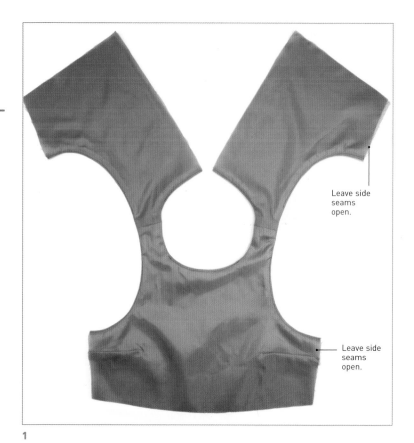

Leave side seams open.

Leave side seams open.

1

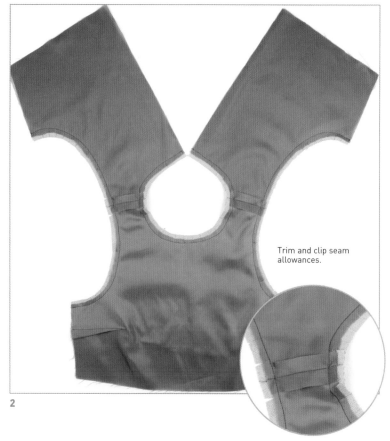

Trim and clip seam allowances.

2

Pull bodice through shoulder seams.

3

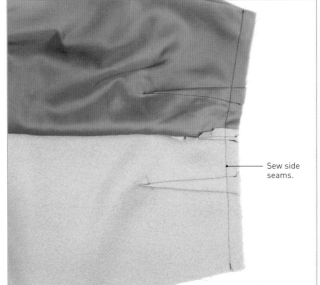

Sew side seams.

4

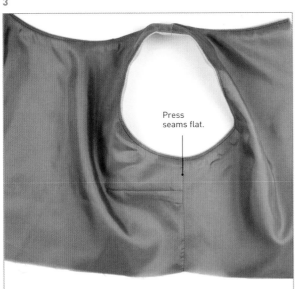

Press seams flat.

5

Baste waist.

6

Resources

ESTIMATING FABRIC REQUIREMENTS

CLOTHING TYPE		FABRIC WIDTH		CLOTHING TYPE		FABRIC WIDTH	
		45 in. (115 cm) wide	60 in. (150 cm) wide			45 in. (115 cm) wide	60 in. (150 cm) wide
Straight skirt (above knee)	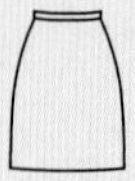	1⅛ yd (1 m)	⅞ yd (0.75 m)	Bodice (waist length)		½–1¼ yd (0.5–1 m)	½–1¼ yd (0.5–1 m)
Straight skirt (knee length)	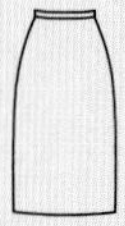	1⅛–1⅗ yd (1–1.5 m)	⅞–1 yd (0.75–1 m)	Bodice (hip length)		¾–1¼ yd (0.75–1 m)	¾–1¼ yd (0.75–1 m)
Straight skirt (calf length)		1–2 yd (0.9–1.75 m)	1–1½ yd (0.75–1.5 m)	Sleeve (short)		½ yd (0.4 m)	½ yd (0.4 m)
Straight skirt (full length)	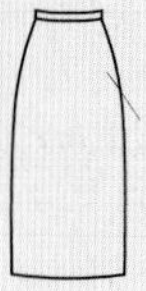	1⅝–2⅛ yd (1.5–2 m)	1⅝–2⅛ yd (1.5–2 m)	Sleeve (¾ length)		½–¾ yd (0.5 m)	½–¾ yd (0.5 m)
Bias skirt (calf length)		2⅛ yd (2 m)	1⅕–2⅛ yd (1.4–2 m)	Sleeve (long)		¾ yd (0.7 m)	¾ yd (0.7 m)
Shift dress (above knee)	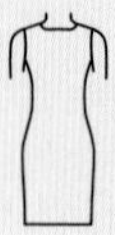	2¾ yd (2.5 m)	1⅝–2⅛ yd (1.5–2 m)	Sleeve with cuff		1 yd (0.8 m)	1 yd (0.8 m)
Shift dress (calf length)	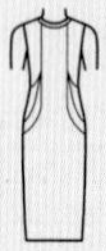	3⅞–4½ yd (3.5–4 m)	3⅞–4½ yd (3.5–4 m)	Sleeve (two piece)		1 yd (0.8 m)	1 yd (0.8 m)
Pants	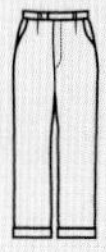	1¾–2¼ yd (1.5–2 m)	1¾–2 yd (1.5–1.75 m)				

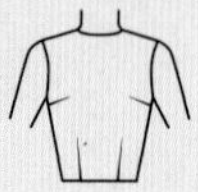

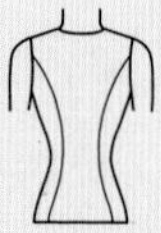

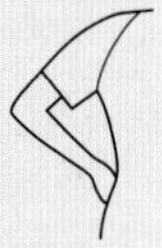

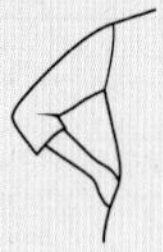

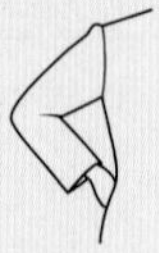

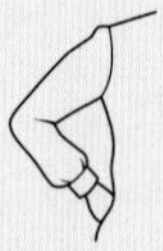

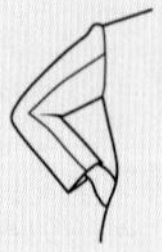

Note: Use this rough guide to help when estimating how much fabric to buy for a particular type of garment. Combine the length (e.g. dress or skirt) with the sleeve type to estimate the yardage/meterage needed.

PRESSING GUIDE

FABRIC	TEMPERATURE	SPECIAL NOTES
Acrylic	Cool to medium	Apply light pressure
Arctic fleece	Do not iron	
Beaded/sequined	Cool	Cover with a thick cotton pressing cloth and treat gently with little pressure
Calico/muslin	Hot	
Corduroy	Hot	Iron from the wrong side
Cotton lawn	Hot	Consider using spray starch to stiffen
Denim	Hot	Iron damp or use plenty of steam
Dressweight cotton	Hot	Protect with a pressing cloth if necessary
Faux fur	Cool	Dry iron with light pressure
Lace	Cool to medium, depending on fiber content	Iron over a towel or padded surface and use steam, hovering the iron above without applying pressure on the lace
Leather/suede	Medium	Dry iron only
Linen	Hot	Iron damp or use plenty of steam
Microfiber	Medium	Dry iron
Organdy	Hot	Use a pressing cloth to protect the surface
Polyester	Medium	
Silk chiffon	Hot	Use a silk organza pressing cloth
Silk dupion	Hot	Use a pressing cloth and dry iron
Silk organza	Hot	
Silk tweed	Hot	Use steam and a pressing cloth with light pressure
Stretch polyester with Lycra (spandex)	Cool to medium	Iron only when necessary
Sweat shirting	Hot	Use steam and apply light pressure
T-shirt cotton	Hot	Use steam and apply light pressure
Toweling	Hot	Use steam and light pressure so as not to flatten the pile
Upholstery	Hot	Use steam and a clapper/basher on stubborn seams
Velvet	Medium for cotton, cool for synthetic velvet	Iron with light pressure from the wrong side and use a velvet board or spare length of velvet
Wool crepe	Medium	Use a length of the wool crepe as a pressing cloth
Wool tweed	Medium	Use steam and light pressure
Worsted wool	Medium	Use a pressing cloth to prevent shining seam ridges

Glossary

Apex
Bust point.

Armscye
This is the armhole measurement.

Bagged lining
A bagged lining is one where the lining is made up and sewn to a garment leaving only a small opening to allow it to be pulled through to the right side. This does away with the need for hand stitching, making for a stronger finish.

Balance points
Dots and marks printed on the pattern to match and join when constructing a garment.

Basic block pattern
This is a basic pattern produced from standard measurements before any style has been incorporated. Designs are made from these basic blocks.

Bias/cross grain of fabric
The diagonal direction of fabric between the warp and the weft threads.

Break point
The turning point where the lapel twists at the center front of a jacket.

Buttonhole twist
Buttonhole twist is a strong, lustrous thread, and is used for hand-worked buttonholes and for sewing on buttons.

CB
Abbreviation used for center back.

CF
Abbreviation used for center front.

Dart
A dart is a wedge of fabric that is pinched out of a garment to allow shaping or to remove excess fabric.

Dress form
A mannequin that is a replica body shape and is used to assist in the fitting of garments.

Ease
Ease refers to the amount of space built into a sewing pattern—in addition to body measurements—to allow movement and to achieve the required garment silhouette.

Facing
A piece of fabric the same shape as the main garment usually used to finish off a waist, neckline, or armhole.

Feed dogs
Teeth that lie under the presser foot and move the fabric to allow the needle to make each stitch.

Finger pressing
Some fabrics (for example, those with natural fibers) respond to handling better than others (for example, those from synthetic fibers) and some small areas or seams are better pressed into place using your finger, as an iron would flatten a whole area or create too sharp a finish.

Fold line
Used to describe the position of pattern pieces to be placed on folded fabric. The fabric is folded (usually lengthwise) so that the selvages are together. A directional arrow on the pattern tissue indicates the edge to place to the folded fabric.

French tack
Thread strands wound with thread, often used to join a lining to a coat hem.

Grain line
The fabric grain is the direction of the woven fibers. Straight or lengthwise grain runs along the warp thread, parallel to the selvages. Crosswise grain runs along the weft, perpendicular to straight grain. Most dressmaking pattern pieces are cut on the lengthwise grain, which has minimal stretch.

Grading
When seam allowances are trimmed to different amounts to reduce bulk. Also known as layering.

High hip
The high hip is approximately 2–4 in. (5–10 cm) below the waist and just above the hip bones.

Hip
The hip is the fullest part of the figure and is approximately 7–9 in. (17.5–23 cm) below the waist.

Interfacing
A stabilizing fabric used on the wrong side to support a piece of a garment, for example a collar or behind a pocket.

Interlining
This is a separate layer of fabric cut the same as the panels of dress fabric and placed to the wrong side. The panels are placed together, then sewn up as one. Using an interlining or underlining changes the characteristics of the original fabric, either to make it heavier, crisper, or less transparent.

Layplan
The manufacturer's guide to laying pattern pieces on fabric in the most economical way and keeping pieces "on grain" or on fold lines, and so on. A number of layouts are provided for different fabric widths and pattern sizes.

Lining
A separate fabric sewn on the inside of a garment to conceal all raw edges and help it to hang well.

Mercerized cotton
A treatment applied to give strength and luster.

Natural fiber
Fiber from a non-synthetic source for example, cotton or flax plant, silk moth, or wool.

Notions
All the bits and pieces you need to make your garment, e.g. thread, buttons, zippers, hook and eyes, etc.

Overlocker
A machine designed to sew and finish edges in one step, although it can produce many other effects too. Also known as a serger.

Pressing cloth
A fine, smooth fabric piece used to protect the surface of a fabric when ironing or pressing.

Princess line
A dress with curved seaming running from the shoulder or the armhole to the hem on the front and back, giving six panels (not including the center back seam).

Quarter pinning
A technique used to arrange tucks (created with elastic) evenly. The elastic and fabric are divided into quarters and pinned at these points. Pull the elastic to match the fabric length and stitch the layers together.

Rouleau turner
A tool made of a length of wire, with a hook and latch at one end for turning narrow tubes of fabric.

Seam allowance
The area between the sewing line and the edge of the cloth, normally ⅝ in. (1.5 cm) but 1 in. (2.5 cm) in couture sewing.

Selvage
The neat edge that runs down both long sides of the fabric. It is created when the horizontal weft threads come to the end and turn back on themselves, woven under and over the vertical warp threads. It has very little give and allows the fabric to hang true and straight.

Sleeve head
Sometimes referred to as a sleeve cap—the upper part of the sleeve that fits into the shoulder. Not to be confused with a cap sleeve, which is a small sleeve covering the very top of the shoulder.

Slip tack
Similar to ladder stitch, where two edges are joined from the right side, taking alternate stitches from each edge but used as a temporary join.

Sloper
This is a template from which patterns are made and also known as a basic pattern block.

Slub
An uneven thread woven into fabric, resulting in an interesting textured surface.

Smocking
Embroidery stitches sewn over the folds of gathered fabric.

Spi
"Stitches per inch" is used to indicate the stitch length. This measurement is often shown in millimeters.

Stabilizer(s)
A material used to support fabric. Often associated with machine embroidery and normally placed under the work.

Staystitching
Stitching used to hold fabric stable and prevent it from stretching.

Stitch in the ditch
Also called "sink stitch," this is where pieces are held together by stitching through an existing seam. Used on waistbands and on Hong Kong finishes.

Stretch stitch
A machine stitch suitable for sewing stretch fabric—either a narrow zigzag or one which includes back stitches in its construction.

Swing needle sewing machine
A machine where the needle moves to the left and right to make stitches, and not simply straight stitches.

Synthetic fiber
Fibers from a non-natural source. Examples are nylon, polyester, and acrylic.

Tailor's dummy
Also known as a dress form. A mannequin used to assist in the making up of garments.

Tailor's ham
A small, hard cushion traditionally filled with sawdust and used as a pressing aid.

Truing a line
This is where a line on a pattern is slightly altered to make it smooth and adjust the fit. Often used when transferring adjustments from a muslin to a pattern.

Understitch
When the seam allowances are stitched to one edge to hold it down, for example, on armhole facing.

Underwrap
The extension on a waistband for the fastening.

Walking foot
This replaces the standard machine foot and walks over the fabric while sewing, so avoiding the fabric "creep" that sometimes occurs.

Zipper foot
An alternative machine foot. It allows the needle to get closer to the teeth of a zipper than a standard machine foot.

Index

Credits

The author would like to thank:

The hardworking team at Sew Me Something, and especially my husband Charlie Budd, for all their help, support, and endless cups of coffee laced with constructive criticism.

Quarto would like to thank and acknowledge the following for their contribution to this book:

Lorna Knight and Lynda Maynard

FashionStock.com, Shutterstock.com, p.58bc; Alexander Gitlits, Shutterstock.com, p.58tr; kojoku, Shutterstock.com, p.58tc; lev radin, Shutterstock.com, p.58tl, 58bl; Nata Sha, Shutterstock.com, p.58br